RUSSIA

MONGOLIA

NORTH
KOREA

Beijing

Bo
Hai

SOUTH
KOREA

Yellow
Sea

Shanghai

East
China Sea

VIETNAM

LAO
ND

D0264065

EYEWITNESS TRAVEL

BEIJING &
SHANGHAI

EYEWITNESS TRAVEL

BEIJING & SHANGHAI

Main Contributor **Peter Neville-Hadley**

DK

LONDON, NEW YORK,
MELBOURNE, MUNICH AND DELHI
www.dk.com

Produced by Brazil Street

Project Editor Andrew Humphreys

Art Editor Gadi Farfour

DORLING KINDERSLEY

Senior Editor Hugh Thompson

DTP Designer Natasha Lu

Picture Researchers Ellen Root

Production Linda Dare

Contributors

Peter Neville-Hadley, Donald Bedford, Christopher Knowles

Photographers

Chen Chao, Colin Sinclair, Linda Whitwam

Illustrators

Gary Cross, Richard Draper, Paul Guest,
Chapel Design & Marketing, John Mullany

Printed in Malaysia

First published in the UK in 2007
by Dorling Kindersley Limited
80 Strand, London WC2R 0RL

16 17 18 19 10 9 8 7 6 5 4 3 2 1

Reprinted with revisions 2009, 2011, 2013, 2016

Copyright 2007, 2016 © Dorling Kindersley Limited, London

A Penguin Random House Company

All rights reserved. No part of this publication may be reproduced, stored in a
retrieval system, or transmitted in any form or by any means, electronic,
mechanical, photocopying, recording or otherwise without the prior written
permission of the copyright owner.

A CIP catalogue record is available from the British Library.

ISBN 978-0-2411-9676-2

Floors are referred to throughout in accordance with
US usage; ie the "first floor" is at ground level.

MIX
Paper from
responsible sources
FSC
www.fsc.org FSC™ C018179

The information in this DK Eyewitness Travel Guide is checked regularly.
Every effort has been made to ensure that this book is as up-to-date as possible at
the time of going to press. Some details, however, such as telephone numbers,
opening hours, prices, gallery hanging arrangements and travel information, are
liable to change. The publishers cannot accept responsibility for any consequences
arising from the use of this book, nor for any material on third party websites, and
cannot guarantee that any website address in this book will be a suitable source of
travel information. We value the views and suggestions of our readers very highly.
Please write to: Publisher, DK Eyewitness Travel Guides, Dorling Kindersley,
80 Strand, London, WC2R 0RL, UK, or email: travelguides@dk.com.

Front cover main image: The futuristic Pudong skyline in Shanghai

◀ The magnificent Temple of Heaven in Beijing

Contents

Gateway, Lama Temple, Beijing

Introducing Beijing and Shanghai

Watchtowers along a steep section of
the Great Wall

Laughing Buddha in the Feilai Feng hills, Hangzhou

Sightseeing boats carrying visitors on one
of Tongli's canals

The Hall of Prayer of Good Harvests,
centerpiece of the Temple of
Heaven, Beijing

HOW TO USE THIS GUIDE

This guide helps you to get the most from your stay in Beijing and Shanghai. It provides detailed practical information and expert recommendations. *Introducing Beijing and Shanghai* locates the cities geographically, sets them firmly in their historical and cultural context, and gives an overview of the main attractions on offer. The individual city chapters start on page 58 with Beijing, followed by Shanghai on page 122. These are the main sightseeing sections, which cover all of the important sights, with photographs, maps and illustrations. The *Farther Afield* sections showcase sights beyond the city limits and each of these is followed by two walking tours. Information about hotels, restaurants, shops, markets and entertainment is found in *Travelers' Needs* while the *Survival Guide* contains useful advice on everything from etiquette to transport.

Beijing and Shanghai

The cities are divided into four sightseeing areas – the central districts of Beijing, Beijing Farther Afield, the central districts of Shanghai and Shanghai Farther Afield. Each area chapter opens with an introduction and a list of sights covered. Central districts have a Street-by-Street map of a particularly interesting part of the area. The sights farther afield have a regional map.

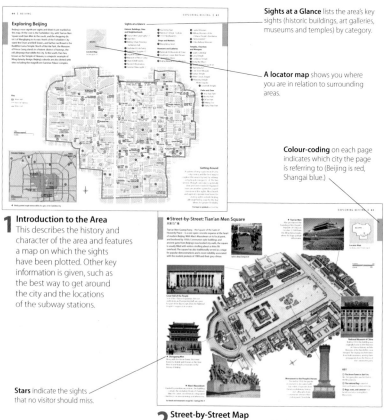

Sights at a Glance lists the area's key sights (historic buildings, art galleries, museums and temples) by category.

A locator map shows you where you are in relation to surrounding areas.

Colour-coding on each page indicates which city the page is referring to (Beijing is red, Shangai blue.)

1 Introduction to the Area
This describes the history and character of the area and features a map on which the sights have been plotted. Other key information is given, such as the best way to get around the city and the locations of the subway stations.

Stars indicate the sights that no visitor should miss.

2 Street-by-Street Map
This gives a bird's-eye view of the heart of each sightseeing area. The numbering of the sights ties in with the area map and the fuller descriptions on the pages that follow.

Beijing and Shanghai Area Map

The coloured areas shown on this map (see inside front cover) are the city areas covered by this guide.

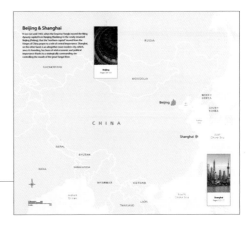

Practical information lists all the information you need to visit every sight, including a map reference to the Street Finder at the end of each chapter.

Numbers refer to each sight's position on the area map and its place in the chapter.

3 Detailed Information on each Sight

All important sights in each area are described in depth in this section. They are listed in order, following the numbering on the *Area Map*. Practical information on opening hours, telephone numbers, websites, admission charges and facilities available is given for each sight. The key to the symbols used can be found on the back flap.

The Visitors' Checklist provides the practical information you need to plan your visit.

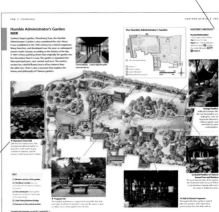

Stars indicate the most interesting architectural details of the sight, and the most important works of art or exhibits on view inside.

4 Major Sights

These are given two or more full pages in the sightseeing area in which they are found. Historic buildings are dissected to reveal their interiors; and museums and galleries have colour-coded floor plans to help you find important exhibits.

INTRODUCING BEIJING & SHANGHAI

GREAT DAYS IN BEIJING AND SHANGHAI

As two of China's most iconic and rapidly redeveloping cities, Beijing and Shanghai change on an almost weekly basis. Whether you are staying for several days, or just wanting a flavor of these great cities, you will need to make the most of your time. Over the following pages, you will find itineraries for some of the best attractions these cities have to offer, from themed days out to five-day

sightseeing extravaganzas. There's a mix of activities, and the schedules are not meant to be rigid – you'll find ample time to explore places that take your fancy. Sights are cross-referenced to the rest of the guide so you can look up more information and tailor the day to suit your needs. Price guides on these pages show the cost for two adults, or a family of four, excluding meals.

Historic Beijing – Empire to Republic

Two adults allow ¥300

- **Experience imperial splendor at the Forbidden City**
- **Stand on the spot where modern China began**
- **Pay your respects to the embalmed Chairman Mao**

Morning
Start early at **Jing Shan Park** *(see p72)* at the east side where the last Ming emperor hanged himself on a tree known as the Guilty Sophora. Climb to the top of the hill for a spectacular view south across the roofscape of the **Forbidden City** *(see pp66–71)*. Just below is the northern entrance to the palace. It would be easy to spend a day here, but for a first taste rent an audio guide and travel south along the main axis, through the emperors' private quarters contained within the Inner Court, and past the Hall of Union and the Palace of Earthly Tranquility *(see p64)*. This simple walk will take up much of the morning. There are numerous snack restaurants

Heroic Socialist sculptures in front of Mao's Mausoleum

dotted around, marked on maps located in the complex.

Afternoon
Leave the palace by the main entrance to pass through the **Tian'an Men** *(see p63)*; buy a ticket that allows you to mount the Ming-era gate and stand where Mao stood to announce the formation of the People's Republic on October 1, 1949. The Chairman's embalmed body lies in his **Mausoleum** *(see p62)*, which is straight ahead at the focal point of the square. Before entering, you must deposit all bags at the dedicated cloakroom

located south of the **National Museum of China** *(see p63)*. The museum presents a manipulated history of China through some of the most famous treasures of the imperial era as well as photos and installations chronicling the Communist rule since 1949. Finish the day by walking to the southern end of Tian'an Men Square and ascending the **Qian Men** *(see p62)*, one of the last relics of the Ming city walls.

Family Beijing – Insects to Acrobats

Family of four allow ¥1,000

- **Visit the Guanyuan market for flowers, birds, fish, and insects**
- **Enjoy the green spaces at the Temple of Heaven**
- **Partake in a traditional tea ceremony**
- **See an acrobatic show**

Morning
Spend a few hours exploring some of Beijing's favorite pastimes: *hua, niao, yu, chong* – flowers, birds, fish, and insects – by taking a taxi to the Guanyuan Market to see all four in action, especially the insect vendors in the alley at the rear. Jump on the subway at nearby Fucheng Men and ride four stops north to Jishuitan. This is the beginning of the **Hou Hai walk** *(see pp104–5)*, which you can follow as far as the restored Mei Lanfang Memorial Hall. At this point, taxi south for a fantastic seafood lunch at **Kong Yiji** *(see p202)*.

Tian'an Men, the imposing gate from which the square takes its name

◄ Detail from *Emperor Hui Tsung (r.1100–26) transporting pierced stones*, from *A History of the Emperors of China* (color on silk)

Practicing *tai ji quan* at the Temple of Heaven

Afternoon
From the restaurant it is a short walk to the magnificent **Temple of Heaven** *(see pp78–81)*, where you can admire the many and varied historial buildings while seeing locals enjoying the green spaces, playing board games, and exercising. Turn back north to pay a visit to the **Purple Vine Teahouse** *(see p112)*, just outside the Forbidden City's west gate, for tea in a traditional setting. In the evening, you have the option of **Beijing Opera** or **traditional acrobatic performances** in historic surroundings at either the Huguang Guildhall or Zhengyici Theater *(see p111)*. Children will definitely prefer the latter.

Alleyways and Avenues of Shanghai

Two adults allow ¥500
- Shop on Nanjing Road
- Explore the bazaars and backstreets of the Old City
- Stroll the historic Bund

Morning
The pedestrianized part of **Nanjing Road**, *(see p128)*, was once known as the best shopping street in China. With everything from "old-school" Chinese stores to global luxury outlets, it remains the city's most atmospheric avenue for shopping and street entertainment. From here, walk or take a taxi to the Old City and the busy **Yu Gardens Bazaar** *(see p134)*. Most of the flying-eaved

buildings here are of recent construction but there is the working City God Temple, the Yu Gardens, and the Huxinting Teahouse as well as lots of shops. Enjoy lunch in one of the dumpling restaurants but be sure to arrive early as they get very busy.

Afternoon
Walk west from the bazaar among the winding alleyways of the Old City to glimpse a vision of the past – old people sit outside their homes playing *mah jong* while the washing billows overhead and bicycles cut through the narrow paths. Pass old temples, mosques, and markets, before cutting north to **Huaihai Middle Road** *(see p136 and 166)* once the grand Avenue Joffre and now where the chic department stores and malls reside. This isn't the place for bargains but it is fun window-shopping alongside the Chinese.

Finish the day by taking a taxi to the **Bund** *(see pp126–7)*, where Nanjing Road meets the river-front. The Bund was known as the "Wall Street of Asia" in the early 19th century and the strip of heritage stone mansions is now home to some of the city's most glamorous dining and drinking establishments – it is the perfect place to enjoy a stroll and a drink as the sun sets.

Gardens of Suzhou

Two adults allow ¥350
- Enjoy a canal boat ride
- Stroll around gardens designed over generations

Morning
Suzhou *(see pp148–53)* is close to Shanghai but an early trip by train, which will take around 30 minutes, is recommended. One of many canal towns, it is nicknamed the "Venice of the East." Begin with a ride in the local equivalent of a gondola, taken from across the road from the railway station, and alight at the **Pan Men Scenic Area** *(see p153)*. Here you can climb up to the Ruiguang Pagoda to enjoy views of the city from 140 ft (43 m). Afterwards head by cab to the **Suzhou Museum** *(see p148)*, which illuminates the area's rich cultural and archaeological history. Next, visit the sprawling **Humble Administrator's Garden** beside the museum *(see pp150–51)*.

Afternoon
Take a taxi north to visit Suzhou's gardens such as the quiet, intimate **Ou Yuan** *(see p148)* or the **Master of the Nets Garden** *(see p152)*, considered the most satisfying for its balance feng shui.

Monks at the City God Temple in the Yu Gardens Bazaar

The Drum Tower, in ancient times used to alert the city-dwellers to danger

Architectural Highlights – 2 Days in Beijing

- **Marvel at the Confucius Temple, which contains China's oldest city map**
- **Explore the timeless imperial splendor of the Forbidden City**
- **See Ai Weiwei's stunning Olympic Stadium**

Day 1
Morning Start your day in Wudaoying Hutong, an increasingly hip neighborhood with courtyard cafés and cool boutiques, before heading in the direction of Guozijian, home of the **Confucius Temple** *(see p75)*. The temple has been a center of learning for hundreds of years and is remarkably well preserved. A 20-minute walk down Gulou East Street will take you to the imposing **Drum** and **Bell Towers** *(see p74)*. The Drum Tower dates back to 1420.

Afternoon Spend a few hours taking in the architectural magnificence of the **Forbidden City** *(see pp66–71)*, a breataking relic of dynastic China.

Day 2
Morning West of Tian'an Men Square, just steps away from the Soviet-style architecture of the **Great Hall of the People** *(see p62)*, is the **National Center for the Performing Arts** *(see p111)*. This beautiful dome structure

overshadows the older building both literally and figuratively, as a new style of architecture takes centre stage. Further west is the **Capital Museum** *(see p83)*, whose design is inspired by ancient Chinese architecture whilst being fiercely modern.

Afternoon A drive past the **CCTV Headquarters** *(see p89)* is well worthwhile: architect Rem Koolhas said he was not sure whether the twisted design was even possible, but the tower seems to be holding itself up nicely and has become one of Beijing's newest landmarks. Finish your day with a visit to the **Olympic Stadium** *(see p89)*, and get up close to the extraordinary bird's-nest structure that in itself was one of the stars of the 2008 Games.

A statue of the great man welcomes visitors to the Confucius Temple

Gourmet Getaway – 2 Days in Beijing

- **Sample the Beijing breakfast of champions**
- **Tuck into world-class crispy duck**
- **Try something different from China's desert west**

Day 1
Breakfast Start your day as Beijingers have for generations with a *jian bing* pancake, from any one of the thousands of street food stalls around the city. It's a pancake wrapped around a *youtiao* – a crispy, deep-fried dough stick – topped with an egg, spring onion and lashings of hot chilli sauce.

Lunch For lunch, head to atmospheric lantern-lined Gui Jie, or Ghost Street, so called because in ancient Beijing this was the only way for dead bodies to be taken out of the city. The street is considered to be cursed and only restaurants are thought to thrive here – so there are plenty to choose from.

Dinner You can't come to the capital without trying the city's eponymous dish – amid a raft of Peking duck restaurants, **Siji Minfu** is number one *(see p197)*, marrying tradition and quality. As custom dictates, the bird itself is served in three stages – first the crispy skin, which is dipped into sugar; then the moist meat, rolled up in pancakes; then the aromatic duck soup that finishes the dish.

Day 2
Breakfast Ease into another day with breakfast at one of the many restaurants in the heart of Sanlitun, which also happens to be one of the city's best destinations for shopping. Spend the rest of the morning cruising the boutiques and visiting **Yaxiu Market** *(see pp108–9)*.

Lunch Head to **Qian Men Dajie** *(see p64)*, famous for restaurants specializing in delicious, tender *jiaozi* (dumplings), served with tasty dipping sauce.

Dinner Seek out a restaurant specializing in the cuisine of Xinjiang province, such as **Crescent Moon** *(see p196)* or one of the other courtyard restaurants. In the far west of China, Xinjiang – only slightly smaller than Mexico – is largely desert. Its people are Uighur Muslims, whose diet is very different from the rest of China, and it's one few Westerners have experienced. Order juicy lamb kebabs sprinkled with cumin and coriander, washed down by Xinjiang-brewed beer.

The Summer Palace, the imperial retreat fom the heat of the city

5 Days in Beijing

- Visit the political, cultural, and spiritual center of China: Tian'an Men Square
- Conquer the hill in Jing Shan Park to enjoy spectacular views of the Forbidden City
- Soak up the atmosphere at the incense-fragrant Lama Temple
- Travel back through the dynasties with a visit to the Great Wall

Day 1
Morning Get up early and head for China's historic center, **Tian'an Men Square** *(see pp62–3)*. If you have time, take the subway there; the experience of climbing the stairs and suddenly finding yourself in such an iconic spot is not to be missed. Depending on your interests, a trip to **Chairman**

Mao's Mausoleum *(see p62)* in the center of the square could be on the cards, as could a tour of China's "parliament", the **Great Hall of the People** *(see p62)* on its west.

Afternoon Join the crowds that flock to the **Forbidden City** *(see pp66–71)*, an unmissable spectacle thanks to its dramatic history and jaw-dropping architecture. The palace is vast, but if you can reach the north end and climb the hill in **Jing Shan Park** *(see p72)*, you will be rewarded with a perfect view of the complex, plus a glimpse of the space-age **National Center of the Performing Arts** *(see p111)* to the right.

Day 2
Morning The Olympics may long be over, but the awesome architecture of the stadia serve as an enduring reminder of the drama and excitement. Take a taxi or the subway to the **Olympic Stadium** *(see p89)* in

the north of the city for a look at its fascinating design. Don't miss the iconic Australian-designed aquatic center known as "The Cube"; its exterior resembles blue bubble-wrap.

Afternoon Head west to the sprawling **Summer Palace** *(see pp84–7)* and see where the imperial family used to spend the warmer months away from the confines of the Forbidden City. Although a popular tourist destination, there are peaceful corners to be found.

Day 3
Morning First thing, take a taxi to the **798 Art District** *(see p89)* and enjoy wandering around the area's many galleries, studios, boutiques and cafés. It's a mecca for serious art collectors; prices are high but there is no charge for looking.

Afternoon After experiencing the energy and color of China's modern art scene, for a great,

Magnificent by day and when illuminated at night, the "bird's nest" Olympic Stadium

Pedestrianized Duolun Road, lined with pretty historic buildings and arts and curio shops

but equally colorful, contrast in style head to the **Lama Temple** *(pp74–5)*, the city's largest and most atmospheric Buddhist temple. Look out for yellow-robed monks and the sandal-wood statue of Maitreya.

Day 4
Morning History enthusiasts and Sinophiles cannot afford to miss the harmonious splendor of the **Temple of Heaven** *(see pp78–81)* in the south of the city. Completed during the Ming dynasty, it is a paradigm of Chinese architectural balance and symbolism. Alongside the dazzling buildings, the wide green spaces make for a refreshing change from the bustle of the city.

Afternoon A short taxi ride away is **Qian Men** *(see p64)*, the city's oldest shopping district and now a lively and interesting place to soak up the sights and sounds of old-meets-modern Beijing. Take the 1930s-style tram, which ferries footsore shoppers the full length of the street.

Day 5
Either book yourself on a tour or hire a car to visit the **Great Wall** *(see pp94–7)*. Mutianyu has the longest fully restored part of the Wall open to tourists, and is less crowded than the Badaling section, but Badaling is easier if you also want to see the **Ming Tombs** *(see pp92–3)*.

Architectural Highlights – 2 Days in Shanghai

- Discover Art Deco gems including the famous Peace Hotel
- See restored traditional *shikumen* houses and peek down the alleyways of old Shanghai
- Stroll along car-free Duolun Road, stopping to explore the many antique shops en route

Day 1
Morning Few cities have as many well-preserved Art Deco gems as Shanghai. Start your day at the **Bund** *(see pp126–7)* to view buildings such as the Bank of China, the Former Bank

The famous Peace Hotel on the Bund, still redolent of its 1930s heyday

---

of Communications, and the grand old Peace Hotel. Art Deco buffs should also check out the **Majestic Theater** *(see p168)* on Nanjing West Road, which is still in use today, and the nearby Park Hotel and its neighbor, the former Chinese YMCA.

Afternoon Explore **Soong Qingling's Former Residence** *(see p142)*, a gracious, *Empire of the Sun*-era villa that was the home of the wife of Dr. Sun Yat Sen. Her limousines, one a gift from Stalin, are still in the garage. Nearby on Henshang Road are the Georgia and Washington apartments, stylish 1930s residential buildings.

Day 2
Morning Start your day in **Xintiandi** *(see p161)*, where one of the elegant *shikumen* houses, the Shikumen Open House Museum, can be explored; its carefully restored two storys are fascinating to wander around. In the lanes surrounding Xintiandi, you can still glimpse timeless vestiges of authentic lane life.

Afternoon Head to **Duolun Road** *(see p165)*, north of the Bund, lined with antique shops and rows of stately brick *shikumen* houses down *long-tang*, or alleyways. This district served as the International Settlement in colonial Shanghai, and many famous artists and writers lived here.

5 Days in Shanghai

- See the city laid out in front of you from the dizzy heights of the Shanghai Tower

- Stroll past the Bund's architectural gems, hints of a bygone age

- People-watch at the leafy French Concession

- See priceless Chinese artifacts at the Shanghai Museum

- Explore China's cutting-edge contemporary art scene at Long Museum

Shanghai Museum, designed in the shape of a *ding* (an ancient bronze cooking vessel)

Day 1

Morning Start your visit up in the clouds – head to the 1,840 ft- (561 m-) high observation deck of the **Shanghai Tower** (see p141). Back on the ground, the walk along the **Pudong Riverside Promenade** (see p127) gives fabulous views of the grand buildings along the Bund and the steady flow of river traffic.

Afternoon Cross the river by subway, tunnel, or ferry, and stroll along the iconic **Bund** (see pp126–7), stopping at classic Art Deco buildings such as the Peace Hotel and the Bank of China.

Day 2

Morning Walk past the elderly people who gather to practice *tai chi* in **People's Square** (see p128–9) and spend a couple of hours at the magnificent **Shanghai Museum** (see

pp130–33). The eleven galleries cover all of the major categories of ancient Chinese art including bronze, jade, ceramics, calligraphy and painting. For something more avant-garde, **MOCA Shanghai**, the Museum of Contemporary Art (see p129) is a 10-minute walk away in neighboring People's Park.

Afternoon Back to People's Square and the **Urban Planning Exhibition Hall** (see p128) to see how Shanghai will look in 2020 and view recreations of its past. While in the neighborhood, a quick walk down pedestrianized **Nanjing Road** (see p128) will astound you with the epic scale of capitalism on show.

Day 3

Morning Stroll along Fangbang Middle Road, lined with shopping and snack stalls. Visit **Yu Gardens and Bazaar** (see pp134–5) early, before the crowds pack in. Refuel with local *xiao long bao* dumplings at one of

the restaurants in the bazaar, then enjoy the tranquillity at the atmospheric **Chenxiangge Nunnery** (see p160) nearby.

Afternoon Catch a cab to the **Mogan Shan Art District** (see p165) near the train station and spend a few hours taking in the most cutting-edge Chinese art. The venerable **Jade Buddha Temple** (see p138), still a working monastery, is also nearby.

Day 4

Morning Walking the **French Concession** (see p136) is a fine way to soak up the city's unique atmosphere. Browse the quaint alleyways, boutiques, and cafés of **Xintiandi** (see p161) and choose a spot for lunch.

Afternoon After a quick stop off at **Fuxing Park** (see p136), a French-style garden, wander down the leafy shopping streets of Xinle Lu, Changle Lu, and Fumin Lu, lined with the small boutiques of local designers.

Day 5

Morning Opened in 2014, the **Long Museum at West Bund** (see p143) is a private art collection. While away the morning admiring the stunning contemporary art inside and the intriguing architecture outside.

Afternoon For a full day of art, head to the **YUZ Museum** (see p143) at Xuhui Riverside. This outstanding institution is made up of former aircraft hangars filled with the best of contemporary Asian art.

Tranquillity among the lakes and greenery of Fuxing Park

Putting Beijing & Shanghai on the Map

Beijing sits on a plain 25 miles (40 kilometers) east of the mountains that once offered protection from the war-like tribes of the provinces beyond. It is one of very few capitals not sited on a major river system. By contrast, Shanghai sits on the banks of the Huangpu River, on silt carried down in the muddy waters of the Yangzi and washed up the Huangpu with the tide. Since rapid development began in the 19th century, constant dredging has been necessary.

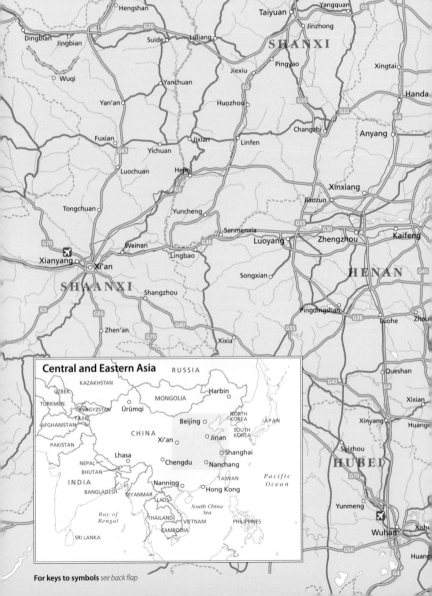

For keys to symbols see back flap

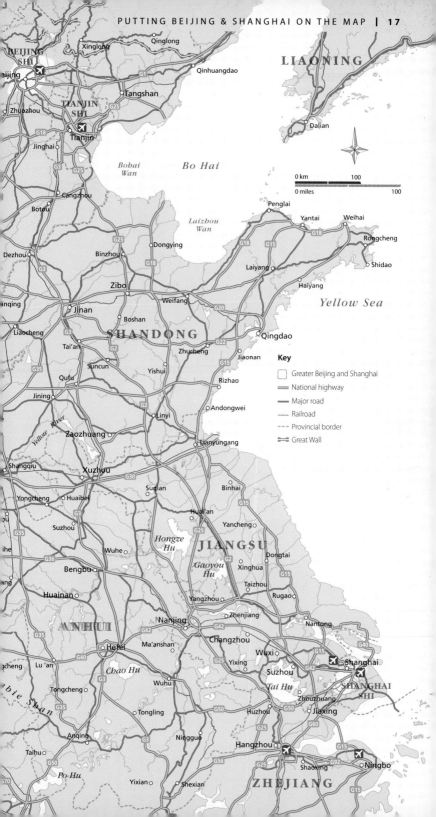

A PORTRAIT OF BEIJING & SHANGHAI

The two cities of Beijing and Shanghai have long loomed large in the Western imagination, one as the capital of an ancient and cultured civilization, all temples and ceremony, and the other as a legendarily louche 19th-century collision of Western and Eastern cultures, famed as the "Paris of the East."

The modern-day realities are rather different. Standing in the shadow of towering glassy skyscrapers and partly obscured by clouds of construction dust and traffic pollution, the two cities seem to be rapidly converging towards a culturally unspecific modernity that already sees Shanghai appearing as an anonymous urban landscape of the future in Western science fiction films. In both cities, boulevards have been driven through narrow alleys, and ancient courtyard housing is disappearing beneath shopping malls and tower blocks. Rapid regeneration of the infrastructure of both Beijing and Shanghai was judged necessary for the Beijing Olympics in

2008 and the 2010 Shanghai World Expo. Change and growth are common to all developing cities, but here they seem to be happening much faster and on a much larger scale than anywhere else. Beyond the similarities are some profound regional differences and historic rivalries – the citizens of Beijing and Shanghai are particularly well-known for needling each other, each with a sense of pride based on their home cities' fundamentally different histories and cultural traditions. Despite the long periods spent under foreign rule, Beijingers see themselves as the truly Chinese inheritors of a rich imperial culture, while Shanghainese are perhaps more future-oriented, and see

Crowded Bin Jiang Avenue, the Bund, Shanghai

◄ Elaborate costume and formalized gestures used in the colorful Beijing Opera

Early morning exercises along the waterfront promenade of the Bund, Shanghai

themselves as the open-minded absorbers and interpreters of foreign culture and commerce to the rest of China. The Shanghainese inevitably look east from the Bund across the river to the gleaming towers of Pudong, a mini-Manhattan where the new 2,070 ft (632 m) Shanghai Tower surpasses even the 101-floor Shanghai World Financial Center. Pudong is a three-dimensional advertisement for Shanghai's booming economy, designed to increase the confidence of foreign investors. Shanghai has the highest average income per household in China, and leads the emergence of a middle class, tiny as a percentage of the overall population of China, but still larger than the populations of many a European nation.

The Political Capital

Beijing's response to Pudong has been to embark on a concerted building program of its own, with a roster of spectacular architecture. There is the Central Business District to either side of the East Third Ring Road, which features the flamboyant CCTV Headquarters building by Holland's Rem Koolhaas, and the 1,000 ft (330 m) China World Trade Center Summit tower, Beijing's tallest building. Elsewhere, Frenchman Paul Andreu's startling egg-shaped National Center for the Performing Arts rises immediately west of Tian'an Men Square, and Briton Norman Foster's dragon-shaped Terminal 3 increases capacity at the international airport. Herzog & de Meuron's Olympic Stadium in the shape of a giant bird's nest located on the city's historic north–south axis, directly north of the Forbidden City, was home to the Beijing Olympic Games in 2008.

And while Shanghai may be the country's commercial center, political shifts register on Beijing's seismometer first. Word-of-mouth from within the government's high-security Zhong Nan Hai compound, the modern equivalent of the Forbidden City, typically fuels whispered debate amongst the city's inhabitants, who see themselves as the closest to power.

On a more personal level, Beijingers consider themselves cultured but laid-back, and both admire and resent the notorious business acumen of their big-city rivals to the south. The former consider the latter *jinjinjijiaode* or calculating. In return, the Shanghainese consider Beijingers to be no less calculating – it's just that they hide it behind a smoothly political exterior. The Shanghainese are proud of their familiarity with foreign things, and foreigners on the street attract less attention there than they do in Beijing. Quentin Tarantino's visit to Beijing for *Kill Bill* caused considerable buzz among the class tuned in to foreign culture. In contrast, Tom Cruise's visit to Shanghai for *Mission: Impossible III* produced only a studied yawn. The 2012 James Bond film *Skyfall* features scenes shot in Shanghai.

Shanghainese often consider Beijingers, and especially any still speaking the outmoded language of politics, as country bumpkins.

City Talk

Beijingers often regard Mandarin, the official national language of China, of administration, and of a classical education, as their own dialect. But the local habit of adding a retroflex "r" suffix to many words gives their pronunciation a non-standard growl, and makes it sound as if they are rolling the language around their mouths like wine-tasters, before spitting it out.

Shanghainese is a language incomprehensible to all other Chinese except

Praying at the Lama Temple, Beijing

some from neighboring Zhejiang and Jiangsu Provinces (the original homes of most Shanghai people or their forebears).

In anticipation of a larger than usual influx of visitors for internationally high-profile events, the government has been calling for increased levels of culture and civilization, sometimes despairing of the citizens of both cities. Some Beijing men have a habit of taking off their shirts and rolling up their trousers above the knee in hot weather, while Shanghainese of both sexes wear Western-style pajamas in the street. Campaigns against such behavior have joined those against spitting and swearing.

But, however much the government strives to dress up both populations and skylines into a uniform readiness to receive visitors, no one should regard either city as representing any more than itself, each with a distinctly different spirit.

One of the large fashion retailers on Shanghai's Nanjing West Road

Language and Script

The Chinese script can be traced back to the oracle bones of the Shang dynasty (16th–11th centuries BC) that were inscribed with symbols representing words and used for divination. Despite changes brought about by different writing materials, Chinese characters have remained remarkably consistent. It is said that to read a newspaper takes knowledge of at least 3,000 characters, but an educated person would be expected to know over 5,000. Since 1913, the official spoken language has been *Putonghua* (Mandarin) but there are many regional dialects. Although people from different parts of China may not be able to understand each other, they can use a shared written script.

Cang Jie, minister of the legendary Yellow Emperor, was supposedly inspired to invent the Chinese script one morning after seeing bird and animal tracks in the snow.

A Beautiful Script

Writing was elevated to an art form considered on a par with painting as a visual aesthetic (see pp30–31). As the process changed from inscribing bone, brass or stone to using a brush on silk and paper, a more fluid writing style became possible.

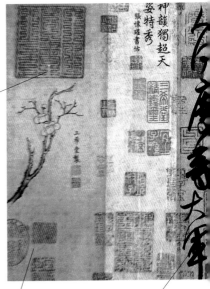

Seal, in red cinnabar – this may be a name seal, or inscribed with other characters.

Oracle bones display China's first examples of seal script. Questions were inscribed on the bones, which were then burnt – the way cracks divided the inscriptions was deemed significant.

Bamboo slats were used from around the 5th century BC. These were tied together to make the earliest type of books. Used for administrative and philosophical texts, the script runs from top to bottom.

Writing materials were silk, stone, or paper, which was first invented around the 2nd century BC.

Cursive script *(cao shu)* has strokes that run into each other. Fluid and dynamic, it allows for great expressiveness.

The Diamond Sutra (AD 868) is the world's first block-printed book to bear a date. Printing was probably invented about a century earlier. Movable block printing was developed in the 11th century but had less social impact than in Europe because of the thousands of symbols required.

Chinese Characters

Characters may be composed of pictographic, ideographic and phonetic elements. The radical (or root), an element that appears on the left or at the top of a character, usually gives a clue as to sense. Here, in the character for "good," pronounced "hao," the radical combines with another meaning element "child." The concept, therefore, is that "woman" plus "child" equals "good."

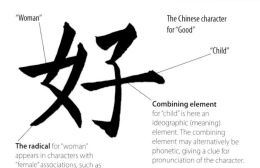

"Woman"

The Chinese character for "Good"

"Child"

Combining element for "child" is here an ideographic (meaning) element. The combining element may alternatively be phonetic, giving a clue for pronunciation of the character.

The radical for "woman" appears in characters with "female" associations, such as "milk," "wife," and "sister."

Pinyin is a Romanization system that was introduced in 1956. While Pinyin will never replace the character forms, it is an easier method for children to start learning the language and useful for input to computers.

Chinese typewriters were very difficult to use. The typist had to find each character in a tray of thousands. Computers have made typing Simplified script much easier – the user types in the Pinyin and gets a sub-menu of several possible characters.

Styles of Calligraphy

Zhuanshu, or seal script, was developed during the Zhou era and used for engraved inscriptions.

Lishu, or clerical script, probably evolved during the Han era and was used for stone inscriptions.

Kaishu, or regular script, developed from Lishu after the Han era, is the basis of modern type.

Cao shu, or cursive script, literally grass script, has strokes that are reduced to abstract curves or dots.

Xingshu, or running script, has strokes that run together, and is a semicursive script.

Simplified script was introduced in 1956 to make it easier for peasants to learn to read.

Chinese Literature

Dating back to the sixth century BC, the earliest Chinese texts were primarily philosophic, such as the Confucian *Analects* and Daoist *Daode Jing*. History as a literary genre was not established until the Han period (206 BC–AD 220) with Sima Qian's *Historical Records*: thereafter each dynasty wrote a history of the preceding one. As for the novel, a fully fledged Chinese example did not appear until the Ming period (1368–1644); the form developed during the Qing dynasty until it was eventually stifled by Communism. Since the 1980s, Chinese authors have been allowed greater freedom of expression, although in 2000, news of exiled writer Gao Xingjian's Nobel Prize for Literature was suppressed.

Confucius, author of the *Analects*, and his disciples

Classics

Post-Qin dynasty, once Confucianism had become the state orthodoxy, five early works were canonized as the Five Classics: the Book of Changes, Book of Documents, Book of Songs, Spring and Autumn Annals *and* Book of Ritual. *These books were established as the basis for Chinese education.*

The scholar class or literati achieved the status of government officials through success in the civil service examinations, based on detailed knowledge of the Classics and accomplishment in writing.

Tang Poets

With early beginnings in the Book of Songs *and* Elegies of Chu, *Chinese poetry reached its height more than twelve hundred years later in the Tang period (618–907). The two greatest Tang poets are considered to be Du Fu and Li Bai. Others include the Buddhist Wang Wei, also 8th-century, and slightly later Bai Juyi (772–846).*

Baoyu prefers to flirt with the women rather than obey his father and study hard to advance his career.

Du Fu (AD c.712–770) wrote of suffering in war, as well as of family life. His keynote is compassion, considered a Confucian virtue. His poems display enormous erudition.

Li Bai (AD c.701–761) was a more ebullient figure. A prolific poet, his favorite subjects were moon gazing and carousing. The theme of freedom from constraint is a Daoist one.

Epic Novels

In the Ming era, the novel developed from folk tales and myths into classics such as Journey to the West, Romance of the Three Kingdoms, *and* The Water Margin – *a tale of the heroic fight against corruption. Later, the Qing novels used a more elevated language and subtle characterization, culminating in the romantic novel,* Dream of the Red Chamber. *These novels contain many characters that reoccur in other cultural contexts from Beijing Opera to popular television serials and films.*

Guandi, God of War, derives from Guan Yu, a general of the state of Shu, portrayed in *Romance of the Three Kingdoms*. This novel was based on historical figures from the Three Kingdoms Era (AD 220–80). A symbol for justice, honesty, and integrity, his figurines are found in temples throughout China.

Journey to the West is a comic fantasy based on the pilgrimage to India of the Buddhist monk Xuanzang. The late Ming novel centers on Monkey, one of the monk's companions, who represents carefree genius, bravery, and loyalty.

Dream of the Red Chamber

Perhaps the greatest Chinese novel, this portrays the decline of an aristocratic Qing household. Infused with a Daoist sense of transcendence, it focuses on the life and loves of the idle Baoyu and twelve perceptively drawn female characters.

20th Century

In the early 20th century, fiction writers and playwrights addressed social issues in a new realist style. However, Communism demanded revolutionary themes. After the persecution of writers during the Cultural Revolution (see pp54–5), experimental forms and styles gradually emerged. However, the books of Chinese authors may still be banned if they are openly critical of the government or are "spiritual pollutants"; nevertheless, pirated versions are often widely available.

Mo Yan is a post-Cultural Revolution fiction writer. Best known for his novel *Red Sorghum* (1986), made into a major film, he writes in a rich style, often graphic, fantastic, and violent.

Lu Xun, early 20th-century writer of short stories and novellas, is known as the father of modern Chinese literature. His realist, satirical style is indebted to such writers as Dickens. He is renowned for his humorous depiction of Ah Q, an illiterate but enthusiastic peasant, done down by the forces of convention.

Religion and Philosophy

Traditionally, the three strands in Chinese religion and philosophy are Confucianism, Daoism, and Buddhism. An eclectic approach to religion allows the three to coexist, often within a single temple. Confucianism, the first to gain real influence, can be seen as a manifestation of the public, socially responsible self. Daoism represents a personal and wilder side; its emphasis on the relativity of things contrasts with Confucian concern for approved roles. Buddhism, a foreign import, is spiritual and otherworldly, offering an alternative to Chinese pragmatism. During the Cultural Revolution, religion was outlawed as contrary to Communist ideas. Today, people are largely able to express their beliefs.

Laozi, Buddha, and Confucius

Confucianism

Originated by Confucius (551–479 BC) and developed by later thinkers, Confucianism advocates a structured society in which people are bound to each other by the moral ties of the five familial relationships: parent-child, ruler-subject, brother-brother, husband-wife, and friend-friend. In Imperial China, Confucianism was the philosophy of the elite scholar-gentleman class. For much of the Communist era, it was reviled as a reactionary philosophy linked to the former ruling aristocracy.

Filial piety, or *xiao*, another Confucian precept, consists of obedience to and reverence for one's parents, and by extension respect for other family members and one's ruler.

Confucius was a thinker and teacher whose philosophy of family obligations and good government is based on the principles of *ren* (benevolence) and *yi* (righteousness). He died unknown, his disciples spreading his teachings.

The paying of respects to one's ancestors is based on filial piety and runs throughout Chinese culture. During the Qing Ming festival in April, Chinese traditionally clean and upkeep their ancestors' tombs.

The birth of Confucius is celebrated in the philosopher's home town of Qufu in late September. Many thousands of his descendants, all surnamed Kong, still live in the city.

Scholars collated the Confucian Classics including the *Lunyu (Analects)*, a series of Confucius's sayings, well after his death. The Classics were the basis of education until 1912.

Daoism

Strongly linked with early folk beliefs, Daoism incorporates the traditional concepts of an ordered universe, yin *and* yang, *and directed energy,* qi. *Over time, Daoism developed into a complex religion with an extensive pantheon. Daoist philosophy encourages following one's intuition and following the grain of the universe by living in accordance with the Dao.*

Laozi, the founder of Daoism, is a shadowy figure, who may have lived in the 6th century BC. The *Daode Jing*, which introduces the idea of Dao or the Way that permeates reality, is attributed to him.

Han Xiangzi, one of the Eight Immortals, a popular group of Daoist adepts, is believed to have fallen from a sacred peach tree, which bestowed eternal life. He is usually shown playing a flute.

Daoist alchemists aimed to find an elixir for eternal life, winning influence with emperors. Daoism influenced scientific development, and contributed to the discovery of gunpowder in the 9th century.

In "Peach Blossom Spring" by Daoist poet Tao Qian, a fisherman chances upon a lost idyllic world and encounters Immortals. Daoist reverence for nature led to the creation of numerous paradises.

Buddhism

In China, the Mahayana school of Buddhism, which promises salvation to anyone who seeks it, is followed. Enlightened ones, bodhisattvas, *remain in this world to help enlighten others. Through deeds and devotion, believers gain merit and maintain their connections with the* bodhisattvas, *bringing them closer to nirvana.*

The Laughing Buddha, or *Milefo*, is an adaptation of the Maitreya, the Future Buddha. His large belly and laughing face are signs of abundance and he is worshiped in the hope of a happy, affluent life.

The Guardian King of the South *(left)* is coiled by a snake; the King of the North holds a parasol. Kings of the four directions guard the entrance to many temples protecting the main deity from evil influences.

Luohans, or *arhats*, are the Buddha's disciples and often appear in temples in groups of 18. Their holiness is thought to enable them to achieve extinction (nirvana) on death.

A Buddhist supplicant burns sticks of incense in aid of prayer. Buddhist temples throb with spiritual energy, as worshipers pray and make offerings to gain merit.

Architecture

For over two thousand years, the Chinese have used the same architectural model for both imperial and religious buildings. This has three elements: a platform, post-and-beam timber frames, and non-loadbearing walls. Standard features of building complexes include a front gate, four-sided enclosures or courtyards, and a series of halls in a linear formation running north. Most Chinese buildings were built of wood, but because wooden buildings tend to catch fire, only a few structures remain; the earliest date from the Tang period.

The Forbidden City viewed from the front, showing the traditional linear layout

Hall

In every context, the Chinese hall, or *tang,* follows the same pattern: a platform of rammed earth or stone, and timber columns arranged in a grid. The front of the hall always has an odd number of bays. Between the columns and beams are brackets (*dougong*), cantilevers that support the structure, allowing the eaves to overhang. The timber is brightly painted, the roof aesthetically curved, and tiled or thatched.

Gate of Heavenly Purity *(see p68)*
An archetypal Chinese hall; the central doorway and uneven number of bays emphasize the processional element.

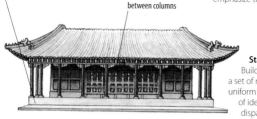

Base gives monumentality

Bay, or space between columns

Standard Hall
Buildings in China conformed to a set of rules about proportions. This uniform architecture created a sense of identity – useful in a large and disparate country.

Storied Building *(Lou)* and Storied Pavilion *(Ge)*

Multistory buildings in China predate pagodas and varied from two-storied private homes to huge seven- or more story towers built to enjoy the scenery. Storied pavilions were used for storage and had doors and windows only at the front. Both types of building kept the standard elements of base, columns, and hanging walls.

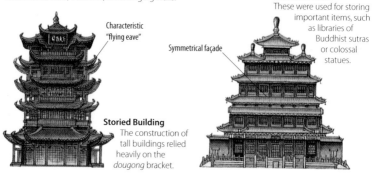

Characteristic "flying eave"

Symmetrical façade

Storied Pavilion
These were used for storing important items, such as libraries of Buddhist sutras or colossal statues.

Storied Building
The construction of tall buildings relied heavily on the *dougong* bracket.

Pagoda

Based on the Indian stupa, the Chinese pagoda, or *ta*, was developed in the first century AD along with the arrival of Buddhism. Multistoried pagodas appeared in Buddhist temple complexes (although later they often stood on their own) and were originally intended to house a religious relic. They were built of brick, stone, or wood.

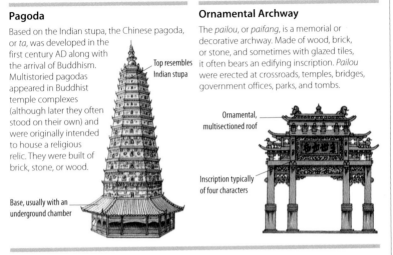

Top resembles Indian stupa

Base, usually with an underground chamber

Ornamental Archway

The *pailou*, or *paifang*, is a memorial or decorative archway. Made of wood, brick, or stone, and sometimes with glazed tiles, it often bears an edifying inscription. *Pailou* were erected at crossroads, temples, bridges, government offices, parks, and tombs.

Ornamental, multisectioned roof

Inscription typically of four characters

City Walls

Early defensive walls, like other early architectural forms, were made of earth – either pounded hard by pestles or moistened to make a clay and pressed around reed frames. Later walls were often built using brick. City walls were traditionally square, with the main gate to the south. The Chinese for "city" (*cheng*) also means "wall."

Easy to defend with a bow

Gate tower, often a two-story *lou*

City Wall and Gate
The towers on top of walls can vary from small buildings to palatial multistory structures.

City Walls
Typically made of rammed earth and brick, ramparts and watchtowers were an effective defense. Both Beijing and Shanghai were originally surrounded by such walls.

Architectural Details

It is interesting to interpret the architectural detail on Chinese buildings. The use of yellow tiles, for example, was reserved for the emperor. The Nine-Dragon Screen, which occurs in the Forbidden City and elsewhere, is also imperial since the dragon symbolizes the *yang*, or male principle, and by extension the emperor.

Chiwen
Able to douse flames with water, the Chiwen often appears at the end of a roof ridge (*see p67*) as a protection against fire.

Dougong
A bracket (*dougong*) transmits the load from roof to column. It is a traditionally complex, nail-free, and ornamental construction method.

Traditional Arts

The earliest Chinese artifacts were found in royal tombs. These include bronzes, ceramics, and jades from the Shang and Zhou period, as well as terracotta warriors from the Qin period. Of the many rich art forms that subsequently developed in China, painting and pottery are perhaps the most important, and have reached the highest aesthetic level. Other significant art forms include sculpture, notably the Buddhist sculpture of Western China. There are also many distinctive and popular forms of Chinese decorative art.

Buddhist sculpture in the Gandharan style

Ritual bronze tripod from an early royal tomb, decorated with a mythical animal design known as a *taotie*.

Wet and dry ink is used to give the detail of the trees.

Pottery

Since inventing porcelain, China developed a huge range of potting, decorating, and glazing techniques that were imitated from Europe to Japan. Chinese ceramics led the world in aesthetic taste and technique up until the demise of the Qing dynasty.

Tang earthenware tomb figure representing a fierce warrior, with typical rough *sancai* (three-color) drip glaze. This was a lead-based glaze, fired at a low temperature.

Textured strokes give the rocks depth.

Song celadon bowl with incised floral design. Celadon was the European name given to the refined gray-green glaze of this type of stoneware and porcelain.

Ming vase in the blue-and-white style known and imitated internationally. The technique involves underglaze painting in cobalt blue before the pot is fired.

Qing famille-rose vase, a delicate porcelain in a distinctive palette. The name comes from the use of bright pink enamel.

Bird-and-flower painting (including the depiction of fruit and insects reveals the Chinese Daoist interest in observing the natural world. Despite the lightness of subject, the paintings have an intense, quasi-scientific depth.

Chinese Painting

Considered the highest traditional art form, Chinese painting is executed on silk or paper using a brush and inks or watercolors. Land-scape painting, associated with the scholar class, reached a high point in the Northern Song and Yuan periods. Huang Gongwang, a master of the Yuan, was admired for his simple calligraphic style (see main image below).

Religious painting first appeared along the Silk Road with the arrival of Buddhism from India. The Chinese soon developed an individual style.

Ink wash is used for the hills in the distance.

Bamboo painting was a genre of the scholar class. Bamboo symbolized the scholar-gentleman who would bend but not break in the face of adversity.

Traditional Crafts

As well as the traditional high art forms of painting and pottery, China has a wealth of beautiful decorative arts. Delicate carvings in lacquer, ivory, and jade are popular, as are colorful cloisonné items, decorated inksticks (or cakes), snuff bottles, and fans.

Snuff bottles were produced in large numbers during the Qing period. Made of glass, jade, mother-of-pearl, or semi-precious stones, they were delicately carved or painted on the inside in exquisite detail.

Lacquer carving is distinctive for its deep red color and floral designs, and is often used on boxes.

Cloisonné is a style of enameling. Individual metal cloisons, usually made of copper, are soldered together and inlaid with different colored enamels. The object is then fired and polished.

Traditional Chinese Gardens

The Chinese garden developed as a synthesis of two concepts linked in Daoist philosophy: scenery and serenity. It was believed that the contemplation of nature in isolated meditation led to enlightenment. Therefore, the educated and wealthy built natural-looking retreats for themselves within an urban environment. The garden creates poetic and painterly concepts, and aims to improve on nature by creating a picture that looks natural but is in fact entirely artificial. For this, the Chinese garden designer used four main elements: rocks, water, plants, and architecture.

Classical Chinese garden design was considered a type of three-dimensional landscape painting or solid poetry.

Rocks: There were two main kinds of rock – the eroded limestones from lakes, often used as sculptures, or the yellow rock piled up to recall mountains and caves to the mind of the viewer. The beauty and realism of the rockery usually determined the success or failure of the garden.

Water: An essential element of life, water also could be used in the garden as a mirror and so appear to increase the size of the garden. Water also serves as a contrasting partner and therefore a balance to the hard stone. Finally, it is a home for goldfish, symbols of good fortune.

Interiors of pavilions were important as the venues for creativity. A lot of care was taken to select an appropriate and poetic name for each building.

Corridors, paths, and bridges link the different areas and give the artist control over how the views are presented to the visitor.

Patterns and mosaics brighten up the garden and are also symbolic. Cranes represent longevity, while the *yin* and *yang* symbol often appears where a path forks in two.

Garden Views

Using these four elements, the garden is like a series of tableaux painted onto a roll of silk. One by one they come before your eyes just as the artist intended them to. As you follow the paths, you see just what he wanted you to see. These may be borrowed views, where the scenery from somewhere else is made to look part of the picture; hidden views, where you round a corner to come upon an unexpected scene; contrasting views, where leafy bamboo softens the view of rock, or opposite views as the yin element water balances the yang element rock.

A moon gate is a round door that neatly frames a view as though it were a picture. Gates can be square-, jar-, or even book-shaped.

Patterned screens allow in a certain amount of light and may be used to cast patterned shadows on white walls. They are also sometimes used to give tempting partial views through to other areas of the garden.

Plants: Plants were used sparingly and usually for their symbolic qualities. Thus the lotus is purity, as it flowers from the mud; bamboo is resolve, as it is difficult to break; plum is vigor, as it blooms in winter; the pine is longevity, because it is evergreen; the imperial peony is wealth.

Buildings: An intrinsic part of the garden, these pavilions and waterside halls provide a place for contemplation and more importantly a specific viewpoint, as well as shelter from the sun and rain. They could range from open kiosks to multistory halls and meeting rooms.

Penjing

Dating as far back as the Tang dynasty (618–907), *penjing* is the art of creating a miniature landscape in a container. Not limited to small trees, the artist may use rocks and specially cultivated plants to portray a scene of natural beauty, as though it were a landscape painting. As well as being beautiful, the harmony in these creations is seen as the spiritual expression of man's relationship with nature, the meeting of the temporal with the omnipresent. Often, part of a Chinese garden will be devoted to the display or cultivation of this delicate art.

The Chinese art of *penjing*, the forerunner to Japanese bonsai

Beijing Opera

One among many hundreds of local operas across China, Beijing Opera began in the Qing dynasty. It is said that Emperor Qianlong (r.1736–96), on a tour of the south, was rather taken by the operas of Anhui and Hebei and brought these troupes back to Beijing, where a new form of opera was established. The Guangxu emperor and Dowager Empress Cixi were also keen devotees and helped develop the art form. Beijing Opera has proved remarkably resilient, surviving the persecution of actors and the banning of most of the plays during the Cultural Revolution.

Emperor Qianlong, credited with the start of Beijing Opera

Beijing Opera

Visually stunning and with a distinct musical style, the plays are based on Chinese history and literature. Beijing Opera is a form of "total theater" with singing, speech, mime, acrobatics, and symbolic visual effects.

Monkey is one of the favorite characters – clever, resourceful, and brave. He appears in Chinese classic literature (*see p25*).

The colors of the painted faces symbolize the individual character's qualities. Red, for example, represents loyalty and courage; purple, solemnity and a sense of justice; green, bravery and irascibility.

Riding a horse is represented by raising a tasseled horsewhip. Other actions and movement on the stage are similarly stylized rather than realistic.

The acrobatics of Beijing Opera combine graceful gymnastics and movements from the martial arts. Training is notoriously hard. The costumes are designed to make the jumps seem more spectacular by billowing out as they spin.

Musical Instruments

Despite the dramatic visual elements of Beijing Opera, the Chinese say that they go to "listen" to opera, not to see it. The importance of the musical elements should not therefore be underestimated. Typically, six or seven instrumentalists accompany the opera. The stringed instruments usually include the *erhu* or Chinese two-stringed violin, *sanxian* or three-stringed lute, and moon guitar, or possibly *pipa* (traditional lute). The main function of the instruments is to accompany the singing. Percussion instruments include clappers, gongs, and drums. These are used largely to punctuate the action; movement and sound are intimately linked. Wind instruments also sometimes feature, such as the Chinese horn, flute, and *suona*.

Gong

Suona   Pipa   Erhu

Mei Lanfang was the foremost interpreter of the female role type, or *dan*, during the opera's heyday in the 1920s and 1930s. Traditionally, all female roles were played by male actors, although that has now changed.

The Four Main Roles

There are four main role types in Beijing Opera: the sheng *(male) and* dan *(female) roles have naturalistic make-up. The* jing *or "painted faces," in contrast, have stylized patterned, colored faces, while the* chou *are comic characters.*

Sheng: these may be young or old, with beard or without.

Chou: with a white patch on his face, the *chou* is usually dim but amusing.

Dan: there are six parts within this role from virtuous girl to old woman.

Jing: the most striking looking, they also have the most forceful personality.

Modern Arts

The birth of modern art in China at the start of the 20th century coincided with greater contact with the West. Experiments with new materials and styles in the visual arts, Western-style music, "spoken drama" *(huaju)*, cinema, and modern literary forms such as free verse all took root at this time. However, after 1949, this creativity was stifled by Soviet-influenced Socialist Realism. During the Cultural Revolution, many artists were even persecuted on the grounds that their works were "reactionary." Since the 1980s, there has been some liberalization in the arts and new, exciting forms have developed.

The Oriental Pearl TV Tower, Pudong, Shanghai is among the buildings that reflect China's high-rise architecture boom since the early 1990s.

Shaven-headed man

This example of performance art is by Cang Xin, a Beijing-based conceptual artist, active since the mid-1990s. The title of this piece, *Unification of Heaven and Man*, alludes to classical Chinese philosophical concepts.

Modern Art

This painting, Series 2 No. 2, is by Fang Lijun, leader of the Cynical Realism school, which came about as a reaction to the demise of the pro-democracy movement in 1989. Rejecting idealism, these artists make fun of the problems of life in China.

Sculpture entitled *Torso*, by Zhan Wang, a Shanghai-based conceptual artist. Zhan uses reflective steel sheets to give the illusion of solidity.

Orchestral and chamber music has been popular in China since the early 20th century. There are many schools specializing in Western-style music, and several high-quality ensembles and artists on the world scene.

Chinese Cinema

From early classics such as Street Angel *(1937), Chinese cinema has scaled new heights of international success, with the work of such directors as Zhang Yimou, who produced the 2008 Beijing Olympics opening ceremony.*

Farewell My Concubine (1993), directed by Chen Kaige, a post-Cultural Revolution filmmaker who gave expression to new moral uncertainties, is set in the world of traditional Beijing Opera.

The Hong Kong film industry followed its own path and became primarily famous for its action movies. Renowned martial arts star Jackie Chan, seen above in an early acting and directorial debut, *Fearless Hyena*, made many films and successfully crossed over from Hong Kong to Hollywood.

Background is a hazy blue, making it appear dream-like

Wei Wei is one of the bestselling pop stars in China today, along with Jay Chou, who also stars in adverts and movies. Rock music only took off in the 1980s: Cui Jian, the "grandad" of Chinese rock, is seen as a rebel by the authorities. Hong Kong's less controversial Canto-pop singers enjoy more freedom.

Anonymous figures seem threatening

Main figure is yelling or yawning – is he angry or just bored?

Ballet in contemporary China mixes traditional Chinese and Western influences. Here, the ballet version of Zhang Yimou's film *Raise the Red Lantern* is performed by members of the National Ballet.

Modern theater provides an expression of Chinese life in the 21st century. Here, a scene from *Toilet* (2004), a black comedy, is performed by the National Theater company in Beijing. The play broke taboos with its frank portrayal of urban life and treatment of homosexuality.

BEIJING & SHANGHAI THROUGH THE YEAR

The dates of traditional Chinese festivals are tied to a lunar calendar, which has 29.5 days a month. This means that festival dates move around in the same manner as the Christian Easter does. Public holidays associated with Communism – National Day and International Labor Day, for example – are fixed on the familiar Gregorian (Western) calendar. Some celebrations of Western origin, such as Christmas, are also observed. Very few Chinese have any sort of discretionary holiday from work, so on the longer public holidays, a large proportion of the population takes to the road all at the same time. At such times it is unwise to attempt much travel, and many tourist attractions may be shut for a day or two *(see p41)*.

Spring

The four seasons are far more clearly marked in Beijing than in Shanghai, which tends to be either cool and humid, or hot and humid, year-round. Spring in Beijing sees seeds from the many scholar trees blown into drifts by winds that clear away the pollution. However, those same winds also sometimes bring scouring clouds of sand from the arid north-west, turning the skies dark and yellow.

A red lantern – lucky symbol

Chinese New Year, is a time when wage packets contain bonuses, debts must be settled, and everyone who can heads for their family home. Many temple fairs take place at this time, especially in Beijing, and these often feature stilt-walkers, acrobats, opera singers, and other traditional entertainments. Museums and most offices are shut for at least three days, many for longer, although a great deal of shopping goes on, commonly encouraged by department store sales.

Lion dancing, performed as part of Spring Festival celebrations

January–February
Spring Festival (Chun Jie) Beijing, Shanghai. This occurs with the first new moon after January 21, which will be February 8 in 2016, January 28 in 2017, February 16 in 2018, and February 5 in 2019. Spring Festival, which is also known as

February–March
Lantern Festival Beijing, Shanghai. Coinciding with a full moon, this festival marks the end of the 15-day Spring Festival period. Lanterns bearing auspicious characters or in animal shapes are hung everywhere. It is also a time for eating the sticky rice balls known as *yuanxiao*.

March
International Women's Day *(March 8)*, Beijing, Shanghai. A holiday, or half-day holiday, for women only; men go to work as usual.

March–April
Peach Blossom Festival Shanghai. This festival takes place among more than 6,175 acres (2,500 hectares) of peach orchards in the Nanhui District outside Shanghai over a two-week period in late March and early April, depending on the progress of the blossom. Visitors come to admire the trees and to eat at local homes that have temporarily become cafés, restaurants, and

Red lanterns form a tunnel in a Beijing park during the Lantern Festival

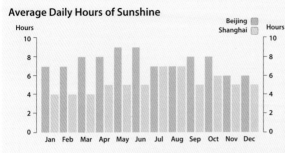

Average Daily Hours of Sunshine

Beijing ▮
Shanghai ▯

guesthouses, in a tradition called *nongjia le*.

April

Clear Brightness Festival (Qing Ming Jie) *(April 5)*, Beijing, Shanghai. Also known as the Tomb-Sweeping Festival, this takes place two weeks after the vernal equinox, usually April 5, but April 4 in leap years. People visit their ancestors' graves to make offerings of snacks and alcohol. Around this time, *qingtuan*, which are green sticky rice balls, are eaten.

Shanghai Formula One Grand Prix Shanghai. This is an entirely foreign event with no Chinese competitors. The 56-lap race takes place around a 3.3 mile (5.5 km) circuit.

Summer

Shanghai steams and drips as the heat steadily rises, and the increased usage of air-conditioning units causes electricity shortages and blackouts. On a more northerly latitude, Beijing is washed clean by intermittent showers, but it is otherwise hot and sticky.

May

International Labor Day *(May 1)*, Beijing, Shanghai. This was shortened from a three-day to a one-day holiday in 2008. It marks the start of the domestic travel season. This is the time of year when all Chinese people visit their families.

Meet in Beijing Beijing. This is a cultural festival running throughout all of May

A dragon boat, with the drummer setting the rhythm for the rowers

with an unpredictable mix of Chinese and foreign elements at a variety of venues around the city.

Art Beijing Beijing. China's biggest contemporary art fair is held in May each year.

June

Dragon Boat Festival (Duanwu Jie) Beijing, Shanghai. Held on the fifth day of the fifth lunar month (usually June), this popular festival features races between colorful dragon-headed boats. On-board drummers set the tempo and keep the twin rows of paddlers in unison. The festival honors the honest official Qu Yuan, who drowned himself after banishment from the court of the Duke of Chu nearly 2,500 years ago.

Shocked citizens threw rice cakes into the water to distract the fish from his body. Rice cakes are eaten today in the form of *zongzi*, pyramids of glutinous rice wrapped in river reeds and tied up with string. Races and pageantry can be seen at Qinglong Hu near the Ming Tombs outside Beijing, and on various lakes and rivers around Shanghai.

Shanghai International Film Festival Shanghai. Held over one week in mid-June, this celebration of celluloid showcases plenty of Chinese cinema unlikely to be seen much in the West – but don't expect anything beyond officially approved projects – along with a selection of unchallenging foreign fare. However, the festival is still important enough for international stars to put in an appearance.

Shanghai International Film Festival poster

Average Monthly Rainfall

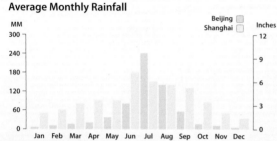

Beijing
Shanghai

Rainfall Chart
Typically for a coastal city, Shanghai is wet throughout the year. Beijing receives its greatest rainfall during the height of summer, when the prolonged and heavy downpours provide a welcome release from the seasonal heat.

Playing with a spinning top in a Beijing park in fall

Fall

The months of September and October are easily the best time to visit Beijing. The summer heat has gone and in its place are warm, dry days, with frequent cool breezes that clear the smog-laden skies. Farther south, the baking temperatures and humidity associated with summers in Shanghai have also dropped to more comfortable levels.

July–August
Qi Xi Beijing, Shanghai. Taking place on the seventh day of the seventh lunar month, which is usually August, Qi Xi celebrates the story of the earthly cowherd and celestial weaving girl who were separated by the gods but who are annually reunited in the heavens by a bridge of magpies. The Chinese equivalent of Valentine's Day, it is going through something of a modern revival, especially in Shanghai, where it involves much shopping for gifts and fully-booked restaurants.

August–September
Mid-Autumn Festival (Zhong Qiu Jie) Beijing, Shanghai. On the 15th day of the eighth lunar month (usually in September), this festival, also known as the Harvest or Moon Festival, is traditionally a time for family reunions. Shops fill with boxes of mooncakes (yuebing), extremely fattening pies filled with bean paste. As of 2008, China has a one-day national holiday on the closest working day to the Mid-Autumn festival.

Mooncake

October
National Day (October 1), Beijing, Shanghai. Marking the anniversary of Mao's speech in which he declared the foundation of the People's

National Day's massed military parades – a throwback to the days of Communist-era China

Average Monthly Temperature

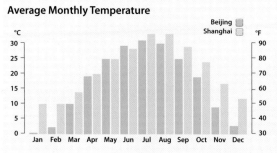

Beijing ▨
Shanghai ▨

Temperature Chart
Beijing annually endures extremes of temperature, with the thermometer often dropping below zero in winter and then threatening to blow in the heat of summer. Shanghai ranges from sultry to sweaty, with the heat exacerbated by humidity.

Republic. Crowds turn out to watch massive parades, particularly at Beijing's Tian'an Men Square. This is another three-day holiday that for most people and businesses expands into a full week. Every city sight and scenic rural tourist destination is crowded to its limits and beyond.

Rolex Shanghai Masters Tennis *(two weeks in October)*, Shanghai. Asia's flagship tennis event takes place at the Qizhong Tennis Center in Shanghai. Established in 2009, the tournament is one of nine ATP Masters 1000 events and the only tennis Masters to take place in Asia. More than 100 tennis professionals, including the world's best players, participate in 99 matches over a nine-day period. Information on court schedules, order of play, and ticket prices is available at www.shanghai rolexmasters.com.

Winter

Beijing winters are not only bitterly cold but dry: the briefest exposure to the arid atmosphere desiccates the face instantly. The dry air and cool temperatures also accentuate the creation of static electricity so be wary reaching for taxi and hotel door handles. By contrast, Shanghai is traditionally deemed to be warm enough year-round for private homes not to be heated, but although temperatures do not drop as low of those of Beijing, the humidity makes the cold more penetrating.

Typical Beijing winter weather – heavy snow and icy roads

Occasional strong winds make viewing Shanghai panoramas from a cosy room in your hotel seem far more attractive than actually venturing out.

December
Christmas Day *(December 25)*, Beijing, Shanghai. Although not a traditional holiday in China, this day has been adopted via Hong Kong, which means, of course, that there is a stress on the commercial aspect. Shopping malls and foreign-run hotels have conspired to press this idea upon the Chinese in major cities to the point that it is now rare for a high-street store not to acknowledge the holiday with images of *Shengdan Laoren*, the Chinese version of Father Christmas.

January
New Year's Day *(January 1)*, Beijing, Shanghai. Although overshadowed by the Spring Festival (Chinese New Year) celebrations that take place soon after *(see p38)*, Western New Year is still a public holiday, celebrated with gusto by the large number of expatriate foreigners living in Beijing and Shanghai.

Public Holidays

New Year's Day (Jan 1)

Spring Festival or Chinese New Year Feb 8, 2016; Jan 28, 2017; Feb 16, 2018; Feb 5, 2019

Tomb-Sweeping Day Apr 4, 2016; Apr 5, 2017; Apr 5, 2018; Apr 5, 2019.

International Labor Day (May 1)

Dragon Boat Festival Jun 9, 2016; 30 May, 2017; Jun 18, 2018; Jun 7, 2019

Mid-Autumn Festival Sep 15, 2016; Oct 4, 2017; Sep 24, 2018; Sep 13, 2019

National Day (Oct 1–3)

Avoid traveling during Spring Festival and the first weeks of May and October. At these times everyone who can afford to takes to the road, either on holiday or to visit relatives. Prices rise, and it is impossible to get a bus or train ticket, or an internal flight. However, traffic in Beijing and Shanghai thins and it can be a pleasant time to spend in either place.

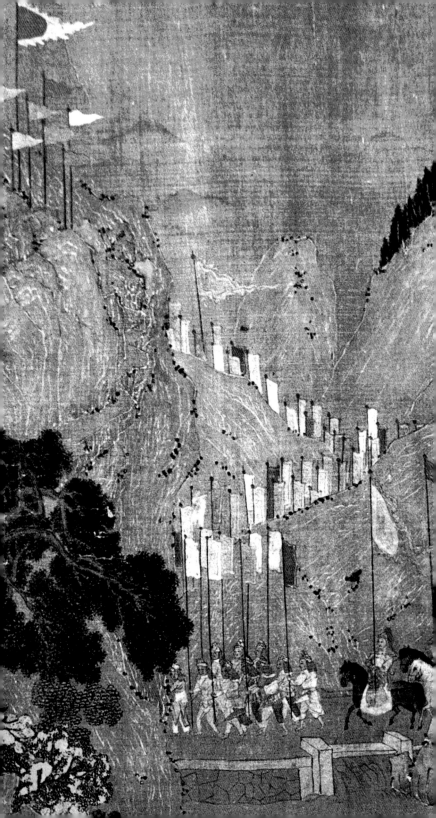

THE HISTORY OF CHINA

China boasts one of the longest single unified civilizations in the world. Its history is characterized by dramatic shifts in power between rival factions, periods of peace and prosperity when foreign ideas were assimilated and absorbed, the disintegration of empire through corruption and political subterfuge, and the cyclical rise of ambitious leaders to found each new empire.

First Settlers

From around 8000 BC, settlements of populations based on a primitive agricultural economy began to emerge in the eastern coastal regions and along the rich river deltas of the Huang He (Yellow River), the Yangzi, and the Wei. These civilizations focused on hunting, gathering, and fishing, and the cultivation of millet in the north and rice in the south. Each civilization is notable for its own distinct style of pottery, such as the bold earthenware of the Yangshao (5000–3000 BC) and the black ceramics of the Longshan (3000–1700 BC).

Bronze Age China and the First Kingdoms

The first dynasty in China was founded by the Shang around 1600 BC. The Shang lived in large, complex societies and were the first to mass-produce cast bronze. Power centered on the ruling elite who acted as shamans of a sort, communicating with their ancestors and gods through diviners. Elaborate bronze food and wine vessels were used both for banqueting and for making ancestral offerings. Inscriptions on oracle bones provide the first evidence of writing, dating from around 1300 BC. In 1066 BC, the Zhou seized power, establishing their western capital at present-day Xi'an. The Western Zhou initially sustained many of the traditions of the Shang, but later reorganized the political system, and replaced the use of oracle bones with inscriptions on bronze and, later, writing on silk and strips of bamboo.

The Eastern Zhou (770–221 BC) is divided into the Spring and Autumn period (770–476 BC) and the Warring States period (475–221 BC). The Eastern Zhou period was dominated by political conflict and social unrest, as rival factions jockeyed for power. It also saw economic expansion and development as the use of iron revolutionized agriculture. It was in this climate of unrest that the philosophical ideologies of Confucianism, Daoism, and Legalism emerged.

				1300 BC First writing on oracle bones	
	5000–3000 BC Yangshao culture based around the Wei river		2200–1600 BC Existence of semimythical first dynasty, the Xia		475–221 BC Eastern Zhou: Warring States
8000–6500 BC Neolithic period				c.551–479 BC Life of Confucius	
8000 BC	**6000 BC**	**4000 BC**	**2000 BC**	**1000 BC**	**500 BC**
	6500–5000 BC Earliest settlements in northern China		1600–1050 BC Shang dynasty	770–476 BC Eastern Zhou: Spring and Autumn period	513 BC First mention of iron casting
		Bronze food vessel, Shang	1066–771 BC Power seized by Zhou		

◄ Detail from "The first Emperor of the Han Dynasty Entering Guandong" by Song painter Chao Pochu

Dynasty Timeline

China was ruled by a succession of dynasties, interrupted by periods of fragmentation and civil war. The emperor's authority was divinely granted through a mandate of heaven and was thus unlimited. Leaders of succeeding dynasties claimed that the previous leadership had displeased the gods and had therefore had its heavenly mandate withdrawn.

Shang Dynasty

1600–1050 BC

The Shang dynasty marked the emergence of Bronze Age China and palace culture. A semi-divine king acted as a shaman and communicated with the gods.

Bronze tripod food vessel, Shang

Western Han

206 BC–AD 9

Gaozu	206–195 BC
Huidi	195–188 BC
Shaodi	188–180 BC
Wendi	180–157 BC
Jingdi	157–141 BC
Wudi	141–87 BC
Zhaodi	87–74 BC
Xuandi	74–49 BC
Yuandi	49–33 BC
Chengdi	33–7 BC
Aidi	7–1 BC
Pingdi	1 BC–AD 6
Ruzi	AD 7–9

Broken terracotta heads found at Jingdi's tomb

Eastern Han

AD 25–220

Guang Wudi	25–57	Shundi	125–144
Mingdi	57–75	Chongdi	144–145
Zhangdi	75–88	Zhidi	145–146
Hedi	88–105	Huandi	146–168
Shangdi	106	Lingdi	168–189
Andi	106–125	Xiandi	189–220

Tang

618–907

Gaozu	618–626	Jingzong	824–827
Taizong	626–649	Wenzong	827–840
Gaozong	649–683	Wuzong	840–846
Zhongzong	684 & 705–710	Xuanzong	846–859
Ruizong	684–690	Yizong	859–873
	& 710–712	Xizong	873–888
Wu Zetian	690–705	Zhaozong	888–904
Xuanzong	712–756	Aidi	904–907
Suzong	756–762		
Daizong	762–779		
Dezong	779–805		
Shunzong	805		
Xianzong	805–820		
Muzong	820–824		

Sancai-glazed dancing tomb figures

Five Dynasties & Ten Kingdoms

907–960

Based north of the Yangzi, five successive dynasties swiftly usurped one another, with no dynasty lasting for more than three reigns. The Ten Kingdoms to the south went through a similarly turbulent period. Throughout this period and most of the Song dynasty, the northern frontiers were dominated by the semi-nomadic Liao dynasty (907–1125) in the east, and by the Western Xia (990–1227) in the west. In 1115, the Liao were overthrown by the Jin (1115–1234), who forced the Song southwards in 1127.

Yuan

1279–1368

Genghis Khan (1162–1227) united numerous Mongol speaking tribes and captured Beijing in 1215. His grandson, Kublai, completed the conquest of China by finally defeating the Southern Song in 1279.

Kublai Khan	1279–1294
Temur Oljeitu	1294–1307
Khaishan	1308–1311
Ayurbarwada	1311–1320
Shidebala	1321–1323
Yesun Temur	1323–1328
Tugh Temur	1328–1329
	1329–1333
Khoshila	1329
Toghon Temur	1333–1368

Ming

1368–1644

Hongwu	1368–1398	Zhengde	1506–1521
Jianwen	1399–1402	Jiajing	1522–1567
Yongle	1403–1424	Longqing	1567–1572
Hongxi	1425	Wanli	1573–1620
Xuande	1426–1435	Taichang	1620
Zhengtong	1436–1449	Tianqi	1621–1627
Jingtai	1450–1457	Chongzhen	1628–1644
Tianshun	1457–1464		
(Zhengtong restored)			
Chenghua	1465–1487		
Hongzhi	1488–1505		

Western Zhou Dynasty

1066–771 BC

The Zhou founded their capital at Chang'an (Xi'an). They continued some Shang traditions, but reorganized the political system, dividing the nobility into grades. The feudal system of the Western Zhou broke down after the capital was sacked and the king slain.

Eastern Zhou Dynasty

770–221 BC

Spring and Autumn
770–475 BC

Warring States
475–221 BC

The Zhou dynasty ruled at its eastern capital of Luoyang alongside numerous rival states. This long period of almost constant warfare was brought to an end when the Qin emerged victorious.

Qin Dynasty

221–206 BC

Qin Shi Huangdi	221–210 BC
Er Shi	210–207 BC

Statue of attendant from the tomb of Qin Shi Huangdi

Period of Disunity

220–589

China was divided into the warring Wei, Wu, and Shu kingdoms. The Wei briefly re-united China under the Western Jin (280–316), the first of the six Southern Dynasties (280–589), with their capital at Jiankang (Nanjing). The north was ruled by a succession of ruling houses – the 16 Kingdoms (304–439). The nomadic Toba Wei set up the Northern Wei dynasty, the first of five Northern Dynasties (386–581) with a capital first at Datong, then at Luoyang.

Sui

581–618

China was once more united by the short and decisive rule of the Sui.

Wendi	581–604
Yangdi	604–617
Gongdi	617–618

Emperor Wendi's flotilla on the Grand Canal

Northern Song

960–1126

Taizu	960–976	Shenzong	1068–1085
Taizong	976–997	Zhezong	1086–1101
Zhenzong	998–1022	Huizong	1101–1125
Renzong	1022–1063	Qinzong	1126–1127
Yingzong	1064–1067		

Painting by Emperor Huizong

Southern Song

1127–1279

Gaozong	1127–1162
Xiaozong	1163–1190
Guangzong	1190–1194
Ningzong	1195–1224
Lizong	1225–1264
Duzong	1265–1274
Gongdi	1275
Duanzong	1276–1278
Di Bing	1279

Emperor Zhengde's love of leisure led to a relaxation of imperial control

Qing

1644–1911

Shunzhi	1644–1661
Kangxi	1661–1722
Yongzheng	1723–1735
Qianlong	1736–1795
Jiaqing	1796–1820
Daoguang	1821–1850
Xianfeng	1851–1861
Tongzhi	1862–1874
Guangxu	1875–1908
Pu Yi	1909–1912

Imperial dragon detail on the back of a eunuch's official court robe

Foundation of Imperial China

The Warring States Period was finally brought to an end as the Qin emerged victorious. In 221 BC, Qin Shi Huangdi pronounced himself the first emperor of China and ruled over a short yet decisive period of history. The Qin state was based on the political theories of Legalism, which established the role of the ruler as paramount and espoused a system of collective responsibility. Following unification, Qin Shi Huangdi conscripted thousands of workers to join together the defensive walls to the north, creating the Great Wall. He standardized the system of money, and weights and measures, and laid the foundations for a legal system. A ruthless ruler, Qin Shi Huangdi died in the belief that his famous terracotta army would protect him in the afterlife from his numerous enemies.

Lance soldier from Qin terracotta army

The founding of the Han dynasty (206 BC–AD 220) heralded a "golden age" in Chinese history. Emperor Gaodi (r.206–195 BC) established the capital of the Western Han (206 BC–AD 9) at Chang'an (Xi'an), and retained much of the centralized administration established by the Qin. Subsequent emperors developed the civil service examination to select able men for state office. Han society was founded on the principles propounded by Confucius, and the Confucian classics formed the basis of the civil service examination. Daoism and *yin-yang* theory coexisted with ancestor worship and would form the basis of indigenous Chinese belief *(see pp26–7)*.

The Han empire expanded with regions of Central Asia, Vietnam, and Korea being brought under Chinese control. In 138 BC, General Zhang Qian was sent to establish diplomatic links with Central Asia and returned with tales of rich pastures and "heavenly horses." The fine thoroughbreds of Ferghana (in modern Uzbekistan) were traded in exchange for Chinese silk, starting the flow of goods along the fabled Silk Road.

Han rule was briefly interrupted as Wang Mang seized power in AD 9, only to be restored by Guang Wudi (r. AD 25–57), who established the Eastern Han capital in Luoyang. Once more, the Han expanded Chinese territory. Paper was by now in use for much official documentation and the first Chinese dictionary was produced. Buddhism began its spread to China with the first Buddhist communities being established in Jiangsu province.

Chariot and footmen, impressed into a tomb's brick, Han

213 BC Burning of the books as part of process of "unification"

206 BC–AD 9 Western Han capital established at Chang'an (Xi'an)

c.139–126 BC Official envoy Zhang Qian establishes first diplomatic and trade links of Silk Road

AD 2 First known census: 57,671,400 individuals

Bronze horse and rider, Han

c.100 First dictionary *Shuo Wen* produced with more than 9,000 characters

200 BC

100 BC

1

AD 100

221–206 BC Qin dynasty under first emperor, Qin Shi Huangdi

Tomb figure, Qin

165 BC First official examinations for the selection of civil servants

25–220 Eastern Han dynasty capital at Luoyang

65 First mention of Buddhist community established at court of Prince Ying of Chu

Sui emperors Yangdi and Wendi in a detail from "Portraits of the 13 Emperors" by Tang painter Yen Li Pen

Period of Division

From the rule of Hedi (r. AD 88–105), the Eastern Han declined. Civil war finally split the country in 220. The next 350 years were characterized by almost constant warfare as China was ruled by over 14 short-lived dynasties and 16 "kingdoms."

China was divided into the Northern and Southern dynasties (265–581), each region taking on its own distinct character. Foreign peoples took control of the North, such as the Toba branch of the Xianbei, who founded the Northern Wei in 386. These rulers were receptive to foreign ideas and religions, creating some of the finest Buddhist cave complexes first at Yungang, near their capital in Datong, and from 494, at Longmen, when they moved their capital to Luoyang.

Apsara from Buddhist cave, Northern Wei

As foreign invaders took control of the North, the Han Chinese retreated south to establish their new capital at Jiankang (Nanjing). In a climate of relative stability, the south became the economic and cultural center as the population shifted to the Yangzi delta. Philosophy and the arts flourished alongside a renewed interest in Daoism and a growing interest in Buddhism.

Unification and Stability

Following military successes against the Liang and the Chen, the Northern Zhou general Yang Jian (541–604) pronounced himself emperor, taking the name Wendi, and founded the Sui dynasty in 581. This brief but significant dynastic rule established political and social stability. He undertook an extensive program of works including extending the Great Wall and the beginnings of the Grand Canal. The second emperor, Yangdi (569–617), restored diplomatic relations with Japan and Taiwan and extended trade to Central Asia.

190 Communications with central Asia are cut

Colossal Buddha at Yungang Caves, Northern Wei

581–618 Sui dynasty, initiated by Wendi's reunification of China

310 Massive exodus of Chinese upper classes to South

| 200 | 300 | 400 | 500 | 600 |

265–581 China divided into Northern and Southern dynasties

386–535 Northern Wei, first of the ruling houses to adopt Buddhism

c. 6th C First true porcelain produced

220 Civil war breaks out between the kingdoms of Wei, Shu, and Wu

c. 7th C Woodblock printing first used in China

Glory of the Tang

The Tang dynasty (AD 618–907) marks a high point in Chinese history. During this golden age, China enjoyed an extended period of peace and prosperity. The arts flourished and were enriched by foreign styles, motifs, and techniques such as silverworking. Foreign religions, such as Nestorian Christianity, were tolerated and co-existed alongside native Daoism and Confucianism. Woodblock printing was invented by the Chinese some time during the 7th century and hastened the spread of Buddhism.

Sancai glazed horse, Tang

Following the An Lushan rebellion of 755, the Tang became increasingly inward looking. The great Buddhist persecution of 841–46 was symptomatic of a dynasty in decline, which finally fell in 907.

The Liao Dynasty (907–1125)

The Liao dynasty, which at its largest covered much of Mongolia, Manchuria, and northern China, was ruled by semi-nomadic and pastoral people, the Qidan. The Liao maintained a dual administration, Qidan and Chinese, and even a prime-ministership, to ensure the survival of their own customs and traditions whilst utilizing the efficiency of Tang structures of government. In 1115, the Qidan were overthrown by another semi-nomadic people, the Ruzhen (Jurchen). With the support of the Northern Song, the Ruzhen took control of the north and founded the Jin dynasty. The Liao were forced westwards to the region of the Tian mountain range in present-day Xinjiang, where they established the Western Liao (1125–1211). The rest of northwest China was dominated by the Western Xia, a Tibetan related people who recognized the Liao as their overlords.

Five Dynasties and Ten Kingdoms (907–960)

While the north of China was dominated by the insurgence of semi-nomadic peoples from the steppe regions, the south was ruled by a series of short military dictatorships. The Song dynasty was founded in 960 by Zhao Kuangyin, a military commander of the later Zhou (951–960), whose imperial name became Shizong. In the Yangzi delta and regions to the south, the Ten Kingdoms existed in relative peace and stability and were reunited by the Song in 979.

Painting of an official celebrating, Five Dynasties (923–938)

618–907 Tang heralds new golden age	690–705 Empress Wu Zetian rules as first empress of China	755–763 An Lushan rebellion drives emperor and court from Chang'an to Sichuan	806 Earliest dated printed manuscript, the Diamond Sutra	907–60 Period of division known as Five Dynasties and Ten Kingdoms	10th c. Gunpowder and firearms first used
	700	**750**	**800**	**850**	**900**
661 Chinese administration in Kashmir, Bokhara, and the borders of eastern Iran	705 Famous poet Li Bai born	*Tang silver*	806–820 First bankers' bill 770 Death of great poet Du Fu	907–1125 Qidan people rule northeastern China as the Liao dynasty, making Beijing their southern capital	

The Song Dynasty (960–1279)

The Song presided over a period of cultural brilliance and unprecedented growth in urban life during which the social makeup of China fundamentally changed. Less territorially ambitious than the Tang, the Song stimulated economic development through improved communications and transport. New industries based on mass production began to emerge, notably the porcelain industry based in Jiangxi province. During the Southern Song, China underwent an industrial revolution producing quantities of raw materials such as salt and iron on a scale that would not be seen in Europe until the 18th century.

Illustration of Song Emperor Huizong, r. 1101–1125

In this buoyant economic climate, a new middle-class emerged, stimulating demand for the new range of consumer goods. Power shifted from the aristocratic elite to government bureaucrats, who spent their spare time practicing the arts of poetry, calligraphy, and painting. Collecting and connoisseurship led to an artistic renaissance and the founding of the first Imperial collections. Emperor Huizong was a great patron of the arts who used ancient precedents and values to buttress his own position. Neo-Confucianism and a renewed interest in Daoism marked a return to indigenous beliefs and traditional structures of power.

The Northern Song repeatedly came under attack from the Western Xia in the northwest and the Jin in the northeast. Only 12 years after joining

Early movable type, Song

forces with the Song against the Liao, the Jin invaded the Northern Song capital at Bianliang (Kaifeng), capturing emperor Qinzong and forcing the court to flee southwards. The capital of the Southern Song (1127–1279) was established at Lin'an (Hangzhou) south of the Yangzi.

Jin Dynasty (1115–1234)

The Jin were a semi-nomadic Tungusic people originating from Manchuria. War with the Song and persistent attacks from the Mongols resulted in a weakening of the Jin state which by the early 13th century formed a buffer state between the Song in the south and the Mongols in the north. In 1227, Mongol and Chinese allied forces defeated the Jin and in 1234, the Jin emperor committed suicide. The Jin state was integrated into the rapidly expanding Mongol empire.

960–1126 Northern Song reunites China and bases capital at Bianliang (Kaifeng)

Detail of painting by Emperor Huizong

1115–1234 Jin dynasty founded in northeast China forcing Liao westwards

1154 First issue of paper money (Jin)

1206–1208 Song and Jin at war

| 950 | 1000 | 1050 | 1100 | 1150 | 1200 |

990–1227 Western Xia people establish kingdom dominating northwest China

1041–8 First attempts at printing with movable type

1090 First attested use of compass on Chinese ships

1127–1279 Southern Song dynasty with capital at Hangzhou, after being forced south by the Jin

1214 Jin move capital from Beijing to Kaifeng in Henan province

Mongol Rule (1279–1368)

The Mongol leader Genghis Khan united the various Mongol-speaking tribes of the steppes and in 1215 conquered northern China. He divided his empire into four kingdoms, each ruled by one of his sons. His grandson Kublai Khan (r.1260–94), ruler of the eastern Great Khanate, finally defeated the Southern Song in 1279 and proclaimed himself emperor of the Yuan dynasty. China now became part of a vast empire which stretched from the East China Sea across Asia as far as Russia, the Ukraine, and Baghdad. Two capitals were maintained at Dadu or Khanbalik (present-day Beijing) and Yuanshangdu (Xanadu). The Silk Routes opened once more, connecting China to the Middle East and Medieval Europe. Direct contact was now made for the first time between the Mongol court and European diplomats, Franciscan missionaries, and merchants. According to the writings of Marco Polo, the Italian merchant spent 21 years in the service of Kublai and his court.

Genghis Khan (c.1162–1227), Persian miniature

Buddhist deity, Yuan

The Mongols ruled through a form of military government, in contrast to the bureaucratic civil service established by the Chinese. Although Chinese and Mongol languages were both used for official business, the Chinese were not encouraged to take up official posts. Muslims from Central and Western Asia took their place, and the Chinese increasingly retreated from official life.

As there were no clear rules for succession, civil war broke out in 1328 between Mongol nobles. The secret societies of the Red Turbans and the White Lotus led peasant rebellions and in 1368 General Zhu Yuanzhang forced the Mongols out of China, becoming the first emperor of the Ming dynasty.

Ming Dynasty (1368–1644)

The Ming (literally "brilliant") dynasty was one of the longest and most stable periods in China's history. The founder of the Ming, Zhu Yuanzhang, rose from humble beginnings to become a general, ruling as emperor Hongwu ("vast military accomplishment"). During his reign, Hongwu introduced radical changes to both central and local government, which he made binding on his successors. The emperor's role became more autocratic as Hongwu dispensed with the position of Prime Minister, taking direct responsibility for overseeing all six ministries himself.

Hongwu appointed his grandson to be his successor. Upon his death, his son the Prince of Yan, who controlled the region

1215 Mongols capture Beijing	1234 Jin emperor commits suicide; Jin integrated into Mongol empire		1368–1644 Ming dynasty, founded by rebel leader General Zhu Yuanzhang	1403 Construction of Great Walls in North China

Mongol on horseback

1250	1300	1350	1400

1227 Genghis Khan dies, having united various Mongol speaking tribes of the steppe	1279–1368 Kublai Khan defeats Southern Song and rules China as emperor of the Yuan dynasty	1328 Civil war breaks out between Mongol nobles	Jade elephant, Ming

The existing battlements of the Great Wall, reinforced and joined together during the Ming dynasty

around Beijing, led an army against his nephew, taking Nanjing and proclaiming himself emperor Yongle ("Eternal Joy"). Yongle (r.1403–24) moved the capital to his power base in Beijing, where he created a new city based on traditional principles of Chinese city planning. At its core lay the Forbidden City (see pp66–71), the imperial palace and offices of government, surrounded by a grid system of streets, with four imperial altars at the cardinal points. The entire city was walled to provide both protection and enclosure. In 1421, Beijing became the official capital and, bar a short interlude during the Nationalist era in the early 20th century, would remain so until the present day.

By the 15th century, China had become a significant maritime power, its ships dwarfing those of contemporary Europe. Blue and white porcelain, silk, and other luxury items were in high demand in the foreign markets of Japan, Southeast Asia, and the Middle East. Yongle sent six maritime expeditions under the Muslim eunuch admiral Zheng He, which

Wedding jewelry, Ming

reached as far as the east coast of Africa. In 1514, Portuguese traders first landed in China, purchasing tea which then became a fashionable drink in European society. Porcelain provided ballast for the ships, and other luxury items were brought back along with the cargo. Trade was dominated by the Dutch in the 17th century, only to be surpassed by the British a hundred years later. Jesuit missionaries, who arrived in the 16th century, claimed few converts but gained access to the emperor and the inner court.

The arts thrived under emperor Xuande (r.1426–35), an artist and poet who patronized the arts, notably the porcelain industry at Jingdezhen. In literature, the late Ming is noted for its great dramas and classical novels, such as Journey to the West (see p25). Philosophy of the time reinforced the Neo-Confucianism of the Song.

The late Ming was dominated by peasant uprisings, incursions by Japanese pirates and Mongolian tribes, and excessive eunuch power. Rebellions within China eventually joined with external forces to end Ming rule.

1426–35 Xuande emperor becomes first Ming emperor to patronize the arts extensively

1514 Portuguese land in China, becoming the first Europeans to trade in tea and porcelain

Gilt bronze bowl, Ming

1573–1620 Wanli reign begins well but dynasty declines as emperor takes little interest in duties

1620 Emperor Taichang poisoned by eunuchs

1450	1500	1550	1600

1420 Construction of the Forbidden City in Beijing completed

Early 16th century Later Ming monarchs neglect duties of government and eunuch power increases

1538 Jesuit Father Matteo Ricci enters southern China and begins missionary duties

1570 Popular novel Journey to the West published

1600s Dutch dominate European trade with China

1601 Jesuit missionary Matteo Ricci allowed to enter Beijing

Qing Rule (1644–1911)

The Manchu leader Nurhachi established the Later Jin in 1616, organizing the scattered tribes of the north into eight banner units. In 1636, the Manchu ruler Abahai changed the name to Qing, literally "pure," and prepared the way for the capture of Beijing in 1644. Under Manchu control, China was once more ruled by a foreign people. The Manchus were keen to adopt the Chinese method of rule, encouraging Chinese scholars into the service of the new empire. Dual administration at national and provincial levels meant Manchu and Chinese bureaucrats worked side by side using first Manchu and later Chinese as the official languages of government. However, despite the close interaction of Manchu and Chinese, the ruling Manchus were careful to maintain a distinct separation in order to protect their own privileges and cultural traditions.

The first emperors of the Qing were enlightened rulers who presided over one of the largest and most populous countries in the world. The territorial aspirations of Emperor Kangxi brought the regions of Central Asia and southern Siberia once more under Chinese control. Kangxi was succeeded by Emperor Yongzheng. It was his fourth son, Emperor Qianlong, "Lasting Eminence," (r. 1736–96) who heralded another golden age.

Emperor Kangxi, r. 1661–1722

An ambitious ruler, Qianlong was determined to extend China's borders beyond those of the Tang, personally leading campaigns to Burma, Vietnam, and Central Asia.

During the 18th century, contact with the west increased through Jesuit missionaries and trade. By the mid-18th century, the Chinese sought to control trade by refusing all official contact with Westerners and opening only Canton to foreign merchants. Pressure from European embassies increased as the British sent Lord Macartney in 1792–94 to establish diplomatic relations and open China to trade. China refused to grant a single concession to the British.

The Decline of the Empire

The 19th century is one of the most turbulent periods of Chinese history, as internal uprisings, natural disasters, and the relentless encroachment of the West culminated in the end of the empire. A succession of weak rulers were

Lord Macartney's massive entourage arriving at Qianlong's tent

1644–1800 Military expansion into Central Asia and Siberia; colonization of new territories Yunnan and Xinjiang

1723–1735 Kangxi's son Yin Zhen seizes power ruling under name of emperor Yongzheng

Emperor Shunzhi, r. 1644–61

1747 Qianlong builds Yuanming Yuan (see p88) in Western style

1650	1675	1700	1725	1750

1650 First Catholic church in Beijing

1661–1722 Rule of Kangxi emperor. Appoints Jesuits to run Board of Astronomy

1757 Chinese restrict all foreign trade to Canton

1644–1911 Manchus establish Qing dynasty

1736–1795 Qianlong, a great patron of the arts, rules over another golden age

A merchant testing tea quality in a Cantonese warehouse

manipulated and controlled by the Dowager Empress Cixi, who ruled for much of the late Qing from "behind the curtain." The Taiping Rebellion of 1850–64 devastated south and central China.

Western powers, frustrated by the reluctance of the Chinese to open to foreign trade, brought the Chinese under increasing pressure. Keen to protect the trade of opium from their colonies in India, the British engaged in the First Opium War (1840–42), which culminated in the Treaty of Nanjing, resulting in the opening of four new ports to trade, the payment of huge indemnities, and the ceding of Hong Kong to Britain. Following the Arrow War (Second Opium War) with Britain and France (1856), the European forces divided China into "spheres of influence" – the British strongest along the Yangzi and in Shanghai, the Germans controlling Shandong province, and the French controlling the borders with Vietnam. In

Sun Yat Sen, 1866–1925

1900, the Boxers allied with imperial troops and attacked the foreign legations in Beijing. An eight-nation army defeated the onslaught, and Cixi fled to Xi'an, blaming everything on the emperor. The Chinese government paid once more for the loss of life and Cixi returned to Beijing until her death in 1908. The child emperor Pu Yi lived in the Forbidden City as the last emperor until his abdication. On January 1, 1912 the Republican leader Sun Yat Sen inaugurated the Chinese Republic.

From Empire to Republic

In the final years of the empire, many Chinese intellectuals recognized the need to modernize. Supporters of the Reform Movement of 1898 propounded the adoption of western technology and education, and, following the Boxer Rebellion, a number of reforms were adopted. Elected regional assemblies were set up, further undermining the power of the Qing. In 1911, the empire collapsed completely. Sun Yat Sen was elected provisional President of China, but was soon forced to resign in favor of general Yuan Shikai, who sought to become emperor. Yuan was forced to back down when governors revolted and he died soon after in 1916. China then came under the control of a series of regional warlords until it was united once more with the founding of the People's Republic of China in 1949.

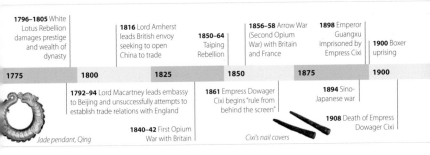

1796–1805 White Lotus Rebellion damages prestige and wealth of dynasty		1816 Lord Amherst leads British envoy seeking to open China to trade		1850–64 Taiping Rebellion	1856–58 Arrow War (Second Opium War) with Britain and France		1898 Emperor Guangxu imprisoned by Empress Cixi	1900 Boxer uprising
1775	**1800**	**1825**		**1850**	**1875**		**1900**	
	1792–94 Lord Macartney leads embassy to Beijing and unsuccessfully attempts to establish trade relations with England		1861 Empress Dowager Cixi begins "rule from behind the screen"		1894 Sino-Japanese war		1908 Death of Empress Dowager Cixi	
		1840–42 First Opium War with Britain				Cixi's nail covers		

Jade pendant, Qing

The Cultural Revolution

In 1965, Mao Zedong set in motion a chain of events that were to unleash the turmoil now known as the Cultural Revolution. Having socialized industry and agriculture, Mao called on the masses to transform society itself – all distinctions between manual and intellectual work were to be abolished and class distinction disappear. The revolution reached its violent peak in 1967, with the Red Guards spreading social unrest. The People's Liberation Army (PLA) finally restored order, but the subsequent years were characterized by fear, violence, and mistrust.

Children were encouraged to take part in the Revolution. Their enthusiasm led to the destruction of family photographs and possessions. In some cases, children denounced their own parents.

The Red Guard

Mao appealed to students to form the Red Guard, in whom he entrusted the fate of the revolution. The movement rapidly gathered momentum and the Red Guard, who raised Mao to godly status, traveled China spreading Mao Zedong "Thoughts," smashing remnants of the past, vandalizing temples, and wreaking havoc.

Mass public meetings were held as part of the Socialist Education Movement, a precursor of the Cultural Revolution intended to reverse "capitalist" and "revisionist" tendencies perceived in social and economic life. Everyone was required to attend.

An injured cadre is carried away after being denounced. Shamings became the benchmark of public meetings. Many politicians and teachers were paraded and accused, leading to job loss and, in some cases, suicide.

The Little Red Book was essential to the Red Guard and issued to every soldier under Lin Biao's command.

Demonstrating their opposition to Soviet-style communism and their support for Maoism, Red Guards change a Beijing street sign in front of the Soviet Embassy from East Yangwei to Fanxiu Lu (Anti-revisionism Road).

Lin Biao spread the study of the "Thoughts of Mao" and compiled the *Little Red Book* which became obligatory reading for his army recruits. As head of the PLA, Lin Biao provided essential military backing and was Mao's named successor. He died in a plane crash over Siberia in 1971 amid rumors of an imminent usurpation.

Model operas were the pet project of Mao's third wife, Jiang Qing. She set about creating a politically correct revolutionary culture. Many artists and intellectuals were sent to the countryside for re-education.

May 7 Cadre Schools were set up by the central government in 1968. 100,000 officials plus 30,000 family members were sent to perform manual labor and undergo ideological re-education. An unknown number of lower-ranking cadres were sent to thousands of other cadre schools.

Liu Shaoqi *(right)*, president from 1959 to 1966, was one of a number of high officials to be denounced, imprisoned, and paraded in "struggle rallies." He died from his experiences.

Gang of Four

The Gang of Four, as they became known, orchestrated attacks on intellectuals and writers, high officials, the party, and the state and were responsible for some of the worst excesses of the Cultural Revolution. Zhang Chunqiao, critic and propagandist, Yao Wenyuan, editor-in-chief of *Shanghai Liberation Army Daily*, Wang Hongwen, a young worker, and Mao's third wife Jiang Qing, an ex-film star, dominated the political center unchallenged until Mao's death in 1976. Millions of Chinese citizens watched their televised trial in 1980–81. Jiang Qing, who was singled out by propagandists and became one of the most hated figures in China, was defiant until the end, railing against her prosecutors throughout the trial. She took her own life in 1991, while serving her life sentence.

Lynched effigies of members of the Gang of Four hanging from a tree

Chiang Kai Shek (1887–1975), leader of the KMT

Communists and Nationalists

After the fall of the empire, the political landscape changed dramatically and became dominated by two forces, the Nationalist Party or Kuomintang (KMT) and the Communist Party, founded in 1921. The Nationalists were led first by Sun Yat Sen from his power base in Guangzhou, then by General Chiang Kai Shek who seized power in 1926. In 1923, the two Parties formed a "united front" against the warlords, but in 1926 the Communists were expelled from the KMT. Chiang Kai Shek led his army to Nanjing where he tried to establish a Nationalist capital, and betrayed the Communist-led workers of Shanghai who were massacred by underworld gangsters. The Communists were driven underground and Mao Zedong retreated to the countryside.

High in the mountains of Jiangxi province, Mao and Zhu De founded the Jiangxi Soviet in 1930. From this inaccessible base, the Communists began to redistribute land to the peasants and institute new marriage laws. In 1934, Chiang Kai Shek drove the Communists from the area, forcing Mao to embark on the legendary Long March. Yan'an, where the march ended, became the new Communist Party headquarters and would remain so until 1945.

Japanese Attack

Domestic turmoil laid China open to attack, and in 1931 the Japanese occupied Manchuria, founding the puppet state of Manchukuo and placing the last Qing emperor, Pu Yi, at its head. By 1937, the Japanese had occupied much of northern China, Shanghai, and the Yangzi valley, ruthlessly taking cities, wreaking death and devastation. The Japanese were finally driven from Chinese soil in 1945, and China was plunged into civil war.

The East is Red

By 1947, the Communist policy of land reform was reaping rewards and gaining the support of people in the countryside. In 1948–9, the Communists gained decisive victories over the KMT. On October 1, 1949 Chairman Mao pronounced the founding of the People's Republic of China. Chiang Kai Shek fled to Taiwan, establishing a Nationalist government and taking with him many

Communist poster depicting Mao surrounded by the masses

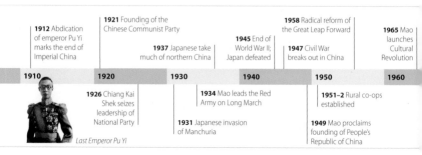

1912 Abdication of emperor Pu Yi marks the end of Imperial China

1921 Founding of the Chinese Communist Party

1926 Chiang Kai Shek seizes leadership of National Party

1937 Japanese take much of northern China

1934 Mao leads the Red Army on Long March

1931 Japanese invasion of Manchuria

1945 End of World War II; Japan defeated

1947 Civil War breaks out in China

1949 Mao proclaims founding of People's Republic of China

1958 Radical reform of the Great Leap Forward

1951–2 Rural co-ops established

1965 Mao launches Cultural Revolution

Last Emperor Pu Yi

1910　1920　1930　1940　1950　1960

Imperial treasures. In the early years of the People's Republic, the Chinese worked hard to rebuild a country devastated by 100 years of turmoil. New laws sought to redress inequities of the past,

Zhou Enlai with President Nixon

redistributing land and outlawing arranged marriages. The Party promptly branded intellectuals as "rightists" and sent them to the countryside for re-education. Frustrated with the slow rate of change, Mao launched the Great Leap Forward in 1958. Large communes providing food and childcare replaced the family, releasing manual labor and improving productivity. But unrealistic productivity targets and the falsification of statistics concealed the disastrous effect of Mao's experiment. Agricultural failure coupled with natural disasters resulted in the starvation of millions.

Having reformed agriculture and industry, Mao sought to transform society and launched the Cultural Revolution in 1965 *(see pp54–5)*. The greatest excesses of the period were over by 1971, but the country was tightly controlled and directed until Mao's death in 1976. Deng Xiaoping emerged as leader, implementing economic reforms which returned land to the peasants and encouraged greater economic freedom.

The economic liberalization of the 1980s stimulated the economy but was unmatched by political freedom. On June 4, 1989, the democracy movement called for political reform and an end to corruption, but was brutally suppressed in Tian'an Men Square.

Whilst many students and intellectuals fled abroad, others remain incarcerated in China's jails. Deng Xiaoping pressed on with economic reform, and the 1990s saw the opening of Special Economic Zones and stock exchanges in most major cities. By 1992, China's economy had become one of the largest in the world.

The unprecedented rate of economic growth in the 1990s was matched by the transformation of the landscape as traditional buildings made way for modern high-rises. The former colonies of Hong Kong and Macau were returned to China and foreign investment flooded in. Entrepreneurs prospered, and the Communist Party has been keen to attract this new class into its ranks. Disbanding the state economy has also spawned inequity, and the gap between rich and poor grows ever wider. How the most populous nation on earth resolves the many issues it faces remains to be seen. The handover of power at the top of the Communist Party in late 2012 saw President Hu

Chinese traders on the Stock Exchange

Jintao and Premier Wen Jiabao pass the reins to a new generation of leaders whose task will be to achieve economic growth while maintaining national unity.

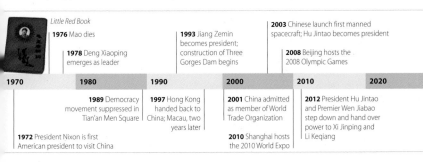

Little Red Book

1976 Mao dies

1978 Deng Xiaoping emerges as leader

1993 Jiang Zemin becomes president; construction of Three Gorges Dam begins

2003 Chinese launch first manned spacecraft; Hu Jintao becomes president

2008 Beijing hosts the 2008 Olympic Games

1970   1980   1990   2000   2010   2020

1989 Democracy movement suppressed in Tian'an Men Square

1997 Hong Kong handed back to China; Macau, two years later

2001 China admitted as member of World Trade Organization

2012 President Hu Jintao and Premier Wen Jiabao step down and hand over power to Xi Jinping and Li Keqiang

1972 President Nixon is first American president to visit China

2010 Shanghai hosts the 2010 World Expo

BEIJING

Exploring Beijing

Beijing's most significant sights and districts are marked on this map. At the core is the Forbidden City, with Tian'an Men Square and Qian Men to the south, and the shopping district of Wangfujing to its east. North of the Forbidden City stand the Drum and Bell Towers, and farther northeast is the Buddhist Lama Temple. North of Bei Hai Park, the Mansion of Prince Gong stands in a historic district of *hutongs*, the old alleyways that riddle the city. To the south, Tian Tan, known as the Temple of Heaven, is a majestic example of Ming dynasty design. Beijing's suburbs are also dotted with sites including the magnificent Summer Palace complex.

BEIJING

Locator Map
See also pp16-17.

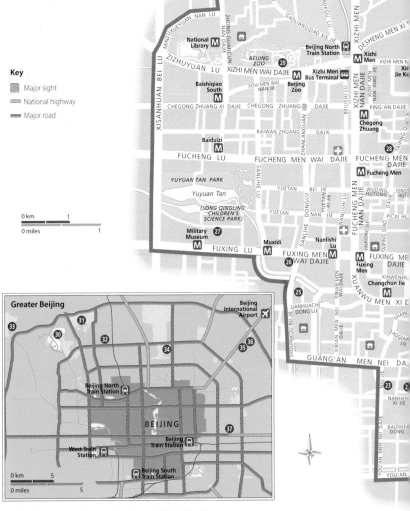

Key

Major sight

National highway

Major road

0 km   1
0 miles   1

National Library

BEIJING ZOO **29**

Beijing North Train Station

Xizhi Men

Baishiqiao South

Xizhi Men Bus Terminal

Beijing Zoo

Baiduizi

YUYUAN TAN PARK

Yuyuan Tan

(SONG QINGLING CHILDREN'S SCIENCE PARK)

Military Museum **27**

Muxidi

Nanlishi Lu

Fucheng Men **28**

Greater Beijing

33 **30** **31** **32** **34** **35** **36** **37** **25** **26** **23**

Beijing International Airport

Beijing North Train Station

BEIJING

West Train Station

Beijing Train Station

Beijing South Train Station

0 km   5
0 miles   5

◀ Vividly painted temple interior within the gates of the Forbidden City

Sights at a Glance

Historic Buildings, Sites and Neighborhoods

1. *Tian'an Men Square pp62–3*
2. Qian Men
3. Beijing Urban Planning Exhibition Hall
4. Dazhalan & Liulichang
6. *Forbidden City pp66–71*
7. Legation Quarter
10. Mansion of Prince Gong
11. Drum & Bell Towers
18. Ancient Observatory
30. *Summer Palace pp84–7*

31. Yuanming Yuan
34. National Olympic Stadium
37. CCTV Headquarters

Shops and Markets

17. Wangfujing Street

Museums and Galleries

16. National Art Museum of China
19. Southeast Corner Watchtower (Dongbian Men)
20. Beijing Natural History Museum

26. Capital Museum
27. Military Museum of the Chinese People's Revolution
35. 798 Art District
36. China Railway Museum

Temples, Churches and Mosques

5. South Cathedral
12. Lama Temple
13. Confucius Temple
15. Dong Yue Miao
21. *Temple of Heaven pp78–81*
22. Xiannong Tan
23. Cow Street Mosque
24. Fayuan Temple
25. White Clouds Temple
28. Miaoying Temple White Dagoba
32. Great Bell Temple

Parks and Zoos

8. Jing Shan Park
9. Bei Hai Park
14. Di Tan Park
29. Beijing Zoo
33. Xiang Shan Park

Getting Around

A system of ring roads encircles the city center, and the best way to explore this area is by taxi, by subway, or by bicycle (see pp222–3). The bus service, though extensive, is generally slow and overcrowded. Organized tours are another option for a quick overview of the sights. Most hotels and agencies operate tour buses for visiting sights outside Beijing, although hiring a taxi for the day allows for greater flexibility.

For keys to symbols *see back flap*

❶ Street-by-Street: Tian'an Men Square
天安门广场

Tian'an Men Guangchang – the Square of the Gate of Heavenly Peace – is a vast open concrete expanse at the heart of modern Beijing. With Mao's Mausoleum at its focal point, and bordered by 1950s Communist-style buildings and ancient gates from Beijing's now leveled city walls, the square is usually filled with visitors strolling about as kites flit overhead. The square has also traditionally served as a stage for popular demonstrations and is most indelibly associated with the student protests of 1989 and their gory climax.

Cyclists along Chang'an Jie

Great Hall of the People
Seat of the Chinese legislature, the vast auditorium and banqueting halls are open for part of the day except when the National People's Congress is in session.

★ **Zhengyang Men**
Along with the Arrow Tower, this tower formed a double gate known as the Qian Men. It now houses a museum on the history of Beijing.

★ **Mao's Mausoleum**
Flanked by revolutionary statues, the building contains the embalmed body of Chairman Mao. His casket, raised from its refrigerated chamber, is on view mornings and afternoons.

QIAN MEN DAJIE

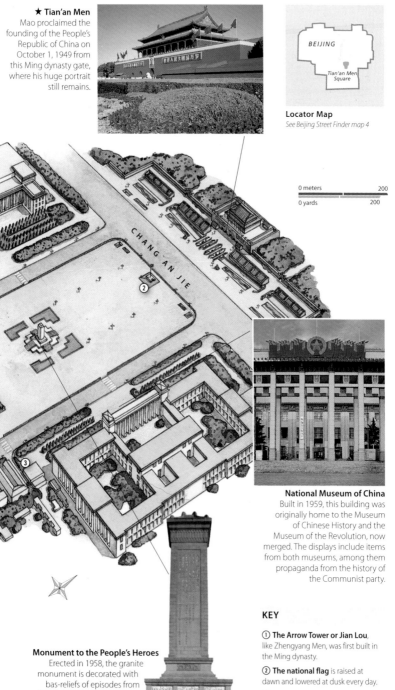

★ **Tian'an Men**
Mao proclaimed the founding of the People's Republic of China on October 1, 1949 from this Ming dynasty gate, where his huge portrait still remains.

Locator Map
See Beijing Street Finder map 4

CHANG AN JIE

0 meters 200
0 yards 200

National Museum of China
Built in 1959, this building was originally home to the Museum of Chinese History and the Museum of the Revolution, now merged. The displays include items from both museums, among them propaganda from the history of the Communist party.

KEY

① **The Arrow Tower or Jian Lou**, like Zhengyang Men, was first built in the Ming dynasty.

② **The national flag** is raised at dawn and lowered at dusk every day.

③ **Bags, coats, and cameras** must be left here before visiting Mao's Mausoleum.

Monument to the People's Heroes
Erected in 1958, the granite monument is decorated with bas-reliefs of episodes from China's revolutionary history and calligraphy from Communist veterans Mao Zedong and Zhou Enlai.

Zhengyang Men, Qian Men – part of Beijing's central fortifications

❷ Qian Men
前门

Qian Men Dajie. **Map** 4 C2. Ⓜ Qian
Men. **Open** 8:30am–4pm daily.

Qian Men, or the Front Gate,
consists of two towers, the
Zhengyang Men, on the
southern edge of Tian'an Men
Square, and the **Jian Lou
Arrow Tower** just to the south.
Zhengyang Men (Facing
the Sun Gate) was the most
imposing of the nine gates of
the inner city wall that divided
Beijing's imperial quarters in
the Forbidden City from the
"Chinese City," where, during
the Manchu Qing dynasty,
the Chinese inhabitants lived.
  Rising 131 ft (40 m), the gate
stands on the north-south axis
that runs through the Tian'an
Men and the Forbidden City. Its
museum has dioramas of the
old city walls, and photographs
of Beijing's old streets.

The 125 ft (38 m) high Jian Lou
(Arrow Tower), originally built
in 1439, has 94 windows that
were used for shooting arrows.
Both the Jian Lou and
Zhengyang Men were badly
damaged by fire during the
Boxer Rebellion. In 1916, the
enceinte, a semi-circular wall
that connected the two
towers, was demolished to
make way for a road. Jian Lou
is now closed to the public.
Across the road to the east, the
Old Railway Station was built
by the British and now houses
a number of shops. The area
around Qian Men, originally
the city's old shopping district,
has received a radical make-
over. Qian Men Dajie is now a
broad, pedestrianized street
flanked by brand boutiques
and mini shopping malls, as
well as cafés and restaurants
housed in ancient Beijing-
themed buildings. A 1930s-
style tram runs up and down

the street, ferrying shoppers
and tourists.

🚇 **Zhengyang Men**
Tel (010) 6511 8110. **Open** daily.

❸ Beijing Urban Planning Exhibition Hall
北京市规划展览馆

20 Qian Men Dong Dajie. **Map** 4 C2.
Ⓜ Qian Men. **Tel** (010) 6701 7074.
Open 9am–5pm Tue–Sun.

Just east of the historic Qian
Men area, this four-story
building traces the history of
Beijing's urban development
through photographs, old
maps, and models. It also offers
a glimpse into what the architecture and urban landscape of
Beijing will look like in the
future. This is dramatically represented through two short 3-D
films, as well as a huge scale
model of what the city should
look like in 2020. A highlight of
the exhibition, the 3,200 sq ft
(300 sq m) model covers most
of the third floor and is also
viewable from a gallery above.

Large scale model at the Beijing Urban
Planning Exhibition Hall

Beijing's City Walls

The earliest defensive walls around Beijing (then called Yanjing, later
Zhongdu) were erected in the Jin dynasty (1115–1234) and modeled
on the wall around Kaifeng. The Mongol Kublai Khan rebuilt
Zhongdu, naming it Dadu, and encompassed it with a 19-mile
(30-km) wall. It was only during the Ming era (1368–1644) that the
walls took on their final shape of an Outer Wall with seven gates, and
an Inner Wall with nine gates. The magnificent Inner Wall was 38 ft
(11.5 m) high and 64 ft (19.5 m) wide. The walls and most of their
gates were unfortunately demolished in the 1950s and '60s to make
way for roads. Of the inner wall, only Qian Men and Desheng Men
survive, while the outer wall retains only Dongbian Men (see p77).
The old gates live on as place names on the second ring road, and
as the names of stations on the Beijing Underground Loop line.

Arrow Tower of Qian Men

Shop selling Communist memorabilia, Dazhalan Jie

❹ Dazhalan & Liulichang
大栅栏和琉璃厂

Map 4 C2. Ⓜ Qian Men.

South of Qian Men are the narrow and lively *hutongs (see p73)* of the old Chinese quarter. The inner city wall and its gates separated the "Inner City" containing the imperial quarters of the Manchu emperors from the "Chinese City," where the Chinese lived apart from their Qing overlords. Today, the district buzzes with shops, cinemas, and restaurants. Running west off the northern end of Qian Men Dajie is Dazhalan Jie (also known locally as Dashilan), whose name, "Big Barrier Street,"

Cyclists on restored Liulichang Jie

refers to the now-demolished gates that were closed every night to fence off the residents from Qian Men and the Inner City. The area was damaged during the Boxer Rebellion and later restored. There are *hutong* tours by rickshaw – drivers just wait in the street in Dazhalan.

The area is a great place for browsing, and has several quaint Qing-era specialty shops. Located down the first alley on the left from Dazhalan Jie is the century-old pickle shop **Liubiju**, selling a vast array of pungent pickles. **Ruifuxiang**, on the right-hand side of Dazhalan, dates from 1893 and is renowned for its silks and traditional Chinese garments. On the south side of Dazhalan Jie is the Chinese medicine shop **Tongrentang Pharmacy**, which has been in business since 1669 and enjoyed imperial patronage. On the same side of the road, the **Zhangyiyuan Chazhuang**, or Zhangyiyuan Teashop, has been supplying fine teas since the early 20th century. To the west of Dazhalan Jie, Liulichang Jie, with its restored buildings and many stores, is a fascinating place to wander around. It has everything from ceramics, bric-a-brac, paintings, lacquerware, and antique Chinese books to Cultural Revolution-era memorabilia. However, beware of so-called "antiques" which should be judiciously examined before buying.

❺ South Cathedral
南堂

141 Qian Men Xi Dajie. **Map** 4 A2.
Ⓜ Xuanwu Men.

The first Catholic church to be built in Beijing, South Cathedral (Nan Tang) stands close to the Xuanwu Men underground station, on the site of Jesuit Matteo Ricci's former residence. Ricci was the first Jesuit missionary to reach Beijing. Arriving in 1601, he sent gifts of European curiosities such as clocks, mathematical instruments, and a world map to the Wanli emperor, thus gaining his goodwill, and eventually given permission to establish a church.

Like many of China's churches, this restored building has suffered much devastation. Construction first began in 1605, and it subsequently burned down in 1775. It was rebuilt a century later, only to be destroyed once again during the Boxer Rebellion of 1900. The cathedral was rebuilt in 1904. Also known as St. Mary's Church, it is the city's largest functioning Catholic cathedral, and has regular services in a variety of languages including Chinese, English, and Latin. Service timings are posted on the noticeboard. A small gift shop is located near the south gate.

Stained glass at the South Cathedral (Nan Tang)

❻ Forbidden City

故宫

Forming the very heart of Beijing, the Forbidden City, officially known as the Palace Museum (Gugong), is China's most magnificent architectural complex and was completed in 1420. The huge palace is a compendium of imperial architecture and a lasting monument of dynastic China, from which 24 emperors ruled for nearly 500 years. The symbolic center of the Chinese universe, the palace was the exclusive domain of the imperial court and dignitaries until the abdication in 1912. It was opened to the public in 1949.

Chinese Lions
Pairs of lions guard the entrances of halls. The male is portrayed with an orb under his paw, while the female has a lion cub.

★ Golden Water
Five marble bridges, symbolizing the five cardinal virtues of Confucianism, cross the Golden Water, which flows from west to east in a course designed to resemble the jade belt worn by officials.

Outer Court
At the center of the Forbidden City, the Outer Court is easily its most impressive part. Most of the other buildings in the complex were there to service this city within a city.

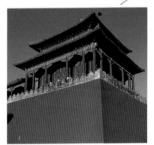

Meridian Gate (Wu Men)
From the balcony the emperor would review his armies and perform ceremonies marking the start of a new calendar.

Gate of Supreme Harmony
Originally used for receiving visitors, the 78 ft (24 m) high, double-eaved hall was later used for banquets during the Qing dynasty (1644–1912).

★ Marble Carriageway
The central ramp carved with dragons chasing pearls among clouds was reserved for the emperor.

VISITORS' CHECKLIST

Practical Information
North of Tian'an Men Square.
Map 2 A4/5. **Tel** (010) 8500 7420.
Open Apr–Oct: 8:30am–5pm daily; Nov–Mar: 8:30am–4:30pm daily. 🎨 🏛 📷 🏛 💻
W dpm.org.cn

★ Hall of Supreme Harmony
The largest hall in the palace, this was used for major occasions such as the enthronement of an emperor. Inside the hall, the ornate throne sits beneath a fabulously colored ceiling.

Roof Guardians
An odd number of these figures, all associated with water, are supposed to protect the building from fire.

KEY

① Offices of the imperial secretariat

② Storehouses

③ Imperial sundial

④ **The Hall of Middle Harmony** received the emperor before official ceremonies.

⑤ **Bronze cauldrons** were filled with water in case of fire.

⑥ Hall of Preserving Harmony

⑦ Gate of Heavenly Purity

Design by Numbers

The harmonious principle of *yin* and *yang* is the key to Chinese design. As odd numbers represent *yang* (the preferred masculine element associated with the emperor), the numbers three, five, seven, and the ultimate odd number, nine, recur in architectural details. It is said that the Forbidden City has 9,999 rooms and, as nine times nine is especially fortunate, the doors for imperial use usually contain 81 brass studs.

Palace door with a lucky number of studs

Exploring the Forbidden City

Magnificent though the Outer Court is, there is still a great deal more to see. A short distance north through the Gate of Heavenly Purity lies the Inner Court with three impressive palaces and the private living quarters of the emperor. Farther on, beyond the Imperial Flower Garden, stands the northern Gate of Divine Prowess and exit into Jing Shan Park *(see p72)*. On the western and eastern flanks of the Inner Court, it is also possible to explore numerous halls, some of which house museum collections (entry fee payable).

The Pavilion of a Thousand Autumns in the Imperial Gardens

🔲 Inner Court
Beyond the Hall of Preserving Harmony *(see pp66–7)* lies a narrow courtyard with gates leading to the open areas east and west of the Outer Court and a main gate, the **Gate of Heavenly Purity**, leading to the Inner Court. Tradition has this gate to be the only building in the whole palace not to have been burned down at least once, and thus the oldest hall of all. The walls to either side that form a boundary between the Outer and Inner Courts only date from the early days of the republic, when the last emperor, Pu Yi *(see p69)* was confined to the rear of the palace until ejected by the Christian warlord Feng Yuxiang in 1924.

To either side of the gate are groups of smaller halls, built on a more human scale and separated by narrow alleys; this area was once the residence of concubines and imperial offspring.

Straight ahead, back on the main axis, stand three splendid palaces, mirroring those of the Outer Court but on a smaller scale. The double-eaved **Palace of Heavenly Purity** was used as the imperial sleeping quarters. It was here that the last Ming emperor, Chongzhen, wrote his final missive in blood, before getting drunk, killing his 15-year-old daughter and his concubines, and then hanging himself on Jing Shan *(see p72)*, just north of the palace, as peasant rebels swarmed through the capital. In the late Qing era it was used for the reception of officials, and after 1900, even foreign ones, who previously had not been allowed inside the palace. The last emperor's wedding ceremony was also held here. Beyond lies the **Hall of Union**, used as a throne room by the empress, and to house the jade seals of imperial authority. Then comes the **Palace of Earthly Tranquility**, living quarters of the Ming empresses.

🔲 Imperial Gardens
The **Imperial Flower Garden**, north of the three inner palaces and the Gate of Earthly Tranquility, dates from the reign of the Ming Yongle emperor. It is symmetrically laid out with pavilions, temples, and halls, as well as a rock garden. On the west and east sides of the garden are the charming **Pavilion of a Thousand Autumns** and **Pavilion of Ten Thousand Springs**, each topped with a circular roof. One of these was the site of the schoolroom used by Sir Reginald Johnston, tutor to the last emperor. Johnston, Pu Yi, and the empress would sometimes have picnics in the gardens.

Positioned centrally in the north of the garden, the **Hall of Imperial Peace** formerly served as a temple, while on top of the lofty rockery in the northeast of the garden the **Imperial View Pavilion** boasts views over the gardens and beyond. During the Qing dynasty, sacrifices were

The intricately carved and painted ceiling in the Hall of Union

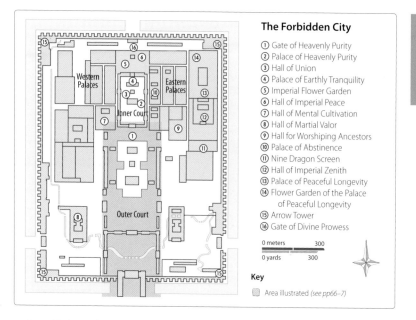

The Forbidden City

① Gate of Heavenly Purity
② Palace of Heavenly Purity
③ Hall of Union
④ Palace of Earthly Tranquility
⑤ Imperial Flower Garden
⑥ Hall of Imperial Peace
⑦ Hall of Mental Cultivation
⑧ Hall of Martial Valor
⑨ Hall for Worshiping Ancestors
⑩ Palace of Abstinence
⑪ Nine Dragon Screen
⑫ Hall of Imperial Zenith
⑬ Palace of Peaceful Longevity
⑭ Flower Garden of the Palace
   of Peaceful Longevity
⑮ Arrow Tower
⑯ Gate of Divine Prowess

| 0 meters | 300 |
| 0 yards | 300 |

Key

☐ Area illustrated *(see pp66–7)*

performed in the gardens on Qi Xi, the seventh day of the seventh lunar month, and the Chinese equivalent of Valentine's Day *(see p40)*. The sacrifices were made by the emperor and empress, and directed to a pair of stars that represent lovers.

Western Palaces

Much of the western flank of the Forbidden City remains closed to visitors, but the halls west of the three inner palaces are accessible. South of these, a network of high-walled alleys links a labyrinth of smaller halls that were the residences of imperial concubines. Particularly fine is the **Palace of Eternal Spring**, where *trompe-l'oeil* paintings at the ends of the passageways make them appear to extend to infinity.

The southernmost accessible hall, the **Hall of Mental Cultivation**, was used by the Yongzheng emperor *(see p97)* for his residence, rather than the Hall of Heavenly Purity, where his father, the Kangxi emperor, had lived for 60 years. The East Warm Chamber of the Hall of Mental Cultivation was the site of the formal abdication of Pu Yi, the

last emperor. The document was signed by his father, who was regent.

There are also further exhibitions in some of the buildings lining the western side of the Outer Court; these include occasionally changing displays of court insignia, and ancient weapons and musical instruments. Before returning to the main Meridian Gate, it is possible to venture farther

west to the **Hall of Martial Valor** (still shown as off-limits on palace maps). The hall was the home of the palace's printing workshop and censors. It now contains a model illustrating the layout of the key central halls in miniature. Other exhibits make much of the Manchu emperors' acceptance of Chinese culture, using the Confucian classics to guide their governance.

The Last Emperor

Aisin Gioro Pu Yi ascended the Qing throne at the age of three in 1908 after the death of his uncle, the Guangxu emperor. His brief reign as the Xuantong emperor was brought to an end on February 12, 1912, when he abdicated the throne in the Forbidden City to make way for the new Republican government. The

Pu Yi (1905–67), China's "Last Emperor"

powerless Pu Yi continued to live in the palace until 1924, before being ejected by a warlord and escaping to the Legation Quarter. He was later installed as the Japanese puppet emperor of Manchukuo, residing in his palace in Changchun. At the end of World War II, he was arrested and handed over to the Chinese Communists, who imprisoned him in 1950. In 1959, Mao granted him amnesty. Pu Yi never returned to the Forbidden City, and he died of cancer, childless and anonymous, in 1967, after working for seven years as a gardener at the Beijing Botanical Gardens.

▦ Eastern Palaces

On the east side of the Inner Court lies a much closer-knit series of smaller palaces and courtyards, formerly used as the residences of imperial concubines. Nowadays, some of these areas serve as museums of jade, paintings, enamels, and other antique collectibles. Among them is the impressive **Clock and Watch Exhibition**, housed in the **Hall for Worshiping Ancestors**, which once held memorial tablets to Qing ancestors. You can walk among the vast pillars, which have now been replaced, the water-damaged coffer ceiling high above revealing why this was necessary. The sizeable and fascinating display of clocks includes elaborate Chinese, British, and French timepieces collected by Qing emperors, from a clumsy giant multi-bucket clepsydra to fragile bejeweled replicas of balloons and steamships, and delicate automata. One piece is topped by a robotic figure that dips his brush in ink and writes eight Chinese characters, as can be seen on an accompanying video. A limited number of the clocks are gently wound and set off at 11am and 2pm daily. On the east side

Decorative gate in the Eastern Palaces quarter

of the Inner Court is the **Palace of Abstinence**, where the emperor would fast before sacrificial ceremonies. Next to it is the **Palace of Prolonging Happiness**, a bizarre and incomplete structure of rusting steel and carved stone, designed to be surrounded by water, begun only two years before the fall of the Qing dynasty. Wings to either side of the palace, which were once the home of some of the museum's research departments, now house regularly changing exhibitions usually involving calligraphy, painting, and ceramics. A little further southeast of the exhibition

halls stands the beautiful **Nine Dragon Screen**, a 100 ft (31 m) long "spirit wall" made from richly glazed tiles and similar to the screen in Bei Hai Park (see p72). Chinese ghosts only travel in straight lines, and this screen blocked the straight route north through the Gate of Imperial Zenith and the Gate of Peaceful Longevity. Displays of jewelry and other treasures begin in a long passage up the west side of the courtyard, and continue in the **Hall of Imperial Zenith**, the **Palace of Peaceful Longevity**, and farther halls to the north. These halls are where the venerable Qianlong emperor (r.1736–95) lived out his retirement.

The infamous Empress Dowager Cixi (see p85) also retired to these same northern halls a century later during the brief period she allowed the Guangxu emperor to take the throne. Their interiors are in striking contrast to other halls, displaying a taste for dark paneling inset with mother-of-pearl, which is also to be seen at Cixi's complex at the Eastern Qing Tombs (see p97). Treasures on display here include scroll paintings and calligraphy, as well as everything from magnificent imperial headdresses with golden dragons disporting themselves among clouds of azure enamel, to vast boulders of jade carved into mountain scenes.

Imperial five-clawed dragons on a glazed Nine Dragon Screen

Chinese Dragons

The Chinese dragon is a curious hybrid of sometimes many animal parts – snake's body, deer horns, bull's ears, hawk's claws and fish scales. Endowed with magical characteristics, it can fly, swim, change into other animals, bring rainfall, and ward off evil spirits. The five-clawed dragon represented the power of the emperor, and therefore could only adorn his imperial buildings. The Chinese dragon is a beneficent beast offering protection and good luck, hence its depiction on screens and marble carriageways, and its significance, even today, in festivals such as Chinese New Year.

🏛 Pleasure Gardens

Both Qianlong and Cixi kept their keenest pleasures close to hand. The retired emperor's was the secluded **Flower Garden of the Palace of Peaceful Longevity** (also known as the Qianlong Garden), which is graced with rockeries, a small theater stage, and, most strikingly, the **Pavilion for Bestowing Wine**. This is where Qianlong and companions would play intellectual drinking games, floating cups of wine along a writhing 88 ft (27 m) long channel in the stone floor, and composing poems.

Cixi's passion was opera, and just to the east of the garden is the three-story **Pavilion of Pleasant Sounds**, a gaudy stage and fly-tower fully equipped with hoists and trap-doors, its ceiling painted with fluffy clouds. In celebration of her 60th birthday, the empress watched some ten consecutive days of performances here. The building opposite, which is where she would sit, contains costumes and scripts used by the imperial troupes.

The less gentle side of Cixi is remembered just to the north at the **Well of the Pearl Concubine**. In 1900, as foreign armies approached to lift the siege of the Legation Quarter *(see p53)*, Cixi prepared to flee for Xi'an, intending that the Guangxu emperor should accompany her. His favorite concubine dared to protest, and was thrown down the well for her temerity.

🏛 Palace Walls and Gates

The fortified wall around the Forbidden City was originally enclosed within a moat. Another wall ran around the grounds of the Imperial City, including what are now Bei Hai Park and Zhong Nan Hai government compound, the "new Forbidden City." The palace's walls are marked at each of its four corners by elaborate **Arrow Towers**, notable for their many eaves. Of the four palace gates, the horseshoe-shaped **Meridian Gate**, or **Wu Men**, *(see p66)*, which is the southern entrance to the Forbidden City, can be climbed to visit the temporary exhibitions on show in the central pavilion. This was the home of some of the first displays of palace treasures during the Nationalist era. It also affords views down into the bustle surrounding the ticket offices, and along the walls.

The northern gate of the palace is called the **Gate of Divine Prowess** or **Shenwu Men**, and originally served as a combined bell and drum tower. It now hosts an exhibition of old photographs and drawings related to the architecture and construction of the palaces and other buildings. Unfortunately the labeling of all items is in Chinese only.

The former City Bank of New York, now Beijing Police Museum

❼ Legation Quarter
东交民巷

Map 5 D1. Ⓜ Qian Men. Beijing Police Museum: **Tel** (010) 8522 5018. **Open** 9am–4pm Tue–Sun.

When the Conventions of Peking ended the Second Opium War in 1860, foreign delegations were permitted to take up residence in a quarter southeast of the Forbidden City. Here, the first modern foreign buildings in Beijing took root.

On the southeast corner of Tian'an Men Square, the distinctive stripey brick building was the first railway station built within the walls of Beijing, constructed by the British in 1901. It is now a shopping mall and theater for Beijing Opera. East of the station, along Dong Jiao Min Xiang, is the former City Bank of New York, now the **Beijing Police Museum**. Displays on the suppression of counter-revolutionaries and drug dealers share space with early tokens of authority from the Jin and Ming eras. There are also live transmissions from a roadside traffic camera.

East again is the Catholic church of **St. Michael's**, built in 1902, and opposite the church, the **former Belgian Legation**, modeled after a villa that belonged to King Leopold II. A rear entrance leads into a square fringed by mock European buildings. Most are now offices, but you can enter the lobby and see traces of the original fittings.

Glazed tile panel from palace gate

The four corners of the palace walls are guarded by Arrow Towers

Bei Hai with Jing Shan's summit in the background

❽ Jing Shan Park
景山

44 Jingshan Xi Jie, Xicheng. **Map** 2 A3.
Ⓜ Tian'an Men West. **Tel** (010) 6404
4071. **Open** 6am–9pm daily. 📷

Situated on Beijing's north-
south axis, Jing Shan Park has
its origins in the Yuan dynasty
(1279–1368). Its hill was created
from earth that was excavated
while building the palace moat
during the reign of the Ming
Yongle emperor. In the early
years of the Ming dynasty, it
was known as Wansui Shan
(Long Life Hill), but was
renamed Jing Shan (View or
Prospect Hill) in the Qing
era. Foreign residents also
referred to it as Coal Hill
(Mei Shan), supposedly
because coal was
stored at the foot of
the hill although other
theories exist.
  Until the fall of the
Qing, Jing Shan was
linked to the Forbidden
City and was restricted
to imperial use. The hill's purpose
was to protect the imperial
palaces within the Forbidden
City from malign northern
influences, which brought death
and destruction according to
classical *feng shui*. However, it
failed to save the last Ming
emperor, Chongzhen, who
hanged himself from a locust
tree *(huaishu)* in the park in
1644 when rebel troops forced
their way into Beijing. Another
tree, planted after the original
tree was cut down, marks the
spot in the park's southeast. The
park is dotted with several
pavilions and halls, but the
highlight of any visit is the
superb view of the Forbidden
City from the hill's Wanchun
Ting (Wanchun Pavilion).

❾ Bei Hai Park
北海公园

1 Wenjin Jie, Xicheng. **Map** 1 F3.
Ⓜ Tian'an Men West. **Tel** (010) 6403
3225. **Open** 6am–9pm daily. 📷

An imperial garden for more
than 1,000 years, Bei Hai Park
was opened to the public in
1925. Filled with artificial hills,
pavilions, and temples, it is
associated with Kublai Khan,
who redesigned it during the
Mongol Yuan dynasty.
The Tuancheng (Round
City) near the south
entrance has a huge,
decorated jade urn
belonging to him. The
park is named after its
extensive lake, **Bei Hai**,
whose southern end
is bordered by the
inaccessible Zhong
Nan Hai, Communist Party
Headquarters. In the middle
of Bei Hai, Jade Island was
supposedly made from the
earth excavated while creating
the lake. It is topped by the
118 ft (36 m) high **White
Dagoba**, a Tibetan-style stupa
built to honor the visit of the
fifth Dalai Lama in 1651.
Beneath the huge dagoba,
Yongan Si comprises a series
of ascending halls. The lake's
northern shore has several
sights, including the massive
Nine Dragon Screen, an 89 ft
(27 m) long spirit wall made
of colorful glazed tiles.

White Dagoba, Bei
Hai Park

Depicting nine intertwining
dragons, it was designed to
obstruct evil spirits. The
Xiaoxitian Temple lies to
the west.

❿ Mansion of Prince Gong
恭王府

17 Qianhai Xi Jie, Xicheng. **Map** 1 F2.
Ⓜ Ping'Anli. **Tel** (010) 8328 8149.
Open 7:30am–4:30pm daily. 📷

Beijing's most complete
example of a historic mansion is
situated in a charming *hutong*
district west of Qian Hai. It was
supposedly the inspiration
behind the residence portrayed
by Cao Xueqin in his classic
18th-century novel *Dream of
the Red Chamber (see pp24–5)*.
Built during the reign of the
Qianlong emperor, the house
is extensive and its charming
garden is a pattern of open
corridors and pavilions, dotted
with pools and gateways.
Originally built for Heshun,
a Manchu official and the
emperor's favorite, the
residence was appropriated by
the imperial household after he
was found guilty of using regal
motifs in his mansion design.
It was later bequeathed to
Prince Gong in the Xianfeng
emperor's reign (r.1851–61).
The house is popular with tour
groups, so early morning is
the best time to visit and
afterwards, the local *hutongs*
can be explored. In summer,
Beijing Opera is performed in
its Grand Opera House.

Elaborate arched gateway, Mansion of
Prince Gong

Beijing's Courtyard Houses

At first glance, Beijing seems a thoroughly modern city, but a stroll through the city's alleyways *(hutongs)* reveals the charm of old Beijing. These *hutongs* – weaving across much of central Beijing – are where many Beijing residents *(Beijingren)* still live. Typically running east to west, *hutongs* are created by the walls of courtyard houses *(siheyuan)*. Formerly the homes of officials and the well-to-do, most are now state-owned. The *hutongs* are very easy to find; for example, try the alleyways between the main streets south of Qian Men, or around Hou Hai and Qian Hai. The modernization of Beijing has destroyed many traditional *siheyuan*, but some have been cleaned up and have again become homes. A few have been converted into hotels *(see pp182–5)*, allowing the visitor a closer look at this disappearing world.

Crowded courtyards
As space became an issue in Beijing, additional buildings filled in the large courtyards. Several families may be living together in one *siheyuan*.

The main hall was the most northerly and usually reserved for the eldest of the family, such as the grandparents.

The wall adds privacy and keeps out spirits as they are unable to turn corners.

The open courtyard lets in both the sunlight and the wind and cold.

The number of halls and courtyards determines the grandeur of the residence.

Walls were important to the Chinese psyche – even in the secure capital, they felt the need to retreat behind them.

The entrance is at the southeastern corner as prescribed by *feng shui*.

Social housing
With several families living together, a strong community spirit is fostered, while the *hutong* outside becomes an extension of the home.

Typical Beijing *hutong*
You can take organized rickshaw tours of the *hutong*s, sometimes with a visit to the Mansion of Prince Gong *(see p72)*, but it can be more fun to explore them by yourself.

A view of the Bell Tower from Beijing's Drum Tower

⓫ Drum and Bell Towers
鼓楼

Northern end of Di'an Men Wai Dajie, Dongcheng. **Map** 2 A2. Ⓜ Gulou Dajie. **Tel** (010) 8403 6706. **Open** daily. 🐾

Located on the north-south meridian that bisects the Forbidden City and Tian'an Men Square, the Drum Tower (Gu Lou) rises up from a historic Beijing *hutong* district (*see p73*). The squat structure seen today was originally built in 1420 during the reign of the Ming Yongle emperor. Visitors can clamber up the steep stairs to look out over the city and inspect the 25 drums there. The one large and 24 smaller drums were beaten to mark the hours of the day. According to the official Chinese accounts, the original drums were destroyed by the foreign soldiers of the international army that relieved Beijing during the Boxer Rebellion.

A short walk north of the Drum Tower, the Bell Tower (Zhong Lou) is an edifice from 1745, which replaced an earlier tower that had burnt down. Suspended within the tower is a 15 ft (4.5 m) high and 42 ton (42,674 kg) bell that was cast in 1420. During Spring Festival (*see pp38–9*), visitors can pay to ring the bell for good luck.

⓬ Lama Temple
雍和宫

12 Yonghe Gong Dajie, Dongcheng. **Map** 2 C1. Ⓜ Yonghe Gong. **Tel** (010) 8419 1919. **Open** 9am–4pm daily. 🐾

Beijing's most beautiful temple complex, the Lama Temple (Yonghegong) was constructed during the 17th century and converted into a Tibetan lamasery in 1744. Its five main halls are a stylistic blend of Han, Mongol, and Tibetan motifs. The first hall has a traditional display – the plump laughing Buddha, Milefo, is back-to-back with Wei Tuo, the Protector of Buddhist Doctrine, and flanked by the Four Heavenly Kings. **Yonghe Hall** beyond has three manifestations of Buddha, flanked by 18 *luohan* – those freed from the cycle of rebirth. Even farther back, the Tibetan-styled **Falun Hall** or Hall of the Wheel of Law contains a statue of Tsongkhapa, the founder of the Yellow Hat sect of Tibetan Buddhism.

The highlight, however, is encapsulated within the towering **Wanfu Pavilion** (Wanfu Ge) – a vast 55 ft (17 m) high statue of Maitreya (the Future Buddha), carved from a single block of sandalwood. The splendid exhibition of

The striking main gateway of the colorful Lama Temple

For hotels and restaurants see pp182–5 and pp196–9

Statue of Confucius at the main entrance, Confucius Temple

Tibetan Buddhist objects at the temple's rear includes statues of the deities Padmasambhava (Guru Rinpoche), and the Tibetan equivalent of Guanyin, Chenresig, alongside ritual objects such as the scepter-like *dorje* (thunderbolt) and *dril bu* (bell), symbols of the male and female energies.

⑬ Confucius Temple
孔庙

13 Guozijian Jie, Dongcheng. **Map** 2 C1. Ⓜ Yonghe Gong. **Tel** (010) 8402 7224. **Open** 7:30am–6pm daily.

The Confucius Temple is the largest in China outside Qufu, the philosopher's birthplace in Shandong province. The alley leading to the temple has a fine *pailou* (decorative archway), few of which survive in Beijing. First built in 1302 during the Mongol Yuan dynasty, the temple was expanded in 1906 in the reign of Emperor Guangxu. It is a tranquil place that offers respite from the city's bustle. Around 200 ancient stelae stand in the silent courtyard in front of the main hall (Dacheng Dian), inscribed with the names of those who successfully passed the imperial civil service exams. Additional stelae are propped up on the backs of *bixi* (a

mythical cross between a tortoise and a dragon), within pavilions surrounded by cypress trees. On a marble terrace in the main hall are statues of Confucius and some of his disciples.

⑭ Di Tan Park
地坛公园

N of the Lama Temple, Dongcheng. **Map** 2 C1. Ⓜ Yonghe Gong. **Tel** (010) 6421 4657. **Open** daily.

An ideal place to stroll amidst trees, Di Tan Park was named after the Temple of Earth (Di Tan), which was the venue for imperial sacrifices. The park's altar (Fangze Tan) dates to the Ming dynasty and its square shape represents the earth. Under the Ming, five main altars were established at the city's cardinal points – Tian Tan (Temple of Heaven) in the south, Di Tan in the north, Ri Tan (Temple of the Sun) in the east, Yue Tan (Temple of the Moon) in the west, and Sheji Tan (Temple of Land and Grain) in the center. Mirroring ancient ceremonies, a lively temple fair (*miaohui*) is held during Chinese New Year (*see pp38–9*), to welcome the spring planting season and appease the gods.

⑮ Dong Yue Miao
东岳庙

141 Chaoyang Men Wai Dajie, Chaoyang. **Map** 3 E4. Ⓜ Chaoyang Men. **Tel** (010) 6551 3883. **Open** 8am–4:30pm Tue–Sun.

On Beijing's eastern side near Chaoyang's Workers' Stadium, the mesmerizing Dong Yue Miao takes its name from the Daoist Eastern Peak, Dong Yue, also known as Tai Shan. It is fronted by a fabulous glazed Ming dynasty *paifang* inscribed with the characters "Zhisi Daizong," meaning "offer sacrifices to Mount Tai (Tai Shan) in good order."

This colorful and active temple, dating to the early 14th century, was restored at considerable cost in 1999, and is tended by Daoist monks. The main courtyard leads into the Hall of Tai Shan, where there are statues of the God of Tai Shan and his attendants. The greatest attractions here are over 70 "Departments," filled with vivid Daoist gods and demons, whose functions are explained in English captions. In Daoist lore, the spirits of the dead go to Tai Shan, and many Departments dwell on the afterlife. The Department for Increasing Wealth and Longevity, for example, offers cheerful advice.

Guardian at entrance, Dong Yue Miao

Corn laid out to form Chinese characters, Temple festival, Di Tan Park

⑯ National Art Museum of China
中国美术馆

1 Wusi Dajie, Dongcheng. **Map** 2 B4.
Ⓜ Dong Si Shi Tiao. **Tel** (010) 6403
4951. **Open** 9am–5pm daily, last entry
4pm. 🚇 Ⓦ **namoc.org/en**

Hosting a number of
exhibitions of Chinese and
international art, as well as
occasional photographic
displays, the National Art
Museum of China (Zhongguo
Meishuguan) has 14 halls
spread over three levels. This
quite ordinary building holds
an exciting range of Chinese
modern art, which suffers less
censorship than other media,
such as film or literature.
Magazines such as *Time Out
Beijing* and *The Beijinger* carry
details of exhibitions.

⑰ Wangfujing Street
王府井

Map 2 B5. Ⓜ Wangfujing. Night Food
Market: **Open** 5:30pm–10pm daily. St.
Joseph's Church: 74 Wang-fujing Dajie.
Open early morning during services.

Bustling Wangfujing Street
(Wangfujing Dajie), Beijing's
main shopping street, has been
undergoing significant
redevelopment since 2008. The
street is now lined with malls
and plazas filled with high
fashion and other retail outlets.
Everything from curios, *objets
d'art*, antiques, clothes, and

The imposing façade of St. Joseph's Church,
Wangfujing Street

books can be found here. The
huge **Foreign Language
Bookstore** is a good place to
buy a more detailed map of
Beijing. The street has a lively
mixture of pharmacies, laundry
and dyeing shops, as
well as stores selling
silk, tea, and shoes.
However, the
street's highlight
is the **Night Food
Market**, with its
endless variety of
traditional Chinese
snacks, including
skewers of beef
and more exotic
morsels such as
scorpions. Other
offerings include
pancakes, fruit,
shrimps, squid, flat
bread, and more. The
Wangfujing Snack Street, south
of the Night Market, also has a
range of colorful restaurants.

The impressive triple-domed
St. Joseph's Church, known
as the East Cathedral, is at
74 Wangfujing Dajie and is one
of the city's most important
churches. It was built on the site
of the former residence of Jesuit
Adam Schall von Bell (1591–
1669) in 1655, and has been
rebuilt a number of times after
being successively destroyed by
earthquake, fire, and then during
the Boxer Rebellion. It is fronted
by an open courtyard and an
arched gateway.

⑱ Ancient Observatory
古观象台

Map 5 F1. Ⓜ Jianguo Men. **Tel** (010)
6524 2202. **Open** 9am–4pm daily. 🚇

Beijing's ancient observatory
(Gu Guanxiangtai) stands on
a platform alongside a
flyover off Jianguo Men
Nei Dajie. Dating to
1442, it is one of the
oldest in the world.
A Yuan dynasty
(1279–1368)
observatory was
also located here,
but the structure that
survives today was
built after the Ming
emperors relocated
their capital from
Nanjing to Beijing.
In the early 17th
century, the Jesuits, led by
Matteo Ricci (1552–1610) and
followed by Adam Schall von
Bell, impressed the emperor
and the imperial astronomers
with their scientific knowledge,
particularly the accuracy of their
predictions of eclipses.
The Belgian Jesuit Father
Verbiest (1623–88) was
appointed to the Imperial
Astronomical Bureau, where he
designed a set of astronomical
instruments in 1674. Several of
these were appropriated by
German soldiers during the
Boxer Rebellion of 1900, and
were only returned after
World War I.
A collection of reproduction
astronomical devices can be
found in the courtyard on the

Ecliptic armillary sphere,
Ancient Observatory

Delicious street food at the Night Food Market, just off Wangfujing Street

For hotels and restaurants see pp182–5 and pp196–9

The atmospheric Red Gate Gallery, Southeast Corner Watchtower

⑳ Beijing Natural History Museum
自然历史博物馆

126 Tianqiao Nan Dajie, Chongwen.
Map 4 C3. **M** Qian Men, then taxi.
Tel (010) 6702 7702. **Open** 9am–5pm
Tue–Sat. 🖼 **W** bmnh.org.cn

Housed in an enormous 1950s building covered in creepers, this museum is the largest of its type in China, with about 5,000 specimens arranged into three collections: zoology, paleontology, and botany. The most interesting collection is found in the Paleontology Hall which displays a selection of the dinosaurs and prehistoric animals that populated China between 500 million and one million years ago. Exhibits to look out for include the large-handed Lufengosaurus from the early Jurassic period, and a skeleton of the spine-nosed Qingdaosaurus (*Tsintaosaurus spinorhinus*) from the late Cretaceous period, whose skull sported a horn-like crest. The zoology section displays an abundance of marine, bird, and plant life to explain and illustrate the course of evolution from simple aquatic to far more complicated land-based forms. There is a also a display devoted to human evolution; many of the braver visitors head for the basement, which houses a macabre display of cross-sections of human cadavers, pickled corpses, limbs, and organs. The botany collection is less impressive but also much less disturbing.

ground floor, some decorated with fantastic Chinese designs including dragons. From here, steps lead to the roof, where there are impressive bronze instruments, including an azimuth theodolite, used to measure the altitude of celestial bodies, and an armillary sphere, for measuring the coordinates of planets and stars.

Southeast Corner Watchtower
(Dongbian Men)

⑲ Southeast Corner Watchtower
东边门箭楼

Off Jianguo Men Nan Dajie,
Chongwen. **Map** 5 F2. **M** Beijing
Zhan. Red Gate Gallery: **Tel** (010)
6525 1005. **Open** 10am–5pm daily.
🖼 for exhibition details visit
W redgategallery.com

A short distance south of the Ancient Observatory, an imposing chunk of the Beijing City Walls (*see p64*) survives in the form of the 15th-century Southeast Corner Watchtower (Dongbian Men). After climbing

onto the Ming dynasty battlements, visitors can walk along the short but impressive stretch of attached wall to admire the towering bastion, pitted with archers' windows, and look down on the city below. The walls of the tower are engraved with graffiti left by soldiers of the international army that marched into the city to liberate the Foreign Legations during the Boxer Rebellion in 1900.

Within its splendid, cavernous interior, accessed from the battlements, the rooms reveal enormous red wooden columns and pillars, crossed with beams. The **Red Gate Gallery**, one of Beijing's most appealing art galleries, is situated within this superb setting on levels 1 and 4. Originally founded in 1991 by an Australian who came to Beijing to learn Chinese, the gallery exhibits works in a wide variety of media by up-and-coming contemporary Chinese artists. Forthcoming exhibitions are listed on the gallery's website.

Dinosaur skeletons in the Paleontology Hall, Natural History Museum

㉑ Temple of Heaven
天坛

Completed during the Ming dynasty, the Temple of Heaven, more correctly known as Tian Tan, is one of the largest temple complexes in China and a paradigm of Chinese architectural balance and symbolism. It was here that the emperor would make sacrifices and pray to heaven and his ancestors at the winter solstice. As the Son of Heaven, the emperor could intercede with the gods, represented by their spirit tablets, on behalf of his people and pray for a good harvest. Off-limits to the common people during the Ming and Qing dynasties, the Temple of Heaven is situated in a large and pleasant park that now attracts thousands of visitors daily.

Qinian Dian, where the emperor prayed for a good harvest

The Temple of Heaven Complex

The main parts of the temple complex are all connected on the favored north-south axis by the Red Step Bridge (an elevated pathway) to form the focal point of the park. The Round Altar is made up of concentric rings of stone slabs in multiples of nine, the most auspicious number. The circular Echo Wall is famed for its supposed ability to carry a whisper from one side of the wall to the other.

① Hall of August Heaven
② Qinian Dian (Hall of Prayer for Good Harvests)
③ Red Step Bridge
④ Echo Wall
⑤ Imperial Vault of Heaven
⑥ Round Altar
⑦ Seven Star Rock
⑧ Hall of Abstinence

0 meters 250
0 yards 250

Key
☐ Area illustrated

North Heavenly Gate

West Heavenly Gate

TEMPLE OF HEAVEN PARK

East Heavenly Gate

South Heavenly Gate

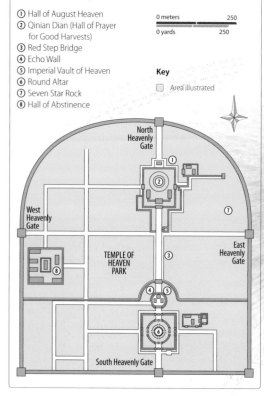

Qinian Dian

Originally built in 1420, the Qinian Dian, or Hall of Prayer for Good Harvests, is often incorrectly called the Temple of Heaven. There is in fact no single temple building as such at Tian Tan, a more literal translation of which is Altar of Heaven referring to the whole complex.

★ **Caisson ceiling**
The splendid circular caisson ceiling has a gilded dragon and phoenix at its center. The hall is entirely built of wood without using a single nail.

VISITORS' CHECKLIST

Practical Information
Tian Tan Dong Lu, Chongwen.
Map 5 D4. **Tel** (010) 6702 8866.
Open 6am–10pm daily. Temple
Buildings: **Open** 8am–5pm daily.

Transport
Ⓜ Qian Men, then taxi.
🚌 34, 6, 35 Park.

★ **Dragon Well pillars**
The roofs of the hall are supported on 28 highly decorated pillars. At the center, the four huge columns, known as Dragon Well pillars, represent the seasons, while the other 24 smaller pillars symbolize the months in a year plus the 12 two-hour time periods in a day.

KEY

① **Dragon and phoenix motifs** inside and out represent the emperor and empress.

② **Red** is an imperial color.

③ **The circular roof** symbolizes the sky.

④ **Name plaques** are often written in the calligraphy of an emperor.

⑤ **The golden finial** is 125 ft (38 m) high and prone to lightning strikes.

⑥ **Blue** represents the color of heaven.

⑦ **Tablets** in memory of his ancestors were worshiped by the emperor.

⑧ **Symbolic offerings**

Marble platform
Three tiers of marble form a circle 300 ft (90 m) in diameter and 20 ft (6 m) high. The balusters on the upper tier are decorated with dragon carvings to signify the imperial nature of the structure.

Exploring the Temple of Heaven

The Temple of Heaven complex (or Tian Tan, which is more correctly translated as Altar of Heaven) is set in one of Beijing's most impressive parks. The temple was the place where earth, signified by square shapes including the bases of the enclosures, communicated with heaven, signified by the rounded top. This motif of square and rounded shapes is repeated in the layout of the park. Today, local retired people, inured both to the magnificence of the buildings and their hordes of visitors, use the site as a public recreational space, practicing *tai ji quan (tai chi)*, various martial arts, and other exercises, flying kites, and rehearsing Beijing Opera, all of which add to the charm.

Triple gates for emperor (east), officials (west), and gods (center)

⛩ The Tian Tan Complex

Entering through the North Heavenly Gate, the first building encountered is the **Hall of August Heaven**. This once held wooden spirit tablets representing imperial ancestors. It is also where preliminary ceremonies would take place.

But the Hall of August Heaven is dwarfed by the **Qinian Dian**, or **Hall of Prayer for Good Harvests**, which has come to symbolize Beijing almost as much as the Tian'an Men. This circular tower, topped by a conical roof of dark blue tiles and a gold knob, is perhaps the most beautiful building in the entire city, standing on a great triple-layered, circular, marble plinth, and painted in blue, green, and gold, with red latticed doors at ground level. One of its many claims to fame is that it was constructed without the use of a single nail. Visitors should lean inside for a view of the dragon and phoenix, which form the centerpiece of the caisson ceiling. This central roundel is mirrored by a natural marble slab in the center of the floor, which is where the emperor would make his prayers for good harvest in the autumn.

The emperor would spend the night before the rituals fasting at the **Hall of Abstinence**, southwest of the Qinian Dian. Prior to this he would have been carried in a yellow palanquin through the shuttered streets of the city in almost complete silence, accompanied by as many as 500 officials and ceremonially dressed eunuchs. The foreign legations who settled in Beijing after 1860 were sent notice to keep away and not disturb the procession. Services to the British-built railway station at Qian Men had to be halted for the duration of the ceremonies. The Abstinence Hall itself is the Forbidden City in miniature, walled and moated, entered by two great gates accessed by bridges.

Running south from the Qinian Dian, the **Red Step Bridge** is the central axis of the whole complex, an elevated walkway of stone and marble leading to the main altar. Before the altar is the **Imperial Vault of Heaven**, a lower round building used for storing ceremonial equipment. This is surrounded by the perfectly circular **Echo Wall**, with the same sonic effects found in some European cathedrals, where even a whisper travels round to a listener on the other side. A handclap made while standing on different stones at the center produces a different number of echoes. However, since this is one of the most-visited sights in Beijing, it's rarely possible to test either effect amid the hubbub of everybody else's efforts. Although the Qinian Dian is

Imperial Vault of Heaven, store for ceremonial equipment

The Round Altar, site of the annual winter solstice sacrifice

㉒ Xiannong Tan
先农坛

West of the Temple of Heaven.
Map 4 C4. **M** Qian Men, then taxi.
Open 9am–4pm daily.

As late as the 1930s, almost half of the land within the southern part of the city walls was still green space, and the Xiannong Tan complex, which was immediately west of Tian Tan, was nearly the same size. Tan is more correctly translated as altar than temple and, as with its better-known neighbor, the emperor came here annually to perform vital ceremonies. On the vernal equinox, he would perform various sacrifices, then dress as a farmer and, with various officials guiding the oxen, would plough three furrows. This ritual was performed here from 1420, when some of the remaining halls were constructed, until 1906.

The World Monuments Fund has restored several halls, some of which now house an exhibition on the rituals, while the **Hall of Jupiter**, second in size only to the Forbidden City's Hall of Middle Harmony, is now home to the **Museum of Ancient Architecture**. This museum provides an excellent introduction to the construction techniques of so much that has been lost, helpfully illuminated with detailed models. A fascinating three-dimensional plan shows the Beijing of 1949, with the magnificent city walls and gates largely intact.

regarded as the star, in fact the focus of the Tian Tan complex is the vast triple-tiered **Round Altar** that dominates the southern part of the site. The altar is made up of marble slabs laid in nine concentric circles with each circle containing a multiple of nine pieces. The center of the altar represents the center of the world. Supposedly, the extraordinary acoustics of the construction magnify the sound made by anyone speaking at the center. This is where the emperor would perform the annual winter solstice sacrifice of a young bullock.

Various minor buildings around the site were for the use of musicians and other attendants, and for preparation and cremation of the sacrifice.

The park's venerable cypresses were important enough to be the subject of poems, while the seeds of the park's elms were traditionally made into cakes. These cakes, along with a certain "dragon-whisker" vegetable from the grounds, were regarded as delicacies, believed to have added spiritual or medicinal qualities. However, the park's flora has not always been so respected – many of the trees were cut down for firewood during the Nationalist era.

Although the original temple enclosure was off-limits to ordinary people, by the 18th century there were merchants' stalls along both the inside and outside of the north wall, some of which reappeared in the late 1980s, only to be cleared away again in recent times.

Yuan Shikai

So important were the ceremonies at the Temple of Heaven in demonstrating the right to rule that not long after the founding of the republic in 1912, first president Yuan Shikai insisted that he should use them to reaffirm his unstable authority. His trip to the Temple of Heaven to perform the rites in 1915 was widely viewed as his first step to becoming emperor, although the solemnity of the occasion was somewhat ruined by his decision to travel in an armored car, and by the presence of cameras there to record the events. Shortly afterwards he organized a petition demanding that he ascend the throne, and began the process of installing himself as the first emperor of a new dynasty. Protest from overseas and revolt amongst his supporters brought this to a halt in March 1916, and by June an exhausted Yuan was dead, leaving China to decades of civil war and Japanese occupation.

Yuan Shikai, 1859–1916

A decorative ceiling roundel at the Museum of Ancient Architecture

㉓ Cow Street Mosque
牛街清真寺

88 Niu Jie, Xuanwu. **Map** 4 A3.
Ⓜ Xuanwu Men, then taxi.
Tel (010) 6353 2564. **Open** 8am–4pm
daily. Avoid Fri (holy day). 🖼

Beijing's oldest and largest
mosque dates back to the
10th century. It is located in
the city's Hui district, near
numerous Muslim restaurants
and shops. The Hui, a Chinese
Muslim minority group mainly
from Ningxia province, are
now scattered throughout
China and number around
200,000 in Beijing. The men
are easily identified by their
beards and characteristic
white hats.

The Cow Street Mosque is an
attractive edifice, with Islamic
motifs and Arabic verses
decorating its halls and stelae.
Its most prized possession is a
300-year-old, hand-written
copy of the Koran (Gulanjing).

Astronomical observations
and lunar calculations were
made from the tower-like
Wangyue Lou. The graves
of two Yuan dynasty Arab
missionaries engraved with
Arabic inscriptions can be seen
here. The courtyard is lush with
greenery, making it an idyllic
escape from Beijing's busy
streets. Visitors are advised
to dress conservatively.
Non-Muslims are not allowed
to enter the prayer hall.

Buddhist statuary in the main hall, Fayuan Temple

㉔ Fayuan Temple
法源寺

7 Fayuan Si Qian Jie, Xuanwu.
Map 4 A3. Ⓜ Xuanwu Men.
Open 8:30am–4pm Mon, Tue
& Thu–Sun. 🖼

A short walk east from Cow
Street Mosque, the Fayuan
Temple dates to AD 696 and is
probably the oldest temple in
Beijing. It was consecrated by
the Tang Taizong emperor
(r. 626–49), to commemorate
the soldiers who perished in an
expedition against the northern
tribes. The original Tang era
buildings were destroyed by a
succession of natural disasters,
and the current structures date
from the Qing era.

The temple's layout is typical of
Buddhist temples. Near the gate,
the incense burner (lu) is flanked
by the Drum and Bell Towers to
the east and west. Beyond, the
Hall of the Heavenly Kings
(Tianwang Dian) is guarded
by a pair of bronze lions, and
has statues of Milefo (the
Laughing Buddha) and his
attendant Heavenly Kings.
Ancient stelae stand in front
of the main hall, where a
gilded statue of Sakyamuni
(the Historical Buddha) is
flanked by bodhisattvas and
luohan – those freed from the
cycle of rebirth.

At the temple's rear, the
Scripture Hall stores sutras,
while another hall contains a
16 ft (5 m) Buddha statue.
The grounds are busy with
monks who attend the
temple's Buddhist College.

㉕ White Clouds Temple
白云寺

6 Baiyuanguan Jie, Xuanwu.
Ⓜ Nanlishi Lu, then taxi. **Tel** (010)
6346 3531. **Open** 8am–5pm daily. 🖼

Home to the China Daoist
Association, the White Clouds
Temple (Baiyun Guan) was
founded in AD 739 and is
Beijing's largest Daoist shrine.
Known as the Temple of
Heavenly Eternity, it was one of
the three ancestral halls of the
Quanzhen School of Daoism,
which focused on right action
and the benefits of good karma.
Built largely of wood, the
temple burned to the ground
in 1166, and since then has
been repeatedly destroyed
and rebuilt. The structures that
survive date largely from the
Ming and Qing dynasties.
A triple-gated Ming pailou
(decorative archway) stands at

Resplendent interior of the Cow Street Mosque

the entrance. It is believed that rubbing the carved monkey on the main gate brings good luck.

The temple grounds are full of Daoist monks with their distinctive topknots. It is most lively during the Chinese New Year *(see pp38–9)*, when a temple fair *(miaohui)* is held.

❷❻ Capital Museum
首都博物馆

16 Fuxingmenwai Dajie. Ⓜ Muxidi. **Tel** (010) 6337 0491. **Open** 9am–5pm Tue–Sun (last adm 4pm). Ⓦ **capitalmuseum.org.cn**

This striking glass and concrete structure houses around 200,000 relics arranged over seven storys, ranging from ancient bronze, porcelain and jade, to calligraphy and paintings. There is also an impressive collection of ancient Buddhist statues on display. Admission is free but book ahead for guaranteed entry.

❷❼ Military Museum of the Chinese People's Revolution
军事博物馆

9 Fuxing Lu, Haidian. Ⓜ Military Museum. **Tel** (010) 6686 6244. **Open** 8:30am–5pm Tue–Sun. Ⓦ **jb.mil.cn**

Topped by a gilded emblem of the People's Liberation Army, the Chinese Military History Museum is devoted to weaponry and revolutionary heroism. It is close to Muxidi, where the People's Liberation Army killed scores of civilians in 1989. Visitors are

Buddhist monks, Miaoying Temple White Dagoba

greeted by paintings of Mao, Marx, Lenin, and Stalin. The ground floor exhibits defunct F-5 and F-7 jet fighter planes, tanks, and surface-to-air missiles. The top floor gallery chronicles many of China's military campaigns.

❷❽ Miaoying Temple White Dagoba
妙应寺

Fucheng Men Nei Dajie, Xicheng. **Map** 1 D3. Ⓜ Fucheng Men. **Tel** (010) 6616 6099. **Open** 9am–4pm daily. 🖼

Celebrated for its distinctive Tibetan-styled, 167 ft (51 m) white dagoba (stupa or funerary mound) designed by a Nepalese architect, the Miaoying Temple (Miaoying Si) dates to 1271, when Beijing was under Mongol rule. In addition to its conventional Drum and Bell Towers, Hall of Heavenly Kings, and Main Halls, this Buddhist temple has a remarkable collection of small Tibetan Buddhist statues and a collection of 18 bronze *luohan* (disciples).

❷❾ Beijing Zoo
北京动物园

137 Xizhi Men Wai Dajie, Haidian. Ⓜ Beijing Zoo. **Tel** (010) 6831 5131. **Open** 7:30am–6pm. 🖼 Ⓦ **bjzoo.com**

West of the Beijing Exhibition Hall, Beijing Zoo is a relic of a bygone era, with outdated concrete and glass cages. The Panda Hall is one of the most popular enclosures, and the bears are at their liveliest in the mornings. There is also a huge aquarium with coral reefs, an array of aquatic mammals, an Amazon rainforest and an impressive shark pool.

F-5 fighter planes, Military Museum of the Chinese People's Revolution

㉚ Summer Palace
颐和园

The sprawling grounds of the Summer Palace (Yihe Yuan) served the Qing dynasty as an imperial retreat from the stifling summer confines of the Forbidden City. Despite existing as an imperial park in earlier dynasties, it was not until the time of Emperor Qianlong, who reigned from 1736 to 1795, that the Summer Palace assumed its current layout. The palace is most associated, however, with the Empress Dowager Cixi, who had it rebuilt twice: once following its destruction by French and English troops in 1860, and again in 1902 after it was plundered during the Boxer Rebellion.

Suzhou Street
A recreation of the shopping street originally built for the Qianlong emperor.

Marble Boat
Cixi paid for this extravagant folly with funds meant for the modernization of the Imperial Navy. The superstructure of the boat is made of wood painted white to look like marble.

KEY

① Boat pier

② **The Bronze Pavilion**, weighing 207 tons (188 tonnes), is a highly detailed metal replica of a timber-framed building.

③ Temple of the Sea of Wisdom

④ Back Lake

⑤ **The Garden of Harmonious Pleasures** was Cixi's favorite spot for fishing.

⑥ East Palace Gate (main entrance).

⑦ Hall of Jade Ripples

⑧ Hall of Happiness and Longevity

★ Longevity Hill
The Tower of the Fragrance of the Buddha dominates this slope covered with impressive religious buildings.

Empress Cixi, 1835–1908

Empress Dowager Cixi

Along with the Tang dynasty, Empress Wu Zetian, Cixi, is remembered as one of China's most powerful women. Having borne the Xianfeng emperor's son as an imperial concubine, Cixi later seized power as regent to both the Tongzhi and Guangxu emperors (her son and nephew respectively). Cixi prevented Guangxu from implementing state reforms and, in her alliance with the Boxer Rebellion, paved the way for the fall of the Qing Dynasty in 1911.

★ **Garden of Virtue and Harmony**
This three-story building served as a theater, where the court's 348-member opera troupe entertained Cixi, who watched from the surrounding gallery.

★ **Long Corridor**
The beams along the length of this 2,388 ft (728 m) walkway are decorated with over 14,000 scenic paintings.

Hall of Benevolence and Longevity
The principal ceremonial hall, this single-eaved building houses the throne upon which Cixi sat.

Exploring the Summer Palace

Following the conventions of Chinese gardens *(see pp32–3)* the palace grounds are arranged as a microcosm of nature, its hills *(shan)* and water *(shui)* creating a natural composition further complemented by bridges, temples, walkways, and ceremonial halls. Even after repeated restoration, the Summer Palace tastefully harmonizes the functional and fanciful, with administrative and residential quarters leading to the pastoral vistas of the grounds, as well as numerous peaceful temples and shrines. Despite the Summer Palace's popularity, a little walking takes you to peaceful corners that are among the most idyllic in Beijing.

A pleasure cruise on Kunming Lake aboard a dragon ferry boat

🔲 Palace Complex

The grounds of the Summer Palace are extensive, but the main buildings can all be visited by those with sufficient energy and time.

The main entrance at the **East Palace Gate** (Gong Dong Men) leads to the official and residential halls of the palace complex. Just inside the main gate stands the **Hall of Benevolence and Longevity** (Renshou Dian), where the Empress Dowager Cixi and her nephew the puppet-emperor Guangxu gave audience. The bronze statues in front of this ceremonial hall include the symbol of Confucian virtue, the mythical *qilin*, a hybrid, cloven-hoofed animal with horns and scales, sometimes incorrectly referred to as China's unicorn.

To the west, by the lakeside, the **Hall of Jade Ripples** (Yulan Tang) is where Cixi incarcerated Guangxu during her extended stays here after he supported the abortive 1898 Reform

Movement betrayed by Yuan Shikai. Cixi's former residence, the **Hall of Happiness and Longevity** (Leshou Tang), is full of Qing-era furniture and supposedly remains as it was at the time of her death in 1908. To the south is the jetty from where Cixi would set sail across the lake; to the east is the **Garden of Virtue and Harmony** (Dehe Yuan) with Cixi's private theater. The theater buildings now contain an exhibition of Qing-era artifacts of daily use, from vehicles to costumes and glassware.

🔲 Longevity Hill

From the Hall of Happiness and Longevity, the **Long Corridor** (Chang Lang), decorated with painted landscapes and other scenes, zigzags along the shore of the lake, interrupted along its length by four pavilions.

At the corridor's halfway point, a series of religious and administrative buildings ascends the slopes of **Longevity Hill** (Wanshou Shan), artificially raised to improve the view in Qianlong's time. The start of the sequence is marked at the lakeside by a fabulous decorative gate *(pailou)*, beyond which stands the **Cloud Dispelling Gate**, with two bronze lions sitting alongside it.

The first main hall, the **Cloud Dispelling Hall** (Paiyun Dian), is a double-eaved structure that was the throne room when the court was at the palace. In the center of the hall is the Empress Dowager's nine-dragon throne, where she sat to receive tribute. Above the hall, rising from a great stone platform, stands the prominent, octagonal, four-eaved **Tower of the Fragrance of the Buddha** (Foxiang Ge). The stiff climb is worth the effort for views from the balcony over the yellow roofs of the halls and pavilions to the lake below.

West of the Tower of the Fragrance of the Buddha is the **Bronze Pavilion**, more properly known as the **Precious Clouds Pavilion** (Baoyun Ge), which imitates the construction of other wooden pavilions, but is built entirely in metal. Dating from the 18th century, the building is one of a handful

Door to the Temple of the Sea of Wisdom with glazed Buddha effigies

Seventeen-Arch Bridge linking South Lake Island to the mainland

that, although damaged, survived the destruction wrought by English and French troops during the Second Opium War. The same is true of the magnificent **Temple of the Sea of Wisdom** (Huihai Si), which is directly behind the Tower of the Fragrance of the Buddha. It has an exterior decorated with green and yellow tiles and façades embellished with glazed Buddhist effigies, many of which have been vandalized. From here, you can look down or descend to the **Back Lake** (Hou Hu) and **Suzhou Street**, a row of recently recreated historical commercial buildings. Here, the Qianlong emperor with his concubines and eunuchs would play at being part of the common herd, acting out the roles of shoppers, shopkeepers, and pickpockets. Today, these buildings house snack vendors and souvenir stalls, with staff dressed in Qing-era costume.

🚣 South Lake

The buildings at the north end of the lake are more than enough to fill a single day, however the southern end of the grounds can be blissfully free of crowds. Boat trips to **South Lake Island** depart from

the jetty near the **Marble Boat**, also known as the Boat of Purity and Ease, which is found at the very westernmost end of the Long Corridor (north of here are the imperial boat-houses). Alternatively, if time will allow, hire a boat for a leisurely row around Kunming Lake, or in muggy summer heat, a slow but battery-powered

The eastern shore's bronze ox

alternative. On South Lake Island, the **Dragon King Temple** (Long-wang Miao) is dedicated to the god of rivers,

seas, and rain. Cixi would come here to pray for rain in times of drought. The island is connected to the eastern shore by the elegant **Seventeen-Arch Bridge** (Shiqi Kong Qiao). A marble lion crowns each of the 544 balusters along the bridge's length, all supposedly individual. A large **bronze ox**, dating back to 1755 but looking entirely modern, reposes on the eastern shore; it was believed to pacify the waters and prevent floods.

Across on the western side of Kunming Lake, steep-sloped **Jade Belt Bridge** links the mainland to the West Causeway, which slices through the lake to its southern point.

Plan of Grounds

The grounds of the Summer Palace cover 716 acres (290 hectares), with Kunming Lake lying to the south of Longevity Hill. South Lake Island is just off the east shore and a stroll around the entire shoreline takes about two hours.

① Jade Belt Bridge
② West Causeway
③ South Lake Island
④ Bronze ox

Longevity Hill

Kunming Lake

West Lake

South Lake

Key

☐ Area illustrated (see pp84–5)

| 0 meters | 800 |
| 0 yards | 800 |

Remnants of the Yuanming Yuan, once said to resemble Versailles

❶ Yuanming Yuan
圆明园

28 Qinghua Xi Lu, Haidian.
Ⓜ Yuanming Yuan Park.
Open 7am–5pm daily.

The Yuanming Yuan (Garden of Perfect Brightness, sometimes called the Old Summer Palace) now sits isolated from the main Summer Palace, but was a collection of princely gardens fused into the main mass by the Qing Qianlong emperor in the mid-18th century. He commissioned Jesuits at his court to design and construct a set of European-style buildings in one corner, which they likened to Versailles. Unfortunately, all the traditional Chinese halls were burned down by British and French troops during the Second Opium War in 1860. Later, the European-style buildings were pulled down, and much of the remains carted away by the locals for building purposes. Chinese narrations of the devastation criticize both the marauding European troops and the ineffectual Qing rulers.

Today, Yuanming Yuan is a jumble of sad yet graceful fragments of stone and marble strewn in the **Eternal Spring Garden** in the park's north-eastern corner. A small museum displays images and models of the palace, depicting its scale and magnificence. The **Palace Maze** has been recreated in concrete to the west of the ruins. The rest of the park is a pleasant expanse of lakes, pavilions, gardens and walks.

❷ Great Bell Temple
大钟寺

31a Beisanhuan Xi Lu, Haidian.
300, 367. **Tel** (010) 6255 0819.
Open 8:30am–4pm daily.

Home to a fascinating collection of bells, the 18th-century Dazhong Si follows a typical Buddhist plan, with the Heavenly Kings Hall, Main Hall, and the Guanyin Bodhisattva Hall. Its highlight is the 46.5 ton (47,246 kg) bell – one of the world's largest – that is housed in the rear tower. The bell was cast between 1403 and 1424, and brought here from Wanshou Temple in the reign of the Qianlong emperor. Buddhist *sutras* in Chinese and Sanskrit embellish its surface. During the Ming and Qing dynasties, the bell was struck 108 times to bring in the New Year, and could be heard for 25 miles (40 km). The gallery above has a display on bell casting, and

Heng, Biyun Temple deity

visitors can toss a coin into a gap at the top of the bell for luck. Hundreds of bells from the Song, Yuan, Ming, and Qing eras can be seen in a separate hall on the west side.

❸ Xiang Shan Park
香山公园

Wofosi Lu, Xiang Shan, Haidian district.
333 from Summer Palace, 360 from Zoo. **Open** 6am–7pm.
Botanical Gardens: **Open** daily.

This wooded parkland area, also known as Fragrant Hills Park, is at its scenic best in the fall, when the maples turn a flaming red. Its main attractions are the fine views from **Incense Burner Peak**, accessible by a chairlift, and the splendid **Biyun Temple**, or Azure Cloud Temple, close to the main gate. The temple is guarded by the menacing deities Heng and Ha in the Mountain Gate Hall. A series of halls leads to the Sun Yat Sen Memorial Hall, where his coffin was stored in 1925 before being taken to Nanjing. At the temple's rear is the distinctive 112 ft (34 m) high Diamond Throne Pagoda. About a mile (2 km) east of Xiang Shan Park are the **Beijing Botanical Gardens**, with pleasant walks and some 3,000 plant species. The gardens' **Sleeping Buddha Temple** is renowned for its magnificent bronze statue of a reclining Buddha. China's last emperor, Pu Yi (see p69), ended his days here as a gardener.

The Great Bell Temple, or Dazhong Si

㉞ National Olympic Stadium
奥林匹克体育中心

Olympic Green. **M** Olympic Park. 🚌 Water Park. **Tel** (010) 8437 3011. **Open** 10am–4pm daily. ♿ **W** n-s.cn

Beijing's National Olympic Stadium was the stunning centerpiece of China's massive building program for the 2008 Olympics. It is part of the city's "Olympic Green" development, which includes a large land-scaped park, an Olympic Village, and many other stadia including the National Indoor Stadium and Water Cube National Aquatics Center.

Swiss architects Herzog & de Meuron won the competition for the stadium, working in combination with Beijing-based artist and architect Ai Weiwei, with a bird's nest-like structure of apparently random, inter-twined ribbons of steel and concrete that simultaneously form both façade and structure. The gaps in the concrete lattice of the roof are filled with tran-slucent inflated bags, making the building waterproof while allowing light to filter down to the spectators within.

In 2010, a vast water park opened at the Water Cube Center. The park features a wavepool, 13 giant slides, and other colorful, high-tech aquatic attractions.

㉟ 798 Art District
七九八艺术区（大山子）

2-4 Juxian Qiao Lu, Da Shan Zi, Chaoyang. 🚌 915 or 918 from Dong Zhi Men to Da Shan Zi, or 420 from Beijing Station. **Open** 10:30am–7:30pm daily. **W** 798district.com

Although it has spilled out of its original home and into neighboring moribund industrial buildings to form the Da Shan Zi Art District, the lively arts scene here is still mostly known for the abandoned No. 798 Electronics Factory. This was the first to be converted into a complex of studios, workshops, and galleries called 798 Space.

Contemporary art meets obsolete industry at 798 Space in Da Shan Zi

Built in the Bauhaus style in the 1950s by East Germans with Soviet funding, the area was once the center of Chinese high-tech, said to have produced parts for China's first nuclear bombs and satellites. Now its industrial chic is put to more peaceful purposes with art in all media for sale both in galleries and directly from the artists themselves. Wandering among the galleries reveals a different and interesting side to the city – there are large Communist-style sculptures making ironic reflections on history and new Mao-kitsch graffiti on the walls next to the original 1950s slogans exhorting workers. Cafés and restaurants have sprung up to add to the allure of the area.

㊱ China Railway Museum
中国铁道博物馆

1 Jiuxiang Qiao Bei Lu, Chaoyang. **Tel** (010) 6438 1317. **Open** 9am–4pm Tue–Sun. ♿ **W** china-rail.org

The last passenger steam services in China came to an end in 2006, but a short taxi ride northeast of the 798 Art District, the Railway Ministry Science and Technology Center has a vast modern hall displaying 53 old locomotives. The collection includes some of the vast black engines imported by the Japanese when they controlled Manchuria, as well as huge Chinese beasts from Datong, and tiny Thomas the Tank Engine-scaled machines that once worked narrow-gauge extensions to French-built lines in Yunnan Province.

㊲ CCTV Headquarters
央视总部

32 E 3rd Ring Road Middle, Chaoyang. **M** Jintaixizhao. **Closed** to the public.

This 768 ft- (234 m)- high Deconstrucivist skyscraper, a remarkable feat of engineering dreamt up by architects Rem Koolhas and Ole Scheeren, houses the China Central Tele-vision offices. Closed to the public, it is worth a visit for the sheer spectacle alone.

Communist-era locomotives at the China Railway Museum

FARTHER AFIELD

Beijing continues to expand, ring road by ring road, but – for now – there is still relief from the crowds to be found in the surprisingly lush landscapes beyond the city limits. The Great Wall meanders across hilly territory to the north, always making for the highest point, and frequently doubling back on itself. There are several official access points with coach parks and souvenir shops, and an unlimited number of unofficial ones.

To the west, ancient temples nestle on green hillsides where rural life goes on much as it has for centuries. A trip out here offers a glimpse of the realities of existence for two-thirds of China's population. This is a world of tiny two-stroke tractors and water buffalo; of orderly patchworks of tiny wheat, corn, and sorghum fields; of bee-keeping and pig husbandry. Most temples have simple guest rooms, while at the well-preserved Ming- and Qing-era village of Cuandixia, you can stay with the villagers themselves.

The countryside also harbors the vast necropolises of the Ming emperors and, more interestingly, the much less visited but more elaborate resting places of the Qing, to the east and southwest of the city. Also to the southwest is the 300-year-old stone Marco Polo Bridge and neighboring Wanping, a rare surviving example of a walled city. Both are an easy suburban bus ride from the city.

Sights at a Glance

Tombs, Temples, and Historic Buildings
1. Ming Tombs pp92–3
2. Great Wall of China pp94–6
3. Eastern Qing Tombs
4. Marco Polo Bridge
5. Tanzhe Temple
6. Jietai Temple

Towns and Villages
7. Shidu
8. Cuandixia

Key
- City limits
- National highway
- Major road
- Minor road
- Railroad
- Great Wall of China
- Beijing Province border

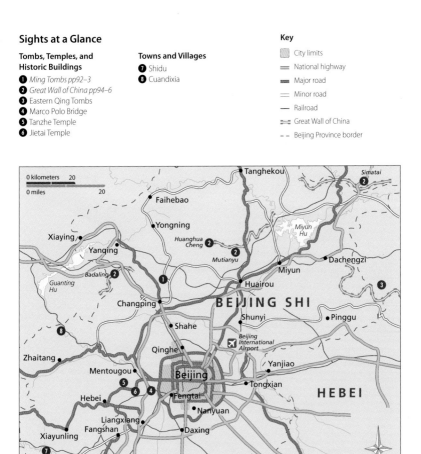

◀ The timeless spectacle of the Great Wall, snaking its way along mountain ridges

For keys to symbols see back flap

❶ Ming Tombs: Chang Ling

明十三陵

The resting place for 13 of the 16 Ming emperors, the Ming Tombs (Shisan Ling) are China's finest example of imperial tomb architecture. The site was originally selected because of its auspicious *feng shui* alignment; a ridge of mountains to the north cradles the tombs on three sides, opening to the south and protecting the dead from the evil spirits carried on the north wind. The resting place of the Yongle emperor (1360–1424), the Chang Ling is the most impressive tomb and the first to be built. It has been beautifully restored, although the burial chamber, where Yongle, his wife, and 16 concubines are thought to be interred, has never been excavated.

★ **Spirit Way**
Part of the 4 mile (7 km) approach to the tombs, the Spirit Way is lined with 36 stone statues of officials, soldiers, animals, and mythical beasts.

★ **Hall of Eminent Favor**
One of China's most impressive surviving Ming buildings, this double-eaved sacrificial hall is erected on a three-tiered terrace.

Reconstruction of Chang Ling
This shows the Chang Ling tomb at the time of the burial of the Yongle emperor in the 15th century.

The Ming Tombs

The 13 tombs are spread over 15 square miles (40 sq km), so are best visited by taxi. Chang Ling, Ding Ling, and Zhao Ling have been restored and are very busy. Unrestored, the rest are open yet quiet.

① Chang Ling (1424)
② Yong Ling (1566)
③ De Ling (1627)
④ Jing Ling (1435)
⑤ Xian Ling (1425)
⑥ Qing Ling (1620)
⑦ Yu Ling (1449)

⑧ Mao Ling (1487)
⑨ Tai Ling (1505)
⑩ Kang Ling (1521)
⑪ Ding Ling (1620)
⑫ Zhao Ling (1572)
⑬ Concubine cemeteries
⑭ Si Ling (1644)

Spirit Way

Pailou
(Archway)

0 kilometers   4

0 miles   4

★ Ding Ling treasures
Artifacts from the Wanli emperor's tomb, such as this threaded-gold crown decorated with two dragons, are on display in the main hall at Chang Ling.

VISITORS' CHECKLIST

Practical Information
30 miles (45 km) NW of Beijing.
Tel (010) 6076 1334.
Open 8:30am–5pm daily.
🚫 ♿ interiors.

Transport
🚌 845 from Xizhi Men (near subway) to Zhengfa Daxue in Changping, then taxi or bus 314 to Da Gong Men. Many tours to the Great Wall (see pp94–6) stop here.

③

④

Cedar columns
Supporting the huge weight of the roof, the colossal 43 foot (13 m) *nanmu* (fragrant cedar) columns are topped with elaborate *dougong* bracket sets.

Statue of the Yongle Emperor
Yongle, the third Ming emperor, moved the capital from Nanjing to Beijing, where he then oversaw the construction of the Forbidden City.

Ding Ling Burial Chamber

Ding Ling, the tomb of the longest reigning Ming emperor, Wanli (r. 1573–1620), is the only burial chamber of the 16 tombs to have been excavated and opened to the public. During the 1950s, archeologists were stunned to find the inner doors of the chamber still intact. Inside they found the treasures of an emperor whose profligate rule began the downfall of the Ming dynasty.

KEY

① **The Stele Pavilion** bears inscriptions dating from the Qing dynasty, which revered the Ming emperors.

② **Gate of Eminent Favor**

③ **The Spirit Tower** marks the entrance to the burial chamber.

④ **An earthen mound**, surrounded by a circular rampart, covers the stone burial chamber.

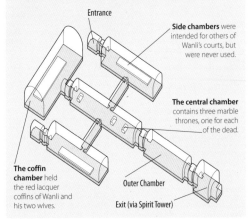

Entrance

Side chambers were intended for others of Wanli's courts, but were never used.

The central chamber contains three marble thrones, one for each of the dead.

The coffin chamber held the red lacquer coffins of Wanli and his two wives.

Outer Chamber

Exit (via Spirit Tower)

❷ Great Wall of China
长城

A symbol of China's historic detachment and sense of vulnerability, the Great Wall snakes through the countryside over deserts, hills, and plains for several thousand miles. Originally a series of disparate earthen ramparts built by individual states, the Great Wall was created only after the unification of China under Qin Shi Huangdi (r. 221–210 BC). Despite impressive battlements, the wall ultimately proved ineffective; it was breached in the 13th century by the Mongols and then, in the 17th century, by the Manchu. Today, only select sections of its crumbling remains have been fully restored.

Crumbling ruin
Most of the wall is still unrestored and has crumbled away leaving only the core remaining.

★ Panoramic views
Because the wall took advantage of the natural terrain for defensive purposes, following the highest points and clinging to ridges, it now offers superb panoramic views.

Reconstruction of the Great Wall

This shows a section of the wall as built by the most prolific wall builders, the Ming dynasty (1368–1644). The section at Badaling, built around 1505, is similar to this and was restored in the 1950s and 1980s.

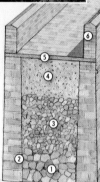

KEY

① **Large, locally quarried rocks**

② **Kiln-fired bricks** were cemented with a mortar of lime and glutinous rice.

③ **Bigger rocks and stones**

④ **Tamped layer of earth and rubble**

⑤ **Surface of stone slabs and bricks**

⑥ **Ramparts** enabled the defending soldiers to fire down on their attackers with impunity.

⑦ **Signal beacons** were used to warn of attack by burning dried wolf dung.

⑧ **The carriageway** is on average 8 m (26 ft) high and 7 m (21 ft) wide.

⑨ **Towers** were spaced two arrow shots apart to leave no part unprotected.

★ Watchtowers
A Ming addition, these served as signal towers, forts, living quarters, and storerooms for provisions.

Cannons
Another Ming addition, cannons were used to defend the wall and summon help.

Tips for Visitors

- The wall is exposed to the elements so be prepared for all conditions: wear layers of clothing and a waterproof top, but also bring sun block.
- Bring plenty of water.
- The wall can be very steep in places, so make sure you have strong footwear with a good grip such as hiking boots or tough waterproof trainers.

Multi-function wall
The wall enabled speedy communications via smoke, flares, drums, and bells, as well as allowing for the rapid transport of troops across the country.

The Great Wall of China (Ming Dynasty)

Most visitors travel to the wall from Beijing *(see p96)*, but it is worth seeing the wall anywhere along its length. Also impressive are the restored forts at Juyong Guan, Jiayu Guan, and Shanhaiguan.

Places to visit

① Jiayu Gua
② Badaling & Juyong Gua
③ Mutianyu & Huanghua Chen
④ Simata
⑤ Shanhaiguan

Exploring the Great Wall of China

A trip to the wall is a must for any visitor to Beijing. Most hotels will be able to organize this for you, usually combined with a visit to the Ming Tombs *(see pp92–3)*. However, be sure to find out whether there are any unwanted diversions planned to cloisonné workshops, jade factories, or Chinese medicine clinics. Small groups can have a more personalized visit, and see the more remote parts of the wall, by hiring a taxi for the day from Beijing and sharing the cost.

Ruins at Huanghua Cheng clinging to the steep hillside

Stall selling tourist paraphernalia at the Great Wall, Badaling

🚇 Badaling

44 miles (70 km) northwest of Beijing. **Tel** (010) 6912 1890. **Open** 6:40am–6:30pm daily. 🚠 🏛️ 🏯 🖼️ 🚌 1 from Qian Men.

Equipped with guardrails, cable car, pristine watchtowers, and tourist facilities, the restored Ming fortification at Badaling is the most popular section of the Great Wall. The reward for coming to Badaling is the breathtaking view of the wall winding its way over the hills. To fully appreciate this, get away from the crowds by walking as far as you can along the wall either east or west of the entrance. The ticket includes admission to the Great Wall Museum. The pass at Juyong Guan is on the way to Badaling and is often quieter than Badaling itself. With unscalable mountains on either side, it is easy to see why this spot was chosen for defense. There are also some authentic Buddhist carvings on a stone platform, or "cloud terrace," in the middle of the pass that date back to the Yuan dynasty (1279–1368).

🚇 Mutianyu

56 miles (90 km) north of Beijing, Mutianyu Town, Huairou County. **Open** 7:30am–6pm daily. 🚠 🏛️ & chair lifts. 🚌 6 from Xuanwu Men.

The appeal of Mutianyu lies in its dramatic hilly setting and less intrusive tourist industry. With a series of watchtowers along its restored length, the wall you can see here dates from 1368 and was built upon the foundations of the wall built during the Northern Qi dynasty (AD 550–77).

🚇 Huanghua Cheng

37 miles (60 km) north of Beijing, Huairou County. **Open** daily. 🚠 🏛️

Situated on the same stretch of wall as Mutianyu, Huanghua is an exhilarating section of Ming wall that is far less developed than other parts of the wall. The great barrier is split into two here by a large reservoir; most travelers take the right hand route on the other side of the reservoir, as the left-hand section is more difficult to reach. Because of its crumbling state and ongoing reconstruction, access has been limited by the authorities and it may not always be possible to visit Huanghua Cheng. If granted access, be careful because the path is devoid of guardrails and the masonry can be uneven and treacherous.

🚇 Simatai

68 miles (110 km) northeast of Beijing, Miyun County. **Open** 6am–6pm daily. 🚠 🏛️ (Apr–Nov). 🚌 6 from Xuanwu Men.

The wall at Simatai has only been partially repaired, affording a more genuine impression of the original wall. The steep and hazardous parts of the wall are also a lot riskier to navigate. Most visitors clamber along the eastern section of wall at Simatai, which leads to much steeper sections of wall and, later, impassable ruins. Despite the tourist trappings, the views are superb here. There is a four-hour trek from Simatai to Jingshanling that provides spectacular vistas, too. Some parts of Simatai are still being renovated, and areas may be cordoned off to visitors.

The restored section of the wall at Badaling, northwest of Beijing

❸ Eastern Qing Tombs
清东陵

77 miles (125 km) east of Beijing,
Zunhua County, Hebei Province.
Open May–Oct: 8am–5:30pm daily;
Nov–Apr: 9am–4:30pm daily. 🖼 🎥

Spirit Way to Emperor Shunzhi's tomb at the Eastern Qing Tombs

The remoteness of the Eastern Qing Tombs east of Beijing and over the border in Hebei province makes them far less popular than the Ming ones (see pp92–3), despite the fact that the setting is even more splendid. In fact, the Eastern Qing tombs make up the largest and most complete imperial cemetery in China, built on as grand a scale as the Forbidden City itself (see pp66–71). Of the many tombs scattered throughout the area, only five

Incense burners in front of a spirit tower at the Eastern Qing Tombs

are the burial places of Qing emperors: the tombs of the Shunzhi emperor (r.1644–61), Kangxi (r.1661–1722), Qianlong (r.1736–95), and Xianfeng (r. 1851–61) are open, while that of the Tongzhi emperor (r. 1862–74), at a distance from the main tomb grouping, is not. A 3 mile (5 km) Spirit Way, an approach lined with guardian figures, leads to Shunzhi's tomb, Xiao Ling, at the heart of the main tomb cluster, while several of the other tombs have their own smaller Spirit Ways. Southwest of here lies Yuling, Qianlong's tomb, with its incredible chamber adorned with Buddhist carvings and Tibetan and Sanskrit scriptures (rare features at imperial and principally Confucian tombs). The devious Empress Cixi

(see p86) is buried at Ding Dong Ling to the west, in the right-hand tomb of a complex of twin tombs, the other being the resting place of Ci'an, eldest wife of the Xianfeng emperor. Although both tombs were built in 1879, Cixi had her magnificent tomb lavishly restored in 1895. The marble carriageway up to the Hall of Eminent Favor features a carving of the phoenix (feng), symbol of the empress, above a carving of the dragon (long), symbol of the emperor. West of Ding Dong Ling, Ding Ling is partially open and approached via a set of stone animal statues. Look for the smaller tombs of imperial concubines, their roofs tiled in green (not the yellow of emperors and empresses).

Emperor Yongzheng

The son of the Kangxi emperor and a maidservant, Yongzheng (r. 1723–35) chose not to be buried at the Eastern Qing Tombs, but perversely started a necropolis as far away as possible in the Western Qing Tombs (Yixian County, Hebei Province). Perhaps, racked with guilt, he could not face burial alongside his father, whose will he had thwarted. For after Kangxi's death, Yongzheng seized the throne from his brother (his father's chosen successor), and declared himself the legitimate heir, ruthlessly eliminating any other brothers and uncles who may have been a threat to his rule. Despite this shaky start, Yongzheng was an able ruler and a devout Buddhist, punishing dishonesty among his officials and seeking to improve the morals and education of his people. Another possible reason for the switch was that he just wasn't satisfied with the Eastern Tombs and chose an area with a better natural setting. Whatever the reason, those keen on Chinese tomb architecture will enjoy the peace of the Western Qing Tombs. Nearby, moved in 1995 to a commercial cemetery, are the remains of Pu Yi, the last emperor of China.

Yongzheng in robes embroidered with symbols of his power

Brick stupas at the Stupa Forest Temple, also known as Talin Si

that led to the Japanese occupation of Beijing and a full-scale war. For those with a keen interest in this period of history, the incident is marked by some gruesome displays in Wanping's **Museum of the War of Resistance against Japan**.

❺ Tanzhe Temple
潭柘寺

Mentougou district. 28 miles (45 km) W of Beijing. Ⓜ to Pingguo Yuan (1 hr), then bus 931 or tourist bus 7. **Tel** (010) 6086 2505. **Open** 8am–6pm daily. 🚻

This enormous temple dates back to the 3rd century AD, when it was known as Jiafu Si. It was later renamed Tanzhe Temple, after the adjacent mountain Tanzhe Shan, which in turn got its name from the nearby Dragon Pool (Long Tan) and the surrounding cudrania (zhe) trees. It has a splendid mountainside setting, and its halls rise up the steep incline. The temple is especially famous for its ancient trees, among which is a huge ginkgo known as the Emperor's Tree. A slightly smaller tree close by is called The Emperor's Wife.

The most fascinating sight, however, is the **Stupa Forest Temple** (Talin Si) near the parking lot, with its marvelous collection of brick stupas hidden among the foliage. Each stupa was constructed in memory of a renowned monk. The towering edifices were built in a variety of designs, including the graceful miyan ta, or dense-eave stupa, characterized by ascending layers of eaves. The earliest among them dates from the Jin dynasty (1115–1234).

❹ Marco Polo Bridge
芦沟桥

Wanping town, Fengtai District. 10 miles (16 km) SW of city center. 🚌 339 from Beijing's Lianhuachi bus station; 309 from WAZI (near Beijing West Railway Station). **Open** 7am–7pm daily. 🚻 Museum of the War of Resistance against Japan: 101 Wanpingcheng Nei Jie. **Tel** (010) 8389 2355 ext 281. **Open** 9am–4pm Tue–Sun. 🚻

Straddling the Yongding River in Wanping town, the 876-ft (267-m) long marble bridge was first built during the Jin dynasty in 1189 but destroyed by a flood. The current structure dates to 1698. Known as Lugou Qiao in Chinese, the bridge acquired its English name after Marco Polo described it in his famous account of his travels. At the bridge's eastern and western ends are stelae inscribed by the Qing emperors, Kangxi and Qianlong. The poetic observation by Qianlong on a stele at the eastern end reads "lugou xiaoyue," meaning "Moon

Stone lion, Marco Polo Bridge

at daybreak at Lugou." The balustrades along the length of the bridge are decorated with more than 400 carved stone lions, each one slightly different in appearance. Local legend has it that these fierce-looking statues come alive at night. Despite the widening and extensive restoration work done over the centuries, a surprising amount of the bridge is original. In addition to its antiquity, it is significant as the site of the disastrous Marco Polo Bridge Incident. This is where, on July 7, 1937, the Japanese Imperial Army and Nationalist Chinese soldiers exchanged fire – an event

The 11-arched Marco Polo Bridge, known locally as Lugou Qiao

The gilded Buddha atop its plinth at Jietai Temple

6 Jietai Temple
戒台寺

Mentougou district, 20 miles (32 km) W of Beijing en route to Tanzhe Temple. **M** to Pingguo Yuan (1 hr), then bus 931 or tourist bus 7. **Open** 8am–6pm daily.

The Jietai (Ordination Terrace) Temple has been used for the ceremony of elevating monks to higher levels of the Buddhist hierarchy as far back as the Liao dynasty (907–1125), and it is well worth a visit on the way to or from the nearby Tanzhe Temple. The "terrace" refered to in the temple's name is a finely carved marble plinth used for the ordination ceremonies. Its three layers feature 113 niched statues. Topped with a gilded Buddha and chairs for three masters and seven witnesses, the plinth stands inside a magnificent and unusual square hall, surrounded by lesser courtyards dotted with pines and cypresses. The temple is located about a half-mile (1 km) walk uphill from the bus stop.

7 Shidu
十渡

Fangshan district. 62 miles (100 km) SW of Beijing. **🚌** bus 917 from Beijing's Tianqiao station to Shidu. **Tel** (010) 6134 9009.

Shidu offers a fabulous escape from the commotion of urban Beijing and a chance to enjoy some stunning natural scenery. Before the new road and bridges were built, travelers

had to cross the Juma River ten times as they journeyed through the gorge between Shidu and nearby Zhangfang village, hence the name Shidu meaning "Ten Ferries" or "Ten Crossings." Pleasant walking trails wind along the riverbank between impressive gorges and jagged limestone formations. Visitors can stop en route to paddle in the shallow river and picnic under the towering peaks. The main sights are around Qingjiang Gou and the lovely Gushan Zhai, marred somewhat by bungee jumping and other entertainment ventures.

8 Cuandixia
川底下

Near Zhaitang town. 56 miles (90 km) NW of Beijing. **M** to Pingguo Yuan (1 hr), then bus 929 to Zhaitang (3 hrs), then taxi. **Open** daily.

Despite the rather laborious expedition required to get here, a trip to the tiny village of Cuandixia (Under the River) is well worth the effort as the crumbling hamlet survives as a living museum of Ming and Qing dynasty village architecture. Situated on a steep mountainside, it is a picturesque outpost of courtyard houses (*siheyuan*) and rural Chinese buildings. Because of the close-knit nature of the original village, all the courtyards were interconnected by small lanes. The entry ticket allows access to the entire village, all of which can be explored within a few hours. Look out for the Maoist graffiti and slogans that survive on the boundary walls; similar graffiti from the Cultural Revolution has been whitewashed in most other Chinese towns.

Cuandixia's population consists of about 70 people spread over a handful of families. Accommodations can be arranged for those wanting to explore the surrounding hills or simply experience the rural hospitality. Alive to the opportunities brought by tourism, quite a few of the old homesteads provide basic facilities at a reasonable price.

Traditional Ming and Qing dynasty houses, Cuandixia village

TWO GUIDED WALKS

Beijing is famous for its centuries-old alleys known as *hutongs*. The *siheyuan* (courtyard houses) that line them were built with their backs turned on the outside world with the main entrance set in otherwise blank walls. But these alleys and their distinctive homes have been disappearing ever more rapidly since 1949. At first they fell victim to Soviet-style edifices celebrating Communist achievements, then to multistory apartment towers, and now to road widening and new crosstown highways. These multi-lane highways and burgeoning traffic problems do not always make Beijing the best place to explore on foot but it is worth giving it a try, as you can see much more detail at walking pace. Look, for example, for the original carved wooden surrounds framing new shop fronts, and the stone "guardians" often found outside the original gates and doors.

Of course, what is charm to some visitors is merely slum living to others. The historic buildings are often almost invisible beneath improvised lean-tos, with windows knocked through external walls to create the tiny and scantily-stocked shops known as *xiaomaibu*.

A walk around Hou Hai *(see pp104–5)* takes in still-standing areas of ancient *hutongs*, some of which are undeniably tatty and some of which have been well renovated. It eventually weaves its way around the Back Lakes and their willow-fringed shores, home to myriad small bars and cafés. Despite the area's popularity, it is always possible to step into a small alleyway and, for the time being at least, be immediately transported back into the past.

If in places things moulder as they have done for centuries, on the walk around Pudu Si *(pp102–3)*, the traditional has been rebuilt from the ground up, and you could cut your finger on the sharp edges of the 20th-century "Ming" brickwork. This walk sandwiches restored *hutongs* between a handful of historical imperial temples and modern-day shopping opportunities.

Key

··· Walk route

Hou Hai
(see pp104–5)

HAIDIAN

East of the
Forbidden City
(see pp106–7)

XI
CHENG

DONG
CHENG

XUANWU

0 kilometers   3
0 miles   1.5

◄ The pretty Silver Ingot Bridge on Hou Hai, the Back Lakes

A 90-Minute Walk East of the Forbidden City

This walk starts at the Imperial Ancestral Temple, a place often overlooked by visitors to the neighboring Forbidden City. Not far from these grand halls lie courtyard houses rebuilt from scratch (after leveling the originals and inserting an underground car park), which now serve as comfortable homes for officials with a taste for the traditional. The route also takes in the very much unpreserved and unreconstructed *hutong* residences of ordinary Beijingers, whose presence at the very heart of the city is surely unlikely to survive much longer. It ends on pedestrianized Wangfujing, the city's premier shopping street.

⑦ Brian McKenna's Courtyard restaurant

① Tian'an Men, gateway to the Forbidden City

Park of the People's Culture

Make your way by subway to Tian'an Men Square. Facing the portrait of Mao that hangs on the **Tian'an Men** ①, turn right and walk east along the Imperial City wall. You soon arrive at an entrance overlooked by almost all. Go through this to the five-bay **Halberd Gate** ② and the Tai Miao, or **Imperial Ancestral Temple** ③, one of the most important in the city. A series of vast halls runs north in mimicry of the main sequence of "Harmony" halls inside the Forbidden City itself. Yet the entire site is usually deserted.

On reaching the canal at the rear of the temple, turn left to exit. This back way in to the complex was opened as a **short cut** ④ for the Qianlong emperor in his old

age. Cross the canal, turn right and follow the dog-leg of the **moat** ⑤ round to the north to reach the **Dong Hua Men** ⑥, or east gate of the Forbidden City (closed to the public).

As you recross the moat by bridge, immediately on the left is the famed restaurant **Brian McKenna @ The Courtyard** ⑦ and its basement gallery. Although this is an ancient courtyard house, the interior has been completely remodeled and internationalized.

Nan Chizi Dajie

Cross over at the first junction and head south down Nan Chizi Dajie. Take the first left into narrow Pudu Si Xi Xiang and follow it round to the right and south for instant relief from traffic noise. There are left turns to explore at whim, but continuing south soon brings you to the magnificent double-eaved hall of the **Mahakala Temple** ⑧, or Pudu Si, raised on a mound to the left. Back in the 15th century the temple was the home of a deposed Ming emperor, and

0 meters 500
0 yards 250

later of the man who led Qing troops into Beijing in 1644. It became a lamasery in the 18th century, and housed a famous statue of Mahakala, whose cult the Qing had absorbed from the Mongols. In modern times, its halls have echoed with the chanted lessons of primary school children. The children are now gone, and the once sagging halls have been made shiny and new in preparation for their occupation by the land tax office.

⑧ Entrance to the little visited Mahakala Temple, or Pudu Si

For hotels and restaurants see pp182–5 and pp196–9

At one time, the area around the temple was filled with the ramshackle residences of ordinary people. These have now been totally rebuilt in a reproduction of antiquity and house local government officials. Security guards patrol the alleys, ready to protect the haves from the have-nots.

Continue south down the east side of the underground car park (the west side will also do) looking for **old pillar bases ⑨** set in the new grey walls. At the end, turn right into **Duanku Hutong ⑩**, the name of which – Satin Warehouse Alley – reveals the use to which the

⑬ Children in the Changpu He Park

Key

• • • Walk route

⑩ Doorway to a courtyard home in Duanku Hutong

surrounding buildings were once put. Follow the alley round to the left; the odd surviving shop sign in green and white **Arabic lettering ⑪** reveals that many in the cloth trade were Muslims. The alley jogs right again to rejoin Nan Chizi Dajie. Resume your progress south and you will encounter the old **Imperial Archive ⑫** a little farther down on the left. Unfortunately, the main hall, which dates back to 1536, is not open but it is still an impressive complex to wander around. Neighboring halls sell made-for-tourist art that recycles the old clichés.

Da Tian Shui Jing Hutong
Continue south down Nan Chizi and you'll soon come to an area where the ancient housing has been removed to create the narrow but pleasant **Changhe Pu Park ⑬**. This park follows the eastward course of the stream that flows in front of the Tian'an Men. Turn left along the stream bank, passing 21st-century **pastiche Qing buildings ⑭** on the left. The park ends at a main road: cross and head north, then turn right where the bicycle route is indicated. This takes you into **Da Tian Shui Jing Hutong ⑮** (Big Sweetwater Well Hutong) – Beijing's wells were notoriously brackish and good water would have been worth noting.

For as long as it lasts, this is real *hutong* life, right in the heart of the city. The lane is

filled with tiny restaurants advertising Chongqing-style hotpot (very spicy) and noodles, all for real Beijing prices – less than ¥5 per dish. After passing a group of video parlors, the alley re-engages with modernity, emerging into **Wangfujing Snack Street ⑯**, a tourist-pleasing but enjoyable food market, where you'll pay five times as much for the same dish as back in the *hutong*.

Turn left to reach the pedestrianized shopping street of **Wangfujing Dajie ⑰** *(see p76)*, with its fashionable shops with permanent sales, and McDonald's and other imports. Those still with some walking in their legs can then enjoy some shopping.

Tips for Walkers

Length: 1.8 miles (3 km).
Getting there: Subway to Tian'an Men Dong.
Galleries at the Imperial Archive: Open 10am–noon & 1pm–6pm daily.
Stopping off points: There are Western and Chinese restaurants around the Nan Chizi crossroads near the Courtyard restaurant. In summer, stands around the Imperial Archive offer cold drinks for sale. The restaurants in Da Tian Shui Jing Hutong are grubby, but authentic and cheap. Otherwise, Wangfujing Dajie and its malls sport numerous Western and local fast food outlets and branches of coffee chains, as well as several superior Chinese and international restaurants.

For keys to symbols *see back flap*

A Two-Hour Walk around Hou Hai

Hou Hai (Back Lakes) is a cluster of three linked bodies of water just over a mile or so north of the Forbidden City. They lie at the heart of a district of labyrinthine old *hutongs* (alleys), studded with a handful of monuments of modest grandeur. This walk takes you through areas of mouldering housing to a renovated courtyard dwelling, and past abandoned mansions to one that has been largely preserved. It meanders through an area undergoing revitalization as a lively nightlife hub before winding up at a couple of ancient towers, which you can ascend to look back over the area which you have just explored.

⑩ Women exercise beside the lake shore at Hou Hai

Xinjiekou Bei Dajie
The walk starts at the Circle Line subway station of Jishuitan. Leave by exit C, turn left down Xinjiekou Bei Dajie, cross the road and continue south past **clothing and shoe shops** ①, all with prices far lower than home. The building set back from the road with a sign on top in green characters, is the **Xu Beihong Memorial Hall** ②. This is worth a look in for the lively watercolors of horses that made Xu (1885–1953) internationally famous.

② Xu Beihong statue

Continue on south past lots more small shops and cross back to the east side of the road at the traffic signals. Note the **model shop** ③ on the corner of Hangkong Hutong with large supplies of hard-to-obtain plastic kits at cheap prices. Walk on past electric guitar shops and jewelers to take the next left turning but one into **Bai Hua Shen Chu** ④.

The name means "in the depths of many flowers," a reference to a time when the *hutong* was famous for its hothouses, which had carefully ducted steam to ensure that the flowers bloomed just in time for the major festivals and temple fairs. One of the biggest such fairs used to be held at the **Protect the Nation Temple** ⑤, or Huguo Si. Take the first right into Huguo Si Xi Xiang, which leads down past ramshackle housing to the temple's sole surviving hall. This was formerly the home of a Yuan dynasty prince, banished for treason in 1355; it was turned into a temple a decade later. The institution was funded by imperial eunuchs and doubled as a retirement home for them. These haunting remains represent the sad state of historic conservation in Beijing: abandonment leading to eventual ruin.

Huguo Si Jie
At the bottom end of Huguo Si Xi Xiang, turn left onto the busier main road of Huguo Si Jie. You will pass take-away snack shops, vegetable and meat vendors, and an art shop, before coming to the **Mei Lanfang Memorial Hall** ⑥. This is a traditional *siheyuan* (courtyard house) in a fine state of preservation, which shows what can be done with old Beijing when tourism income is anticipated. This was the home of Beijing Opera's greatest performer (1894–1961) *(see pp34–5)*. The rear rooms have been left with their traditional

⑥ Street entrance to the Mei Lanfang Memorial Hall

furniture, exactly as they were when Mei died. Other rooms contain hagiographic accounts of his life, diagrams of the stylized movements required by the form, and a video of Mei, already 61, but still playing the young girl roles for which he was famous.

Crossing the next junction, which is with busy Desheng Men Nei Dajie, look in the next gate on the left for a glimpse of part of the former **Mansion of Prince Qing** ⑦, which has not fared as well as Mei Lanfang's residence. Continue east, cross Songshu Jie, and turn left along

⑪ The Silver Ingot Bridge between Hou Hai and Qian Hai

the outer wall of the **Mansion of Prince Gong** ⑧ (see p72). It is worth making time for a look around this extensive former royal residence with its beautiful gardens. The sad fact is that this is the last intact house of its kind in an area that once held several similarly grand mansions.

The Back Lakes

On exiting Prince Gong's mansion, turn right and follow the compound wall around to the right and into **Da Xiang Feng Hutong** ⑨, looking for drum stones, carved panels, and door guardians adorning the fronts of the old houses. Just before the end of the *hutong*, you'll catch a glimpse of the waters of **Hou Hai** ⑩ down a narrow left turn: head this way. You now hit tourist territory. The shores of the lake are hugely popular with both foreign visitors and locals and are lined with Chinese karaoke and faux-Western bars and restaurants. The hub of all activity is the bottleneck of the **Silver Ingot Bridge** ⑪, which arches over the narrow channel between the Hou Hai and Qian Hai, and gives modestly pretty views in two directions.

Once over the bridge, go straight ahead and jink left then right into **Yandai Xiejie** ⑫, a terrifically vibrant small street with corner street-food sellers and an odd mix of gift

shops and bars mixed in with the practical, such as a bicycle repair shop. Look up for glimpses of finely carved wood here and there that belongs to ancient façades to which modern shop fronts have been attached. There is a former bathhouse here that's now a boutique and a temple that's now a café.

Turn left at the end onto main Di'an Men Wai Dajie, to see the **Drum Tower** ⑬ rearing up ahead; the **Bell Tower** ⑭ is just behind. The balconies of both give views back across the labyrinth you've just navigated.

0 meters 300
0 yards 300

GULOU
HOUHAI BEI YAN
XI DAJIE
JIUGULOU DAJIE
Hou Hai
HOUHAI NAN YAN
LIUYIN JIE
DA XIANG FENG HUTONG
⑩
⑨
⑪ ⑫
⑭
⑬
Shichahai Ⓜ
⑧
QIANHAI BEI YAN
Qian Hai
QIANHAI NAN YAN
DI'AN MEN WAI DAJIE
LONGTOUJING JIE
hai North Ⓜ
DI'AN MEN XI DAJIE (PING'AN DA DAO)

Key

••• Walk route

⑧ Shrine with offerings at the Mansion of Prince Gong

Tips for Walkers

Length: 2.5 miles (4 km).
Getting there: Subway to Jishuitan.
Xu Beihong Memorial Hall: Open 9am–4pm Tue–Sun.
Mei Lanfang Memorial Hall: Open 9am–4pm Tue–Sun, but closed for a month in Jan–Feb.
Mansion of Prince Gong: Open 8:30am–4:30pm daily.
Bell Tower and Drum Tower: Open 9am–5pm daily.
Stopping-off points: After turning left onto Huguo Si Jie, turn right at the next crossroads down Hucang Hutong, to find Jing Wei Lou on the right at the corner with the major avenue, Ping'an Da Dao. This is a bustling restaurant with a picture menu of dishes. Just before the entrance to Prince Gong's Mansion is Sichuan Fandian, one of Beijing's oldest restaurants, serving excellent fiery Sichuan food. Some bars along the lake shore offer dishes that faintly resemble the Western foods for which they are named.

SHOPPING IN BEIJING

From some of the world's biggest and glitziest shopping malls selling global brands, to thriving street markets where everything from counterfeit designer goods to reproduction antiques can be found, there is almost nothing you can't buy in Beijing. A new Ferrari? There has been a dealership in Beijing since 1994. Tiffany, the New York jeweler, opened its first branch in the city in 2001. But, as with the likes of Japanese electronics and Swiss watches, severe import duties ensure these foreign products all cost substantially more here than they would at home. Beijing should certainly not be mistaken for the duty-free haven of Hong Kong.

Traditionally, Wangfujing Dajie and its side turnings are the heart of Beijing's shopping, along with Taikoo Li mall and plaza in Sanlitun, which was opened for the 2008 Olympics. But Beijing's historic symmetry means there's a similar concentration west of the Forbidden City at Xi Dan. There are also department stores and markets scattered throughout the city's residential quarters, many with far better prices than the central locations.

Shopping Etiquette

The frantic sanitization of Beijing has removed many of the traditional small side-street markets, and has driven all the better-known larger markets under the cover of purpose-built sites. If you do come across any surviving street markets on your travels – you may still encounter them in residential areas – then they are always worth browsing for cheap prices.

Always bargain hard, not just at markets, but also at supposedly fixed price shops too, just as the Chinese do. Or, try to buy from stalls where you can see people making and selling craft items, as this will benefit the local residents.

Wherever you go, shop with caution. If you are told that something is supposedly old, rare, or intrinsically expensive, it is most likely a fake. China is not

Stallholder selling silks and fabrics at Hong Qiao Market

Caged birds for sale at a traditional Beijing street market

the place to shop for valuable antiques, gems, or jewelry (including jade and pearls) unless you really are an expert. Nothing with an internationally traded value can be bought cheaply in either Beijing or Shanghai. Famous brand-name goods, from Louis Vuitton bags and Calvin Klein apparel to Apple iPods, are all commonly faked. At the very least with high-value locally made items like carpets, considerable time should first be spent visiting carpet dealers and learning about quality, manufacturing methods, and prices.

At the end of the day if you like the item and it seems a reasonable deal to you, go ahead and buy it, but don't assume you have got a real bargain or something of great value cheaply.

Antiques, Crafts, and Curios

Genuine antiques are almost impossible to find, and all purchases should be made on the assumption that what is being bought is fake. Objects dating between 1795 and 1939 cannot officially be taken out of the country without a certificate, something any honest dealer with a genuinely ancient item would help you to acquire. Anything older may not be exported at all. The most interesting market for so-called antiques and curios is **Panjiayuan Market** in the southeast of town, but even vendors admit that 80 percent of what is on sale is fake. However, there is nowhere better to do all your gift shopping in one go, although you may find yourself hoarse by the end of the day from bargaining for items such as Russian optical equipment, gramophones, stuffed deer heads, framed calligraphy, and bamboo-and-bone mah jong sets. Even for anybody who doesn't like shopping, Panjiayuan is worth visiting as a sight in its own right. Neighboring **Beijing Curio City** also has a vast array of ceramics, furniture, jewelry, and Tibetan art on several floors, although authenticity is equally suspect.

The large **Hong Qiao Market** near the Temple of Heaven has an odd range of clothing, souvenirs, and low-quality (or fake) pearls up on the third and fourth floors.

Spend a few hours browsing through the pleasant little shops of **Liulichang** (see p65), which specialize in lacquerware, ceramics, paintings, and assorted crafts. China has a long tradition of making excellent furniture and **Huayi Classical Furniture** sells classical antique, restored, and reproduction furniture, some of which, at least, is clearly marked as being what it is. The trendy store **Sattva**, near the Lama Temple, sells hand-dyed rugs and furniture sourced personally by the owner from Tibet and Qinghai. Assorted extras include drums, art, and jewelry. Another hip store is **Lost & Found**, which sells good-quality furniture, porcelain, clothing, and home accessories.

Perhaps the most unusual curios are those connected with

Traditional-style painting on parchment – a popular souvenir

Curios and reproduction antique furniture at Panjiayuan Market

Beijing's four traditional pastimes of flowers, birds, fish, and insects (hua, niao, yu, chong). While the animals cannot be exported to your home country, some of the associated paraphernalia – ornate bird cages, tiny feeding dishes, gourd homes for insects, and perhaps even tapes for teaching your mynah Mandarin – will certainly make excellent conversation pieces and are genuine souvenirs of Beijing. Even for those who don't like shopping, the **Huasheng Tian Qiao Market** offers a compelling aural and visual feast, as the chirrups and clicks of the insects compete with the wider-ranging whistles of the birds.

Art and Calligraphy

Paintings executed in traditional styles and of traditional subjects can be found at all curio markets and souvenir shops, and hundreds if not thousands of copies will be painted of anything foreigners find appealing. Modern painting in Western styles also tends to choose tourist-pleasing subject matter, attaching prices that show an understanding of Western art markets – although such pieces could rarely be sold on for anything like the same

price outside of China. There is tourist kitsch aplenty at the galleries in the **Imperial Archive** (see p103); for more serious efforts, but still often conscious of Western preferences and beliefs about China, try the **Red Gate Gallery** (see p77) and the **CourtYard Gallery**, attached to the restaurant of the same name. Serious art shoppers should consider visiting the dozens of artists' studios and galleries that make up the **798 Art District** (see p89). Prices will be prohibitive to all but the most committed and deep-pocketed of collectors, but there is no charge for looking. The Caochangdi Art Village is also a great place for art enthusiasts. Chinese artist Ai Weiwei has a studio here and top galleries such as **Pekin Fine Arts** and **Platform China** are located in the area. A good place for affordable Chinese contemporary art is **Surge Art**, which sells both online and from its office near the Confucius Temple.

Books

Take your own reading material when traveling to China, as the choice of imported and English-language fiction in Beijing is limited. The best selection is on the top floor at the **Foreign Languages Bookshop** on Wangfujing. However, English books on cultural and travel topics and coffee-table photography books on Chinese themes are plentiful (although often marked up in price for the foreign market). The best selection can be found at **Page One**. **The Bookworm**, also in Sanlitun, offers a good range too. Specialist art bookshops can be found in and around the **National Art Museum of China** (see p76).

Hanging scroll painted with elegant script

Detail from a traditional embroidered men's robe

Carpets, Textiles, and Clothing

Beijing's markets sell a wide variety of traditional, ornate carpets from Tibet, Gansu, and Xinjiang. Try the **Qian Men Carpet Company**, which has antique, imitation antique, and new carpets for sale. It also very helpfully arranges shipping so you do not have to worry about getting your goods home.

The Beijing Silk Store is the best starting point for silk and related fabrics at local prices. Large tour groups are often taken to the popular **Yuanlong Silk Corporation**, which has fabrics and a large selection of ready-made silk garments. What is known as the **Xiushui Silk Market**, is in fact almost entirely free of silk – its four floors of vendors mostly stock counterfeit designer goods. None of this stops it from reportedly being one of the city's biggest tourist attractions after the Forbidden City and Great Wall. Sanlitun's **Yaxiu Market** (sometimes written Yashow) also has four floors of clothes, fabric, and curios, plus a tailoring services for those who want a figure-hugging *qipao* (cheongsam).

For hip modern Chinese homewares such as funky tea sets and chopsticks, gorgeous printed silk clothing and fabrics, and more unusual contemporary artisanal gifts, **Guangfu Museum Shop**, the cool store owned by local art collector Ma Weidu, is an in-the-know local hotspot.

Department Stores and Shopping Malls

In the west of the city, the **Season's Place** mall is big, glitzy, and modern, with brands like Lane Crawford and Louis Vuitton, plus an excellent basement supermarket and several restaurants. **Taikoo Li** at Sanlitun is the city's busiest mall, with a broad open plaza and plenty of brands including an Apple Store, Nike, Adidas, Agnès B, and Diesel, as well as several cafés, restaurants, and bars. Other large and popular malls are **The Place** on Guanghua Lu, which has a lot of brand shopping, and **Parkview Green Fangcaodi** on Dongdaqiao Road, with its eye-catching collection of contemporary art installations plus hip stores, cafes and restaurants. The **Oriental Plaza** on Dong Chang'an Jie boasts a glittering array of international names, from Paul Smith and Armani to an Apple computer store. The basement level has a large Watson's pharmacy and an excellent Southeast Asian-style food court. Watch the capital's wealthy fashionistas shopping for European styles at **Galeries Lafayette**, the legendary Paris department store on up-and-coming Xidan North Street (Xidan Bei Dajie).

Electronics

Despite what you might think, China is not a good source of cheap electronics. If the equipment is imported, then it is going to be more expensive than in the West; if it is locally made, then it usually comes with a Chinese operating system, pirated software, and a guarantee that is no use outside China. However, China is excellent value for accessories such as cables and converters, and media such as blank disks. Zhongguang Cun in the northwest district of Haidian is the place, but it is a long way to travel. A better option is the **Bai Nao Hui** computer market, which is more central. Apple Store is at Taikoo Li in Sanlitun as well as at the Oriental Plaza.

Anywhere tourists go to shop or play, vendors will be found with fake DVDs of Hollywood movies. Setting aside legal issues, copies may be of foreign language versions with no English option, subtitles may be for a different film altogether, the disc may stop playing partway through, and copies of recent titles will have been made by placing a camera at the back of a movie theater. The authorities in China are cracking down on this piracy, and occasionally there are arrests and fines.

Wangfujing Dajie, Beijing's modern, mall-lined main shopping street

But it is such a big industry and there is such a gap between the cost of legitimate goods and the average wage in China that the trade will be impossible to stamp out completely. At around as little as US$1 per disk, pirated DVDs are understandably still very popular.

Tea

Malian Dao Lu has all the teas in China, available from endless rows of tiny shops on either side of the street, and from the four stories of the **Malian Dao Cha Cheng** with dozens of stalls. Rare and expensive teas should be

Chinese children's kite

avoided unless you're an expert, but few foreigners come here, and most stalls have thimble-sized cups to give you a taste. Packaging is often very ornate, and bricks

of the cheapest tea, pounded into a mould with an assortment of patterns, make attractive, if slightly heavy, souvenirs.

Toys

You can find everything from the Chinese edition of Monopoly to Gameboys, jigsaw puzzles, and radio-controlled cars, all at bargain prices under one roof at the **Hong Qiao Toy City**. **Jack's Toys** is also good, and more toys can be found at China's first flagship **LEGO** store, which stocks the whole LEGO™ series and limited edition collections.

DIRECTORY

Antiques, Crafts, and Curios

Beijing Curio City
21 Dongsanhuan Nan Lu.
Tel (010) 6773 6098.

Hong Qiao Market
16 Hong Qiao Lu. **Map** 5
E3. **Tel** (010) 6711 7429.

Huasheng Tian Qiao Market
E of Shili He Bridge.

Huayi Classical Furniture
89 Xiaodian Dongwei Lu.
Tel (010) 8431 1836.

Lost & Found
42 & 57 Guozijian. **Map** 2
B2. **Tel** (010) 6401 1855.

Panjiayuan Market
Panjiayuan Lu, off
Dongsanhuan Nan Lu.

Sattva
60 Wudaoying Hutong,
Dongcheng district.
Map 2 B1. **Tel** 138 1116
9101.

Art and Calligraphy

798 Art District
2–4 Jiuxian Qiao Lu, Da
Shan Zi.

CourtYard Gallery
95 Donghua Men Dajie.
Map 2 B5.
Tel (010) 6526 8882.

Imperial Archive
Nan Chizi Dajie. **Map** 2 B5.

Pekin Fine Arts
241 Caochangdi Village.
Tel (010) 5127 3220.

Platform China
319-1, East End Art Zone
A, Caochangdi Village.
Tel (010) 6432 0091.

Red Gate Gallery
Southeast Corner Watch-
tower, off Jianguo Men
Nan Dajie. **Map** 5 F2.
Tel (010) 6525 1005.

Surge Art
6 Babaokeng Hutong.
Map 2 C2.
Tel (010) 6407 5314.

Books

The Bookworm
4 Sanlitun South Rd.
Map 3 F3.
Tel (010) 6586 9507.

Foreign Languages Bookshop
235 Wangfujing Dajie.
Map 2 B5.
Tel (010) 6512 6917.

National Art Museum of China
1 Wusi Dajie. **Map** 2 B4.
Tel (010) 6400 6326.

Page One
S2-14a-b, 1-2F, Taikoo Li,
No.19 Sanlitun Road.
Map 3 F3.

Carpets, Textiles, and Clothing

Beijing Silk Store
5 Zhubaoshi, off Qian
Men Dajie. **Map** 4 C2.
Tel (010) 6301 6658.

Guangfu Museum Shop
51-17 Di'anmen Xi Dajie,
(inside Hehua Market),
Xicheng District. **Map** 2 A3.
Tel (010) 8322 8818.

Qian Men Carpet Company
44 Xingfu Dajie. **Map** 5
F3.
Tel (010) 6715 1687.

Xiushui Silk Market
Xiushui Dong Jie.
Map 3 E5.

Yaxiu Market
58 Gongren Tiyuchang
Bei Lu. **Map** 3 F3.

Yuanlong Silk Corporation
15 Yongding Men Dong
Jie. **Map** 5 D4.

Department Stores and Malls

Galeries Lafayette
110 Xidan Bei Dajie,
Xicheng District.
Map 1 E5. **Tel** (010) 5962
9888.

Oriental Plaza
1 Dong Chang'an Jie.
Map 2 B5.

Parkview Green Fangcaodi
9 Dongdaqiao Road.
Map 3 E5.

The Place
9 Guanghua Lu,
Chaoyang. **Map** 3 F5.

Season's Place
2 Jinchengfang Street,
Xicheng. **Map** 1 D4.
Tel (010) 6622 0888.

Taikoo Li
Sanlitun Road. **Map** 3 F3.

Electronics

Bai Nao Hui
Chaoyang Men Wai Dajie.
Map 3 E4.

Tea

Malian Dao Cha Cheng
11 Malian Dao Lu.
Map 4 C2.
Tel (010) 6346 1811.

Toys

Jack's Toys
Pinnacle Plaza, Tianzhu
Real Estate Development
Zone (near the airport).
Tel (010) 8046 3217.

LEGO
NB136, China World Mall,
1 Jianguo Men Wai Dajie.
Map 3 F5.
Tel (010) 6505 1603.

Toy City
See Hong Qiao Market.

ENTERTAINMENT IN BEIJING

Literary and cultured, but still too much under the thumb of a highly conservative government to be truly progressive, Beijing nevertheless offers entertainment that includes the tourist-pleasing, the traditional, and the reasonably recherché. This is, of course, the home of the world-famous Beijing Opera, which continues to be performed at venues across the city on a nightly basis, although the majority of these shows cater for foreign visitors.

The same is true of the various acrobatic performances that take place. The rock and pop scene, on the other hand, is vibrant and wholly targeted at a young, local audience. Performing arts in general have received a shot in the arm thanks to the National Center for the Performing Arts. This vast mercury bubble of a building, controversially designed by French architect Paul Andreu, is worth a visit for the spectacle of the structure itself.

Practical information

For details of performances – from stadium rock concerts to dance troupes appearing on handkerchief-sized stages – see the listings in expat-produced magazines such as *The Beijinger*, *City Weekend*, and *Time Out Beijing*. These free bi-weekly and monthly publications are available in hotels, bars, and restaurants, and together with savvy online lifestyle publication Smartbeijing.com, keeps locals and visitors updated with frantic schedules, rapid changes in fashion, and mayfly existence of venues that close almost as soon as they've opened.

Tickets are generally bought at the venue box offices and paid for in cash. At small music clubs, pay on the door. Most hotel concierges can usually help in securing seats.

French style at Enoterra wine bar on Sanlitun Road

Bars and Clubs

Sanlitun is the one district that all Beijing expats know intimately. Sanlitun Road (once

Seating area of Atmosphere in the China World Summit Tower

known as Sanlitun Bar Street) was redeveloped in time for the 2008 Olympics and includes Taikoo Li and Nali Patio, home to some of the city's best bars. Chic wine bar **Enoterra** is here, which sees Shanghai's favorite French-owned wine bar making a similar success in the capital, with a similarly well-priced wine menu, specials board, and light French cuisine. Also at Nali Patio is **Migas**, which serves beers and cocktails on its 6th-floor rooftop terrace. Nearby is edgy-chic cocktail lounge **Mesh**, which occupies a ground floor spot at the hip Opposite House boutique hotel and has a street-side terrace for summer sipping. A block away, **The Tree**, a long-standing favorite, marries draft beer with wood-fired pizza and remains a popular spot. Also on Sanlitun Road, south of the junction with Gongti Bei Lu is the Courtyard 4 bar and dining mini-district, home to cocktail

hangout **D Lounge** and **Janes and Hooch**, a Lower Manhattan style urban saloon that serves delicious cocktails for a local hipster crowd. **The Hutong** and **Riverbank Café** are two hip café-bars that double as mini-cultural centers, showing movies and hosting dance and theater performances.

New bars and cafés are springing up all the time along the eastern shore of Hou Hai, where the pick of the bunch is the understated and wholly original **No Name Bar**. The first bar to open in the area, it benefits from a wonderful waterside site just south of Silver Ingot Bridge. Across the lake on the western shore is Lotus Lane, a developer's attempt to recreate Sanlitun, but the bars and clubs here are a little tawdry and suffer from a lack of inspiration. Instead, head north and east into the *hutongs*. Nearby, Bei Luogu Xiang is an up-and-coming area with boutiques, cafés, and bars, including **Mai**, a popular cocktail lounge and jazz venue.

Beer in a local bar can cost as little as ¥5, but in foreigner-frequented venues it will more commonly be anything from ¥15–¥30. You also pay inflated prices for imported pleasures such as cocktails. Also pricey is the fashionable **Atmosphere**, a Beijing hotspot located on the 80th floor of the China World Summit Tower. This is the capital's highest bar and a place to "see and be seen" but the views are exceptional. For another great view, the cocktail terrace at **Capital M** overlooks Tian'an Men Square. This upscale restaurant and lounge bar is the sibling of M on the Bund in Shanghai.

For late-night high jinks, **Yugong Yishan** remains Beijing's most eclectic and down-to-earth club, offering live music and alternative DJs most nights of the week. Beijing's coolest late-night party crowd gathers at **Dada**, an understated bar/club hybrid in the shadows of the Drum and Bell Towers. Don't expect VIP rooms or superstar DJs, rather the capital's most eclectic musical mélange – from Chinese hip-hop to garage and dubstep – fused with subcultural 3-D imagery and China's edgiest street fashions.

Beijing Opera

For most non-Chinese, Beijing Opera *(see pp34–5)* is a taste not easily acquired. Incomprehensible plots, unfamiliar sounds, and performances lasting up to three hours can make for uncomfortable viewing. However, there's no denying the acrobatic ability and dramatic splendor of the event, so everyone should try it once. Performances are best seen in the splendid Ming-dynasty **Zhengyici Theater** or Qing-dynasty **Huguang Guildhall**. During the warmer months, there are evening shows at the **Mansion of Prince Gong** *(see p72)* at 7:30pm. Given the choice, you should opt for any of these over the **Liyuan Theater** in the Qian Men Hotel, which is where tour groups are taken.

Cinema

Government-imposed restrictions mean that cinemas show a very limited number of imported English-language films. **Culture Yard**, an independent movie club, shows mostly Chinese movies, while **Riverbank Café** screens classic movies from around the world. For the latest international movies on huge screens, head for **Wanda International Cinema Complex**.

Beijing Opera – difficult to follow, but the color is dazzling

There is also a games arcade and a few cafés here. **The Hutong** culture center also shows international films. During the summer months, keep a look out for movies screened outdoors in various park locations.

Classical Concerts

Take the chance to see and hear a Chinese orchestra, if at all possible. Sections of unfamiliar plucked string, bowed string, woodwind, and percussion instruments compete for attention in swirling arrangements.

The **National Center for the Performing Arts**, just one block west of Tian'an Men Square, is a spectacular multi-purpose venue that puts on classical concerts, ballet, and opera, as well as providing space for art exhibitions. Its central location and impressive architecture alone certainly merit a visit.

Beijing Opera star

National Center for the Performing Arts – or, as it is more commonly known, "the Egg"

Popstars performing an outdoor concert in Beijing

Rock and Pop

The question of which city has the best tunes provokes regular shouting matches between the youth of Beijing and Shanghai, but there is no argument really: Beijing wins.

Beijing-based Cui Jian, the Bob Dylan-like old man of Chinese rock, became the first famous indigenous name in rock with his protest songs, including "Nothing to My Name," with its references to the events in Tian'an Men Square of 1989. As a result he was forbidden to play large venues until 2006.

But the once lone voice of rock is now drowned out by the innumerable punk bands for which Beijing is famous, and Chinese versions of every kind of popular music. Most of the new generation think Cui Jian should retire, although he played small venues across North America in 2005, and was the support act for the Rolling Stones when they played Shanghai in 2006.

Many Chinese rock and pop musicians take Western music genres as a starting point, on to which they then overlay Chinese characteristics. Singing in Mandarin isn't enough: they will also perhaps add an electrified *erhu (see p35)* to the line-up, or use vocal styles from Chinese opera. The results range from appalling to appealing, but there's no lack of talent and enthusiasm.

Sanlitun's **Workers' Stadium** is the usual venue for large-scale rock, filled regularly by Taiwanese and Hong Kong stars, but also by a few mainland pan-Asia mega-stars such as the infinitely talented Wang Fei (Faye Wong to her Cantonese-speaking fans). Tickets are always hard to get, and there is always a thriving trade for them on the black market.

Among the many smaller venues for live music, all with rosters of rock, blues, jazz, punk, and anything else that seems likely to bring in the masses, the **Yugong Yishan** bar is the current favorite for its cheap drinks and eclectic programing policy. Also popular is the rocking student venue, **Mao Livehouse**, which attracts both local and international live acts from across the underground music spectrum (it is part-owned by a Japanese record label). There are sibling Mao Livehouse venues in Shanghai, Chongqing and Kunming.

Teahouses

China's long history of growing and drinking tea has led to considerable refinement in its production, preparation, and serving. A very elaborate tea ceremony may include the use of a sniffing cup into which a small amount of tea is poured and then emptied before the residual aroma is savored. In fact, most ceremonies involve a lot of filling and spilling, or tipping away – the aim is to provide a good number of exquisitely small cups of perfect tea, all at the same strength, from one pot of tea leaves. Teahouses such as the **Purple Vine** near the west gate of the Forbidden City, offer calm interiors with antique furnishings, and a respite from the city's bedlam. The **Xi Hua Yuan Teahouse**, which is across the street from Purple Vine, adds a Chinese-speaking mynah bird to the attractions. The **Ji Gu Ge Teahouse** offers a wide selection of traditional teas and also boasts a small gallery and shop.

At such establishments the prices of various teas are clearly given on a menu, and a demonstration of the traditional preparation of tea is included in the cost of the more expensive ones.

Watch out for English-speaking Chinese who strike up conversations at tourist sites. Sometimes the visitor is asked whether they have ever seen a Chinese tea ceremony? A short walk to a tucked-away teahouse, and a few samples of tea later, a bill that is the equivalent of well over a hundred US dollars or more is presented. Your new Chinese friends will profess to be horrified, as they had no idea it would be so expensive, but of course they are party to the con.

The elaborate art of tea drinking

Puppet Theater and Acrobatics

When it comes to theater, language truly is a barrier. However, there is always traditional Chinese puppet theater. Plays with wooden puppets *(mu'ouxi)* involve elaborate and colorfully dressed marionettes. The fun is as much in admiring the craftsmanship and dexterity as attempting to work out the plot; see what's on at the **China Puppet Art Theater**.

Enterprising entrepreneurs have also put together performances of "teahouse art," which may include acrobatics, storytelling, singers, jugglers, and short extracts from Beijing

Chinese acrobatic troupe performing with bicycles

Opera. These bite-sized cultural morsels are usually served in recreated period atmosphere with tea and a meal. Try the **Lao**

She Teahouse (which has shows at 7:50pm daily), just south of Tian'an Men Square, and the **Tian Qiao Happy Teahouse**.

China has a worldwide reputation for its gymnasts who perform breathtaking routines that showcase their unnerving flexibility. Displays of balance often involve props such as chairs and plates, with one of the most popular tricks being to pile 20 or so acrobats on a bicycle. Venues include the **Chaoyang Theater** and **Tiandi Theater**, both with nightly shows, and occasionally the **Poly Theater**. All of these theaters are in the eastern district of Sanlitun.

DIRECTORY

Bars and Clubs

Atmosphere
80/F, China World Summit Tower, 1 Jianguo Men Wai Dajie. **Map** 3 F5. **Tel** (010) 6505 2299 ext. 6433.

Capital M
3/F, Qianmen Dajie, Chongwen. **Map** 4 C2. **Tel** (010) 6702 2727.

D Lounge
Courtyard 4, Gongti Bei Lu, Chaoyang. **Map** 3 F3. **Tel** (010) 6593 7710.

Dada
206 Gulou Dong Dajie, Dongcheng **Map** 2 A2. **Tel** 183 1108 0818.

Enoterra
D405 Nali Patio, 81 Sanlitun North Road. **Map** 3 F3. **Tel** (010) 5208 6076.

The Hutong
1 Jiu Dao Wan Zhong Xiang. **Map** 2 C2. **Tel** (159) 0104 6127.

Janes and Hooch
Courtyard 4, Gongti Bei Lu, Chaoyang. **Map** 3 F3. **Tel** (010) 6503 2757.

Mai
40 Bei Luogu Xiang. **Map** 2 B2. **Tel** (0138) 1125 2641.

Mesh
Opposite House Hotel, 11 Sanlitun Road. **Map** 3 F3. **Tel** (010) 6417 7688.

Migas
Nali Patio, 81 Sanlitun Road, Chaoyang. **Map** 3 F3. **Tel** (010) 5208 6061.

No Name Bar
Qianhai Dong Yan, S. of Silver Ingot Bridge. **Map** 2 A2. **Tel** (010) 6401 8541.

Riverbank Café
Ground Floor, FX Hotel, 39 Maizidianxi Jie. **Tel** (010) 6506 8277.

Stone Boat
Southwest corner of Ri Tan Park. **Map** 3 E5. **Tel** (010) 6501 9986.

The Tree
43 Sanlitun Bei Lu. **Map** 3 F3. **Tel** (010) 6415 1954.

Yugong Yishan
3–2 Zhangzizhong Lu, Gulou. **Map** 2 B3. **Tel** (010) 6404 2711.

Beijing Opera

Huguang Guildhall
3 Hufang Lu. **Map** 4 B3. **Tel** (010) 6351 8284.

Liyuan Theater
Qian Men Hotel, 175 Yong an Road, Xuan Wu. **Map** 4 B3. **Tel** (010) 6301 6688.

Mansion of Prince Gong
14 Liuyin Jie, off Hou Hai Nan Yan. **Map** 2 A2. **Tel** (010) 6616 8149.

Zhengyici Theater
220 Xiheyan Dajie. **Map** 4 B2. **Tel** (010) 8315 1649.

Cinema

Culture Yard
10 Shique Hutong. **Map** 2 C2. **Tel** (010) 8404 4166.

Wanda International Cinema Complex
3/F, Building 8, Wanda Plaza, 93 Jianguo Lu, Chaoyang. **Map** 3 F5. **Tel** (010) 5960 3399.

Music

Mao Livehouse
111 Gulou Dong Dajie, Dongcheng. **Map** 2 B2. **Tel** (010) 6402 5080.

National Center for the Performing Arts
Xi Chang'an Jie, W. of Great Hall of the People. **Map** 4 C1. **Tel** (010) 6655 0000.

Workers' Stadium
Gongren Tiyuchang Bei Lu. **Map** 3 E3. **Tel** (010) 6501 6655.

Teahouses

Ji Gu Ge Teahouse
132-6 Liulichang Dong Jie. **Map** 4 B2. **Tel** (010) 6301 7849.

Purple Vine
2 Nan Chang Jie. **Map** 2 A5. **Tel** (010) 6606 6614.

Xi Hua Yuan Teahouse
Bei Chang Jie, across from west gate of Forbidden City. **Map** 2 A5. **Tel** (010) 6603 8534.

Puppet Theater and Acrobatics

Chaoyang Theater
36 Dongsanhuan Bei Lu. **Map** 3 F4. **Tel** (010) 6507 2421.

China Puppet Art Theater
A1 Anhua Xi Li. **Tel** (010) 6424 3698.

Lao She Teahouse
3 Qian Men Xi Dajie. **Map** 4 C2. **Tel** (010) 6301 7454.

Poly Theater
Poly Plaza, 14 Dong Zhi Men Nan Dajie. **Map** 3 D3. **Tel** (010) 6500 1188.

Tiandi Theater
10 Dong Zhi Men Nan Dajie. **Map** 3 D3. **Tel** (010) 6502 3984.

Tian Qiao Happy Teahouse
1 Bei Wei Lu. **Map** 4 C3. **Tel** (010) 6304 0617.

BEIJING STREET FINDER

The map references given with all sights, hotels, restaurants, shops, and entertainment venues described in this chapter refer to the following maps only. The first figure of the map reference indicates which map to turn to, and the letter and number that follow are the grid reference. The key map below shows which parts of Beijing's city center are covered in this Street Finder. A complete index of street names follows the maps. Note that there are different ways of presenting Chinese names, so, for example, the main street Jianguo Men Nai Dajie might appear on signs in Beijing as Jianguomennai Dajie. For more on street names see page 172. Modern Beijing has extended a long way beyond the main city center zone depicted below and outlying areas are shown on the Beijing Farther Afield map on page 91.

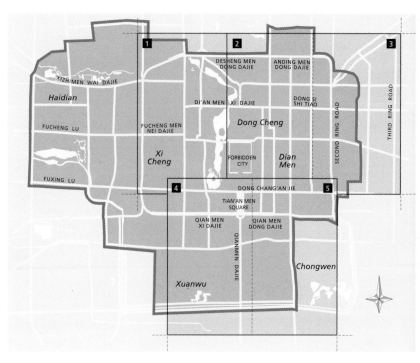

Key to Street Finder

- Major sight
- Place of interest
- Other important building
- Train station
- Bus station
- Subway station
- Tourist information
- Hospital
- Temple
- Church
- Mosque

Scale of map above

0 kilometers 2
0 miles 2

Scale of maps 1–5

0 meters 500
0 yards 500

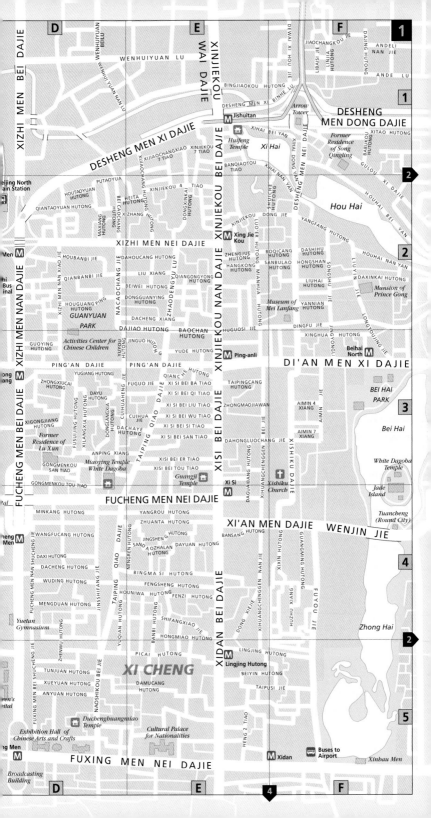

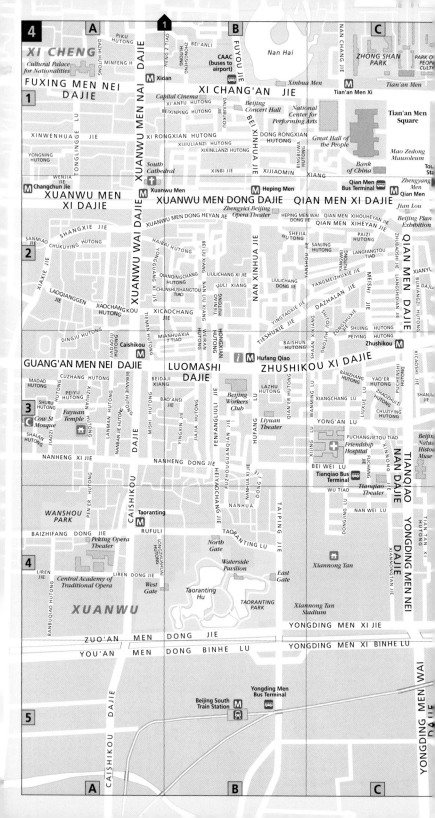

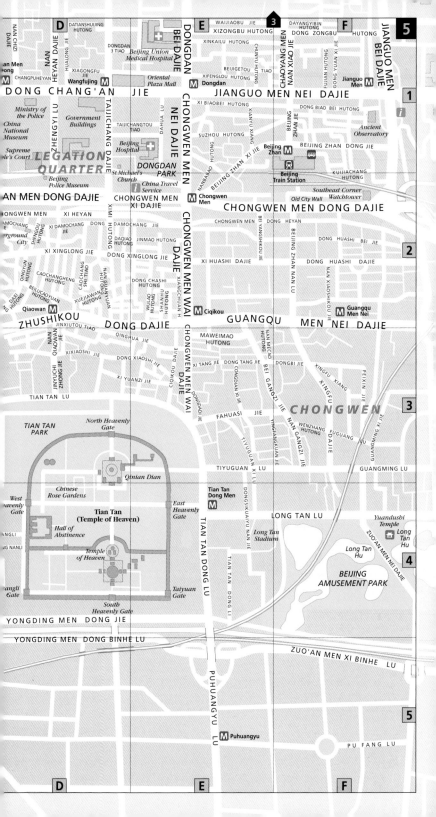

Beijing Street Finder Index

SHANGHAI

Exploring Shanghai

Shanghai has three main areas of interest to the visitor. The Old City is typically Chinese, with alleys, markets, and temples. It is also home to the beautiful Yu Gardens. The former concession areas, once under the direct rule of the French, British, and Americans, boast the Bund, the riverside avenue lined with grand colonial buildings, as well as the city's two main shopping streets, Nanjing Road and Huaihai Road. Pudong, Shanghai's newest district, on the Huangpu's east bank, is an immense business and residential zone, with a clutch of museums and some of the highest buildings in the world. The Shanghai Street Finder on p172–7 provides detailed maps of the central area.

Locator Map
See also pp16–17.

Sights at a Glance

Historic Buildings, Sites, and Neighborhoods

❶ *The Bund pp126–7*
❷ Nanjing Road
❻ Site of the First National Congress of the Chinese Communist Party
❽ French Concession
❾ Shanghai Exhibition Center
⓬ Bund Sightseeing Tunnel
⓭ Oriental Pearl TV Tower
⓯ IFC Tower
⓰ Jinmao Tower
⓱ Shanghai World Financial Center
⓲ The Shanghai Tower
㉑ Soong Qingling's Former Residence
㉓ Longhua Cemetery of Martyrs
㉔ World Expo Site (2010)

Temples and Churches

❿ Jing'an Temple
⓫ Jade Buddha Temple
㉒ Xujiahui Catholic Cathedral

Parks and Gardens

❸ People's Park & Square
❺ *Yu Gardens & Bazaar pp134–5*
❼ Fuxing Park
⓳ Century Park
⓴ Hongkou Park

Museums

❹ *Shanghai Museum pp130–33*
⓮ Shanghai Ocean Aquarium
㉖ The Long Museum
㉗ YUZ Museum

Towns and Areas of Natural Beauty

㉕ She Shan

Key

- ▬▬ National highway
- ▬▬ Major road
- — Railroad

Getting Around

The subway is the best way to get around Shanghai. At the time of writing, there are thirteen lines and the network is still expanding *(see p222)*. Taxis are also convenient, cheap, and plentiful. Buses tend to be extremely crowded and slow due to traffic congestion, especially during the morning and evening rush hours. Road tunnels link the east and west banks of the Huangpu River but it's more fun to take a ferry.

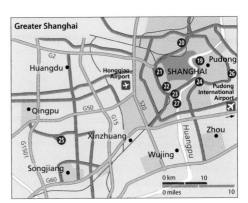

Greater Shanghai

❶ The Bund

外滩

Some places are forever associated with a single landmark and in the case of Shanghai it is surely the Bund. Also known as Zhongshan East No.1 Road, the Bund was at the heart of colonial Shanghai, flanked on one side by the Huangpu River and on the other by the hotels, banks, offices, and clubs that were the grandiose symbols of western commercial power. Most of the old buildings are still in place and a walk along here can easily absorb a couple of pleasant hours. The Bund was extensively relandscaped for the World Expo 2010.

The Bund, at its peak the third biggest financial center in world

★ **Shanghai Pudong Development Bank**
Built in 1921 when it was vaunted to be the most beautiful building in Asia, it boasts delightful murals.

★ **Customs House**
The entrance hall is decorated with some handsome marine mosaics.

★ **River promenade**
On the river side of the Bund is a wide pavement, a wonderful place to stroll and watch locals practising *tai ji quan* (tai chi). It is also a great spot for photographing the Pudong skyline.

KEY

① **The bronze lions'** paws and head are rubbed for good luck.

② **Former Bank of Communications**

③ **Russo-Asiatic Bank Building**

④ **Former Bank of Taiwan**

⑤ **North China Daily News Building**

⑥ **Chartered Bank Building** of India, Australia, and China.

For hotels and restaurants see pp182–5 and pp200–202

★ View from the Bund
The grand old buildings of the Bund face one of China's most futuristic skylines, the Pudong business district. The pagoda-stepped Jinmao Tower and shardlike Shanghai World Financial Centre, in their day the city's tallest buildings, are now seemingly dwarfed by the Shanghai Tower.

Bank of China
Blending 1920s American and traditional Chinese styles, this impressive block was built by a rival of Sassoon, H H Kung.

Former Palace Hotel
The Palace Hotel was built in 1906 and was for a long time one of the best hotels in Shanghai. It is now the Swatch Art Peace Hotel.

Fairmont Peace Hotel
Originally the Cathay Hotel, built in 1930 by Sir Victor Sassoon, this is now a lavish hotel with impressive views of the Huangpu River. The jazz bar is still at the heart of its events.

Chen Yi's statue
The bronze statue looking down the Bund is not Chairman Mao but Chen Yi, revolutionary commander and first mayor of Shanghai after 1949.

❷ Nanjing Road
南京路

Map 1 D3/E3/F2 & 2 A2/B2/C2.
M Nanjing East Road (for pedestrian shopping street), Nanjing West Road (for People's Square).

Nanjing Road has traditionally been Shanghai's foremost shopping street, although since the 1990s it has faced increasing competition from Huaihai Road in the French Concession. The street is divided into two distinct halves: Nanjing East Road stretches between the Bund and People's Park; Nanjing West Road runs from People's Park out past Jing'an Temple. Together, the two parts total close to six miles (10 km).

The "shopper's paradise" has always been **Nanjing East Road**. Before 1949, all the major stores were located here. One of them, the Sun Department Store, is now the **Shanghai No. 1 Department Store**, which continues to attract thousands of customers every day with its exotic window displays. Many of the other department stores have been replaced with modern malls, but it is worth a walk down the street by night because, once the sun has

Statues on Nanjing Dong Lu

The Park Hotel, formerly one of the most fashionable addresses in town

gone down, Nanjing East Road resembles a Chinese version of Las Vegas, with its shop fronts illuminated by a multitude of garish neon signs.

Nanjing West Road once went by the charming name of Bubbling Well Road, after the well near Jing'an Temple (see p138). A grand relic of those times survives in the **Park Hotel**, across from People's Square, which when built in 1934 was the tallest building in Shanghai – a record it held until 1988 – not to mention one of the most fashionable addresses. Beside the Park, **Huanghe Road** is a great place for street food. **Wujiang Road**, which loops off Nanjing Road west of People's Square, now has an impressive and popular shopping plaza.

Beyond the point at which it is rejoined by Wujiang Road, Nanjing West Road is lined by a series of exclusive shopping and commercial centers such as the Westgate Mall, CITIC Square, and the **Jing'an Kerry Center** (see pp166–7), all filled with multiple levels of designer shops, including names such as Armani, Louis Vuitton, and Cartier, with prices even higher than at home. A little farther along is the **Shanghai Center**, one of the earliest such developments, with several good restaurants, a popular bar, and airline offices clustered around the Portman Ritz-Carlton Hotel.

Birds for sale at the Fish & Flower Market on Jiangyin Road

❸ People's Park & Square
人民广场

Nanjing West Road. **Map** 2 A2 & A3.
M People's Square.

What used to be a racecourse (see p129) is now occupied by the pleasantly landscaped People's Park (Renmin Gong Yuan) in the northern half, and People's Square and the **Shanghai Museum** (see pp130–33) in the southern section. Locals visit the park to walk, gossip, exercise, or fly kites but, in addition to the museum, there are several other sights and cultural monuments to attract the visitor. Quite literally overshadowed by the gleaming glass and steel skyscrapers that surround it, **Mu'en Tang**, the Merciful Baptism Church, lies on the eastern side of the square. It was built in 1929 as the American Baptist Church. An interdenominational survivor of China's many revolutions, it is open to all, although the services are in Chinese only.

On the northeast side of the square, the building with four inverted tents for a roof is the **Urban Planning Exhibition Hall**. The Yangzi River delta is the world's fastest-growing urban area and that is reflected here with the world's largest model. The model, which can be viewed from a gallery above, sprawls across 100 square meters, and depicts the

Shanghai of the not-too-distant future. This, unsurprisingly, takes the form of a forest of skyscrapers, all lovingly detailed at a scale of 1:2000. Other floors have maps of more construction to come, and exhibitions on the city's signature *shikumen* housing and colonial-era Shanghai. The top floor houses a quiet café.

The elegant glass box of **MOCA Shanghai**, the Museum of Contemporary Art, opened in 2005. Its two floors house regularly changing exhibitions of cutting-edge art and design, which have included work by Alexander Calder, David Hockney, Jenny Holzer, and Matazo Koyama, and the 80th-anniversary showcase of the Salvatore Ferragamo couture house. Located beside a small lake near the entrance to MOCA Shanghai is Barbarossa, a hip Moroccan-themed bar and restaurant with an al fresco terrace that affords superb skyline views.

At the northwest corner of the park is the Former Shanghai Jockey Club, an elegant old racecourse clubhouse. The lavish marbled interiors of this 1930s Neo-Classical building are particularly impressive. This beautiful building was once the home of the eclectic Shanghai Art Museum, which has now moved to the World Expo Site (2010) *(see p143)*.

The Old Racecourse

The old racecourse was the center of Shanghai social life in the early 20th century, and its Race Club was one of the most profitable corporations in China. It also boasted a swimming pool and a cricket pitch. After the Communists came to power in 1949, the course became a symbol of Western decadence, and was turned into a park and an adjacent square that was used for political rallies. It was later landscaped to accommodate the Shanghai Museum. When the grandstand became the Shanghai Art Museum, all that remained of the racecourse was its old grandstand clock on the park's west side.

View of Shanghai's racecourse pictured prior to 1949

Behind the Former Shanghai Jockey Club is the striking modern building housing the **Shanghai Grand Theater**, made almost entirely of glass and topped by a spectacular convex roof. It is definitely worth a visit, for a meal or a coffee with a view or just to look around; official tours are also available.

🛕 **Mu'en Tang**
315 Xizang Middle Road. **Open** for five daily services, see noticeboard at entrance for times.

🏛 **MOCA Shanghai**
People's Park, 231 Nanjing West Road. **Open** 10am–9:30pm daily.
🅦 **mocashanghai.org**

🎭 **Shanghai Grand Theater**
People's Square.
Open 10:30am–5:30pm daily.

🏛 **Urban Planning Exhibition Hall**
100 People's Avenue.
Open 9am–4pm Mon–Thu, 9am–5pm Fri–Sun. ¥30.
🅦 **supec.org**

Ornamental flower display in the beautifully maintained People's Park, at the heart of Shanghai

❹ Shanghai Museum
上海博物馆

With a collection of over 120,000 pieces, the Shanghai Museum displays some of the best cultural relics from China's neolithic period to the Qing dynasty, a span of over 5,000 years. While the highlights are the bronze ware, ceramics, calligraphy, and painting, it also has excellent displays of jade, furniture, coins, and Chinese seals, or "chops." The museum was established in 1952, and the current building opened in 1995 with a design that recalls some of the exhibits and symbolizes "a round heaven and a square earth."

Shanghai Museum, reminiscent of a Shang-dynasty bronze *ding* pot

Calligraphy

To the Chinese, calligraphy is more than mere communication, it is one of the highest art forms. This cursive script *(see pp22–3)* was painted by Huai Su (AD 737) in typically wild movements that combine delicate and forceful strokes.

Third floor

★ Sancai pottery figures

The major technical advance of the Tang dynasty (618–907) in ceramics was the development of *sancai* (three-color) pottery. This grave figure is a superb piece of polychrome pottery.

Celadon ware

Celadon's simple beauty and strength made it highly desirable. This example of Longquan ware from the Southern Song dynasty (1127–1279) elegantly captures the movement of the coiled dragon.

Second floor

Key to Floorplan

- ☐ Bronzes
- ☐ Sculpture
- ☐ Ceramics
- ☐ Zande Lou ceramics
- ☐ Paintings
- ☐ Calligraphy
- ☐ Seals
- ☐ Jade
- ☐ Furniture
- ☐ Coins
- ☐ Ethnic minorities gallery
- ☐ Temporary exhibitions
- ☐ Non-exhibition space

Zande Lou ceramics is a privately donated collection of 130 pieces and includes some outstanding Qing imperial items.

For hotels and restaurants see pp182–5 and pp200–202

Fourth floor

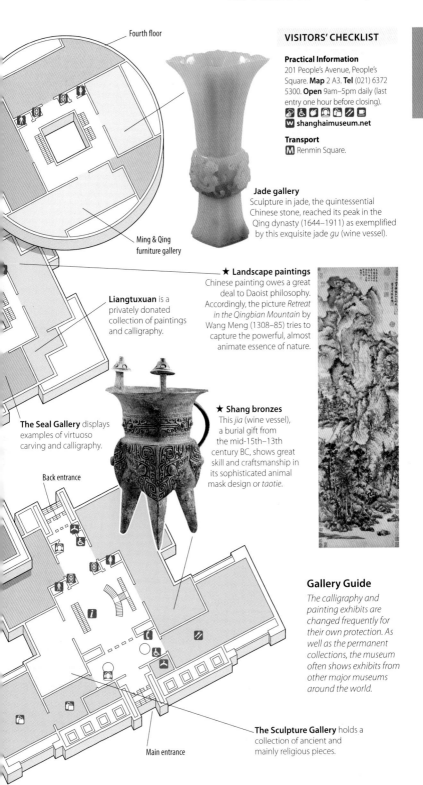

VISITORS' CHECKLIST

Practical Information
201 People's Avenue, People's
Square. **Map** 2 A3. **Tel** (021) 6372
5300. **Open** 9am–5pm daily (last
entry one hour before closing).

w shanghaimuseum.net

Transport
M Renmin Square.

Jade gallery
Sculpture in jade, the quintessential
Chinese stone, reached its peak in the
Qing dynasty (1644–1911) as exemplified
by this exquisite jade *gu* (wine vessel).

Ming & Qing
furniture gallery

★ **Landscape paintings**
Chinese painting owes a great
deal to Daoist philosophy.
Accordingly, the picture *Retreat
in the Qingbian Mountain* by
Wang Meng (1308–85) tries to
capture the powerful, almost
animate essence of nature.

Liangtuxuan is a
privately donated
collection of paintings
and calligraphy.

★ **Shang bronzes**
This *jia* (wine vessel),
a burial gift from
the mid-15th–13th
century BC, shows great
skill and craftsmanship in
its sophisticated animal
mask design or *taotie*.

The Seal Gallery displays
examples of virtuoso
carving and calligraphy.

Back entrance

Gallery Guide

*The calligraphy and
painting exhibits are
changed frequently for
their own protection. As
well as the permanent
collections, the museum
often shows exhibits from
other major museums
around the world.*

The Sculpture Gallery holds a
collection of ancient and
mainly religious pieces.

Main entrance

Exploring the Shanghai Museum

Eleven galleries display a selection from the museum's permanent collection and three others are used to show temporary exhibitions from around the world. The scope and quality of the exhibits mean that one visit may not be enough for the interested visitor. The displays and interpretation are probably the best in China and, as such, should be savored. There's also an excellent shop within the museum with one of the best selections of books on China that you are likely to find anywhere.

Bronze *ding* (food vessel), mid-Western Zhou (10th century BC)

Bronzes

China's Bronze Age (18th to 3rd century BC) is represented by an extraordinary collection of wine vessels, three-legged *ding* (cooking vessels), and bells, all cast in bronze using ceramic moulds. Particularly attractive are the *zun* wine vessels, such as one in the shape of a sturdy ox, 2,500 years old, complete with horns and nose-ring and covered in incised decoration. The intricacy of the metalwork – quite impractical for everyday items – is evidence that these beautiful works of art were used for ritual offerings of food and wine, and that the society that created them was possessed of a sophisticated level of technology. It would also have taken powerful rulers, great organization, and vast amounts of manpower to mine, transport, and refine such large amounts of metal ore and then create these wonderful pieces, setting a precedent for Chinese societies to come.

Sculpture

Buddhism's arrival in China and its gradual absorption into the mainstream is reflected in over 120 pieces of bronze, wood, stone, and pottery dating from around 475 BC to AD 1644, the end of the Ming dynasty. Gradually, the high-cheekboned slender figures of a North Indian and Central Asian aesthetic take on the plumper, moon-faced shapes of the Chinese. There are also legions of tomb figurines from different dynasties, and fine examples of the polychrome equestrian figures that characterize sculpture during the Tang dynasty period.

Gilt bronze Buddha

Painting

A lighting system in each display cabinet that only comes on as visitors approach helps to protect the 120 delicate exhibits on display in the museum's third-floor painting gallery. Some of the pieces date back as far as the Tang dynasty (618–907). Despite the concrete and bedlam of modern Shanghai just outside, here's a reminder of the Chinese delight in nature and wildlife that goes back centuries. Waterfalls plunge down mountains topped with gnarled pines and inhabited by pheasants and other wild birds. Notable treasures include the only surviving original painting by Sun Wei of the Tang dynasty, showing seven hermits disporting themselves in a bamboo forest.

Calligraphy

Calligraphy in China is said to have already atttained maturity by the time of the Eastern Zhou dynasty (770–221 BC). However, the art's greatest exponent is often said to be Wang Xizhi (c.AD 303–361), who is known as the "Sage of Calligraphy". Few Chinese these days can understand much of the classical script of these scrolls, and perhaps the foreign visitor's appreciation of their beauty is enhanced because it is undistracted by any flashes of meaning, allowing concentration on the shapes alone. Stylistic differences can be identified even by the non-specialist, such as the difference between the running style and the more flamboyant cursive style, while the characters adorning the seals seem from another language altogether.

Hermits, a hand scroll by Sun Wei, Tang dynasty (AD 618–907)

Polychrome glazed pottery, Tang dynasty (AD 618–907)

Ceramics

The museum is particularly proud of its display of 500 pieces from all over China, which together illustrate 8,000 years of ceramic production. Some are incredibly rare and were deemed too delicate for public presentation until the current modern facility was built. It is visibly a long journey from the clumsy solidity of some of the early pots displayed here to the *famille verte* of the Qing Kangxi emperor's era, delicately painted with traditional scenes, and the *famille rose* of his successors with their flowery over-decoration and rococo elements designed to pander to the Orientalism of European markets. Better than either is the fine, white-glaze porcelain of the Jin dynasty. Also notable are the delicate celadon hues of Song dynasty wares and the charm of the underglaze paintings of fish and flowers in blue or red of the Ming dynasty. This one gallery alone makes a visit to Shanghai worthwhile.

Jade

The precious substance most closely linked with China, at least by foreigners, is jade, a word the Chinese use to describe a variety of different stones of various hues, but principally the bluish-green nephrite and jadeite. Never particularly abundant in China, stocks are now largely exhausted. Some of the jade objects here are described as dating back to the 51st-century BC. These early examples were symbols of status, as the dense stone requires a great deal of effort to shape. In the late Zhou period, around 2,500 years ago, jade's symbolic value was augmented by an appreciation of its beauty. The stone began to be used for ornaments such as wine cups and brooches. The museum's collection includes examples carved into dragons, turtles, and tigers of marvellous delicacy.

Porcelain vase of Jingdezhen origin

Furniture

Up on the topmost floor of the museum is the furniture gallery, where Ming-dynasty constructions of elegant simplicity sit alongside over-elaborately decorated later Qing pieces. Should any of these items take your fancy, most can be found copied in "antique" furniture stores in both Shanghai and Beijing.

Two beautiful brick-floored rooms contain recreations of the layouts of studies of both eras. Perhaps best of all are the miniature wooden furniture sets, together with a procession of wooden figurines, retrieved from Ming tombs.

Seals

Seals, or chops, as they are also known, remain essential when important documents are signed, even in modern China. They are easily purchased, coming in straightforward plastic and rubber forms. But those in the museum's collection of more than 500 include miniature works of art in ivory, jade, and soapstone. Some are in the shapes of animals or mythical creatures, and some are carved with tiny landscapes. This is rightly regarded as the best such collection in China, although anyone visiting Hangzhou may also want to visit the museum of the Seal Engravers Society (*see pp156–7*).

Other Displays

Other displays include pottery, costume, embroidery, and lacquerware from a few of the 55 or so ethnic minorities that make up the peoples of China. Also, as one of the first countries to systematically use coins and then notes, there's an extensive collection of these items from throughout China's history.

Sandalwood Qing-dynasty throne chair with carved cloud and dragon design

❺ Yu Gardens and Bazaar

豫园

The old-style buildings of the Yu Gardens bazaar are not really old, but the fanciful roofs are nevertheless very appealing. The shops here peddle everything from tourist souvenirs to traditional medicines and, despite inflated prices, the area is incredibly popular. It is best to arrive early and go straight to the beautiful and relatively peaceful Ming-dynasty Yu Gardens (Yu Yuan). A dumpling lunch will set you up for a hectic afternoon of shopping and haggling, followed by a cup of tea in the quaint Huxinting teahouse, or a restorative visit to the tranquil Chenxiangge Nunnery.

Visitors pay their respects before the Buddha at Chenxiangge Nunnery

Yu Gardens Bazaar
Despite being a bit of a tourist trap, there is plenty of fun to be had wandering among the stalls and haggling over prices.

Street performers
Every now and then, a colorful troupe of performers appears bearing young children on top of poles to entertain the thronging crowds.

★ City God Temple
Dating back to the Ming era, the temple once housed the patron god of Shanghai and encompassed an area as large as the bazaar. Now this small restored temple is very popular with tourists.

KEY

① **Shanghai Old Street** (Fangbang Road) and an entrance to the Bazaar

② **Restaurants** surround the lake – you can see the dumplings being made in the morning.

Locator Map
See Shanghai Street Finder map 2

★ **Huxinting Teahouse**
This charming building, built in 1784 by cotton merchants, only became a teahouse in the late 19th century. The zigzag bridge protects the structure, as it is believed that evil spirits can't turn corners.

★ **Huge rockery**
Reputed to be one of the best Ming rockeries, it is surely one of the largest. It recalls the peaks, caves, and gorges of southern China.

Garden entrance

Dragon wall
The white walls in the garden are topped by an undulating dragon. Note it only has four claws and not five like an imperial dragon, so as not to incur the emperor's wrath.

Yu Gardens scenic areas
The walls divide the garden into six scenic areas, which makes it feel like a maze and seem larger than it really is. As a result, the garden gets very busy in the afternoon and on weekends.

Entrance to the First National Congress of the Chinese Communist Party

❻ Site of the First National Congress of the Chinese Communist Party
中共一大会址纪念馆

374 Huangpi South Road. **Map** 2 A4. Ⓜ Huangpi South Road. **Open** 9am–4pm.

This house in the French Concession was the venue for a historic meeting, where representatives of China's Communist cells met to form a national party on July 23, 1921. Officially, there were 12 participants including Mao Zedong, but it is believed that many others also attended. The police discovered the meeting and the delegates were forced to escape to a boat on Lake Nan, in Zhejiang. The house has a reconstruction of the meeting, with the original chairs and teacups used by the delegates. The exhibition hall tells the history of the Chinese Communist Party.

❼ Fuxing Park
复兴公园

Fuxing Middle Road. **Map** 1 F4. Ⓜ Xintiandi. Sun Yat Sen Memorial Residence: 7 Xingshan Road. **Tel** (021) 6372 6083. **Open** 6am–6pm daily. Zhou Enlai's Former Residence: 73 Sinan Road. **Open** 9am–4pm daily.

The French bought this private garden, located in the French Concession, in 1908. It was known then as the "French Park," and has elements of a formal Parisian *jardin*, with meandering paths flanked by cherry trees. It was renamed Fuxing, meaning "revival," in 1949.

Close by on Xiangshan Road is the **Sun Yat Sen Memorial Residence**, a typical Shanghai villa where the leader and his wife, Soong Qingling, lived between 1918 and 1924. The interior is just as it was in Sun's time, with many of his personal items such as his gramophone and books. South of the park, 73 Rue Massenet (now Sinan Road) is the **Former Residence of Zhou Enlai**, who lived here when he was head of the city's Communist Party in the 1940s. It is another excellent example of a European-style Shanghai villa.

❽ French Concession
法国花园

Ⓜ Shaanxi South Road. **Map** 1 E4.

The former French Concession, stretching from the western edge of the Old City to Avenue Haig (Huashan Road), comprises boulevards, shops, and cafés, and its residents were mainly White Russians and Chinese. It had its own electoral system, judiciary, and police force, whose highest-ranking officer, "Pockmarked Huang," was the leader of the infamous Green Gang which controlled the opium trade.

Statue of Sun Yat Sen, Sun Yat Sen Memorial

Today, the Concession is centered on **Huaihai Road** – a vibrant street lined with boutiques, candy stores, hair salons, and bars – and the charming **Jinjiang Hotel** on Maoming Road. The hotel's compound includes the Grosvenor Residence, pre-war Shanghai's most exclusive property. The VIP Club, in the hotel's old wing, retains its 1920s architecture. The adjacent street, Maoming Road, is currently under redevelopment. Another interesting building is the **Ruijin Guesthouse** at the corner of Fuxing Middle Road and Shaanxi South Road. This Tudor-style manor is now an inn set in a quiet compound. **The Children's Palace** at the western end of Yan'an Road was part of an early 1920s estate, and is now a children's arts center. The tourist office arranges tours to watch its singing and dancing shows.

The European-style villa that was Zhou Enlai's residence

The Huangpu River

The Huangpu River is a mere 68 miles (110 km) in length from its source, Dianshan Lake, to its junction with the Yangzi River, 17 miles (28 km) downstream from Shanghai. As a spectacle, however, it is fascinating and there is much for the eye to take in, from the majestic but elderly waterfront at the Bund and burgeoning modern metropolis on Pudong to the bustling docks that line the Huangpu all the way to the mouth of the Yangzi. Boat tours depart from the wharves on the Bund between Nanjing Road and Yan'an Road *(see pp124–5)*. The three-and-a-half hour trip goes all the way to the Yangzi River, but if time is short, there is also a one-hour trip just as far as the Yangpu Bridge.

⑦ The Yangzi River
The color of the water changes markedly here, as the oily Huangpu meets the muddy and turbulent Yangzi. A lighthouse marks the confluence of the two.

④ Shanghai Docks
The Shanghainese proudly claim that nearly a third of all China's international trade enters via the perennially busy Huangpu river.

⑥ Wusong Fort
The site of a decisive battle against the British in 1842, it consisted of a crescent-shaped fort with ten imported cannons.

③ Yangpu Bridge
Built in 1993, this is one of the world's longest cable-stay bridges – cables are anchored to each tower.

⑤ Gongqing Forest Park
This large and pleasantly landscaped park was reclaimed from marshland and is popular with the Shanghainese on weekends.

② Huangpu Park
At the northern tip of the Bund, this park is home to the Monument to the People's Heroes.

Huangpu River

• Pudong

0 kilometres   6
0 miles   3

① The Bund
The best way to enjoy the Bund's grandiose skyline is from a boat, which also gives the visitor a view of the city that would have greeted all expatriates on their arrival here before 1949.

Boat Trip Tips

Length: 37 miles (60 km).
One-hour trip: 10 miles (16 km).
Boat trips: The boats vary in size and facilities, so make sure you know what you are getting. The more expensive trips offer food and even entertainment of sorts.
Times: 9am, 2pm, 7pm Mon–Fri, 11am, 3:30pm, 8pm Sat & Sun. The one-hour trips leave more frequently (times can vary).

The striking Soviet-style Shanghai Exhibition Center

❾ Shanghai Exhibition Center
上海展览中心

1000 Yan'an Middle Road. **Map** 1 E3. **Tel** (021) 2216 2216. **M** Jing'an Temple. **Open** 8am–5pm daily.

The enormous Shanghai Exhibition Center is one of the few reminders of the influence the Soviet Union once had in Shanghai. Built in 1954, it was known as the Palace of Sino-Soviet Friendship, and was designed as a place for exhibiting China's technological and agricultural advances since the founding of the People's Republic in 1949. Ironically, the building stands on the site of the estate of millionaire Silas Hardoon – Shanghai's biggest capitalist in the 1920s. The Center is worth seeing for its grimly florid Soviet-style architecture. It has an impressively ornate entrance, with columns decorated with red stars, and a gilded spire. Today, it is a gigantic mall, filled with shops selling furniture and souvenirs.

Nearby on Xinle Road, in the former French Concession, is the old **Russian Orthodox Church** with its distinctive onion-shaped domes. It served thousands of refugees from the Russian Revolution in 1917. The area around Julu Road and Changle Road nearby has a number of interesting Art Deco and early 20th-century villas and mansions constructed by Shanghai's wealthy residents.

❿ Jing'an Temple
静安寺

1686 Nanjing West Road (near Huashan Road). **Map** 1 D3. **M** Jing'an Temple. **Open** 7:30am–5pm daily.

Located opposite the attractive Jing'an Park, which contains the old Bubbling Well Cemetery, Jing'an Temple (Temple of Tranquility) is one of the city's most revered places for ancestor worship. Originally founded in the Three Kingdoms Period, the current structure dates to 2007 when the temple was completely rebuilt. In the 1930s, it was Shanghai's wealthiest Buddhist temple, headed by the influencial abbot Khi Vehdu, who was also a gangster with a harem of concubines and White Russian body-guards. It is said that his bodyguards went with him every-where, carrying bullet-proof briefcases as shields in the event of an attack. The temple was closed during the Cultural Revolution, but has reopened to become one of the best examples of an active Buddhist shrine in the city. It is a popular place to offer coins and pray for financial success.

Wall detail, Jade Buddha Temple

⓫ Jade Buddha Temple
玉佛寺

170 Anyuan Road. **Map** 1 D1. **Tel** (021) 6266 3668. **M** Hanzhong Road then taxi. **Open** 8am–4:30pm daily.

The most famous of Shanghai's temples, also known as Yufo Si, lies in the northwest part of the city. It was built in 1882 to enshrine two beautiful jade Buddha statues that were brought from Burma by the abbot Wei Ken. The temple was originally located elsewhere, but shifted here in 1918, after a fire damaged the earlier structure. After being closed for almost 30 years, it reopened in 1980, and today has some 100 monks. Built in the southern Song dynasty style, it has sharply curved eaves and figurines on the roof. Its three main halls are connected by two courts. The first hall is the **Heavenly King Hall**, where the four Heavenly Kings line the walls. The **Grand Hall of Magnificence** houses three incarnations of the Buddha, while the **Jade Buddha Chamber** contains the first jade statue – that of a large reclining Buddha. The finer of the two statues lies upstairs. Carved from a single piece of jade, this jewel-encrusted seated Buddha is exqui-site. Visitors should note that photography is forbidden here.

Golden Buddhas in the Jade Buddha Temple

Old Shanghai

Until 1842, Shanghai was a minor Chinese river port, worthy of a protective rampart but otherwise undistinguished. In that year, the Chinese government capitulated to western demands for trade concessions resulting in a number of ports along China's eastern seaboard, including Shanghai, becoming essentially European outposts. Their key feature was that of extra-territoriality – foreign residents were answerable only to the laws of their own country. Thus the Americans, British, and French had their own "concessions" – exclusive areas within the city with their own police forces and judiciary – a situation that attracted not only entrepreneurs, but refugees, criminals, and revolutionaries. This mix was a potent one and Shanghai's reputation for glamor and excess derives from the politically combustible period between the two World Wars. It all came to an end in the 1940s when foreigners gave up their rights in the face of growing Chinese opposition.

The Bund, also known as Zhongshan East No. 1 Road, was the wide thoroughfare running along Huangpu River. This was where all the major players in Shanghai commerce built their offices and created the distinctively grandiose skyline that still greets the river-going traveler today.

The Great World was a quintessential Shanghai creation, a mixture of freakishness, fashion, sex, and theater under one roof, owned by the gangster Pockmarked Huang.

The Race Course, located in the area of today's People's Park, was an indispensable part of expatriate life, where, just as in the numerous clubs and institutions for non-Chinese, expats were able to socialize as if they were at home.

Opium, trafficked commercially with claims for free trade by British companies like Jardine Matheson, was the foundation of Shanghai's prosperity and dens dotted the city. When the mercantile veneer was jettisoned, opium became the currency of Shanghai's gangster underworld.

Nanking Road, as it was then known, was, and still is, Shanghai's retail hub. Divided in two parts (the western end then known as Bubbling Well Road), it was home to China's first department stores, where Chinese and expatriates mixed on an equal footing.

Shanghai Ocean Aquarium

⓱ Bund Sightseeing Tunnel
外滩观光随道

The Bund at Beijing East Road, and near the foot of the Oriental Pearl TV Tower in Pudong. **Map** 3 D2. **Tel** (021) 5888 6000. Ⓜ Nanjing West Road (Bund) or Lujiazui (Pudong). **Open** 8am–10:30pm daily (8am–10pm winter).

Part high-tech, computer-controlled subway ride, part low-tech, fairground haunted house, and wholly ridiculous, the oddly named Sightseeing Tunnel offers a brief but surreal 2,132 ft (650 m) jaunt beneath the Huangpu river. Passenger cars zip down a tunnel assailed en route by a neon and laser light show, with inflatable figures and

The psychedelic experience that is the Bund Sightseeing Tunnel

an accompanying soundtrack. Official government promotional materials imaginatively describe the experience as *pavonine* (peacock-like). You may just consider it kitsch. However, it is a very Shanghai experience and something that should be done at least once. For the return journey, consider taking the ferry: at ¥2 it costs a fifteenth of the fare on the Sightseeing Tunnel and it delivers rather better sightseeing opportunities.

⓲ Oriental Pearl TV Tower
东方明珠广播电视塔

1 Century Avenue. **Map** 3 E2. **Tel** (021) 5879 1888. Ⓜ Lujiazui. **Open** Tower and Shanghai History Museum 8am–9pm daily.

One of the first modern towers to rise above the rubble of the peasant homes that once fringed the river on the Pudong side. When it was completed in 1994, the 1,500 ft (457m) Oriental Pearl instantly became China's most recognizable modern icon. Despite all the high-rises that have gone up since, it is still one of the most striking buildings in Shanghai. It houses an assortment of entertainments, including viewing platforms at various heights, rotating restaurants,

and, in the basement, the **Shanghai History Museum**. This museum uses ingenious technology to conjure up recreations of long-vanished city life. Models of early Shanghai street scenes ring with the traditional cries of vendors, and projected figures re-enact episodes of Shanghai domestic life. The museum also displays the original bronze lions made to guard the Shanghai Pudong Development Bank *(see p126)* – the pair on the Bund are replicas.

⓴ Shanghai Ocean Aquarium
上海海洋水族馆

1388 Lujiazui Ring Road, east of the Oriental Pearl TV Tower. **Map** 3 E2. **Tel** (021) 5877 9988. Ⓜ Lujiazui. **Open** 9am–6pm daily. Ⓦ sh-soa.com

Rated by enthusiasts as one of the best in the world, this vast, US$55 million aquarium features more than 10,000 temperate and tropical fish representing more than 300 species, as well as turtles and other sea creatures. It boasts 480 feet (150 m) or so of underwater, clear viewing tunnels that even include a submarine escalator to bring visitors up close to the marine life. There are also careful recreations of different aquatic environments from around the world, including Antarctica, Africa, and the Amazon, as well as displays highlighting the endangered aquatic species native to China. Feeding sessions take place mid-morning and mid-afternoon.

⓯ IFC Tower
上海国金中心

8 Century Avenue. **Map** 3 E3. **Tel** (021) 2020 7000. Ⓜ Lujiazui. Ⓦ shanghaiifc.com.cn

The glassy, 58-story Shanghai IFC Tower – the sibling of the two IFC towers in central Hong Kong – makes an impressive mark on the Pudong skyline. Opened in 2010, the lower floors comprise a glitzy mall featuring 180 leading name retailers, including several luxury flagship stores, an Apple store, and a vast basement supermarket. There are several restaurants, a six-screen cinema, and direct access to subway lines 2 and 14. On the upper floors is the luxury Ritz-Carlton Shanghai Pudong hotel.

⓰ Jinmao Tower
金茂大厦

88 Century Avenue. **Map** 3 E3. **Tel** (021) 5047 6688. Ⓜ Lujiazui. 🚌 **Open** 8:30am–9pm daily (observation deck). 📷 🚻

The fine-looking 88 story, 1,379 ft (421 m) Jinmao Tower was for a time the tallest building in China. It has a basement food court, 42 floors of offices, and, above them, the luxurious Grand Hyatt hotel. The 88th floor is an enclosed viewing gallery.

The tower is known as the "Golden Prosperity Building" and has a silver exterior, wrapped with rails, which narrows in steps, pagoda-like, to a sharp point. According to the US architects, the building is a pen, the curved roof of the attached exhibition hall a book, and the Huangpu itself the ink. Express elevators to the viewing gallery and the more comfortable Sky Lounge are in the basement, but equally breathtaking is the view up the 33 story interior atrium from the Grand Hyatt's 56th-floor reception.

The enormous, silver, pagoda-like form of the Jinmao Tower

The Maglev Train
This is, for the moment at least, the fastest you'll ever travel without flying. Shanghai's German-built "magnetically levitated" train travels the roughly 18.6 miles (30 km) from Long Yang Road metro station in Shanghai's eastern suburbs to Pudong Airport in under eight minutes, briefly reaching a speed in

A super-fast Maglev train slows as it approaches the terminus

excess of 267 mph (430 kph) with considerable smoothness and limited noise. An LED display in each carriage tells you how fast you are actually going. The service is very regular from early morning to late evening, and the trains are often packed – especially with smartphone-wielding travellers hoping to capture a selfie with the display momentarily flashing up the "magic number" of 431 kph.

⓱ Shanghai World Financial Center
上海环球金融中心

100 Century Avenue. **Map** 3 E3. **Tel** (4001) 100 555. Ⓜ Lujiazui or Dongchang Road. 🚌 **Open** Observatory 8am–11pm daily. 📷 🚻 🖥 Ⓦ swfc-observatory.com

Built by Japan's Mori Corporation and opened in 2008, the 101-story, 1,614 ft (492 m) Shanghai World Financial Center was designed by architects Kohn Pederson Fox. The signature feature of the tower for most visitors – which some say resembles a standing bottle-opener owing to the aperture at its peak – is the Skywalk 100, an 180 ft (55 m) long glass corridor observatory which soars 1,555 ft (474 m) above the ground, providing breathtaking views of the Huang Pu River and downtown Shanghai below. There is another observatory platform on the 97th floor, which features a retractable roof. It is also home to the Park Hyatt Shanghai.

⓲ Shanghai Tower
上海中心大厦

Lujiazui Financial Center. **Map** 3 E3. Ⓜ Lujiazui. 🚌 🖥 📷 🏛

The dizzying, twisting, 2,073 ft (632 m) Shanghai Tower is the city's tallest building. It was

constructed as a stack of nine cylindrical buildings, enclosed by a double-walled glass façade. Between these walls are public spaces with gardens, art exhibits, cafés, restaurants, and shops, and 360-degree views of the city. The core is occupied by offices and a luxury hotel; above the 121st story is an observatory, reached in less than a minute by the world's fastest elevators.

⓳ Century Park
世纪广场

Century Avenue and Yanggao Middle Road intersection. **Tel** (021) 6892 2000. Ⓜ Shanghai Science and Technology Museum. Science and Technology Museum: **Open** 9am–5pm Tue–Sun (last ticket sold at 4:30pm). 📷

Shanghai's largest square is dominated by a giant sculpture called "Oriental Light" that features an arrow piercing a disk that looks a bit like a sundial; it is meant to signify time. The square is graced by flower beds spelling out the characters of its name – Shiji Guangchang, in Chinese – as well as assorted sculpture and water features. It is flanked by the striking **Oriental Arts Center**, designed in the form of a blooming magnolia (the city flower of Shanghai), and the **Science and Technology Museum**, with IMAX cinemas and an IWERKS 4-D theater.

Brightly colored boats alongside the lake pier at Hongkou Park (Lu Xun Park)

honorary Communist heroine. She lived in Shanghai after her husband's death, initially in the house they had shared in the former French Concession (see p136), before moving to this villa. She died in Beijing in 1981.

The house is a charming example of a mid-20th-century Shanghai villa. It has some wonderful wood paneling and lacquerwork. Her limousines are still parked in the garage, and some of her personal items are also displayed.

⓴ Hongkou Park
虹口公园

146 East Jiangwan Road.
Ⓜ Hongkou. **Open** daily.

To the north of Suzhou Creek and Waibaidu Bridge lies the Japanese section of the former International Settlement, which once had a Zen temple, a Japanese school, and Japanese shops. The most interesting spot is Hongkou Park, which is a pleasant place to pass the time and watch the Chinese taking boat rides on the lake, playing chess, practicing *tai ji quan* or simply relaxing. It is also known as Lu Xun Park due to its strong associations with the great Chinese novelist Lu Xun (1881–1936), who lived nearby. Lu Xun was also an early proponent of the *baihua*, or plain speech movement, which championed the simplification of the Chinese script and the use of spoken Chinese in literature. **Lu Xun's Tomb** is also in the park. To the right of the park's main entrance lies a **Memorial Hall** dedicated to the novelist, where visitors can view early editions of his work and his correspondence with intellectuals including George Bernard Shaw. Just south of Hongkou Park is **Lu Xun's Former Residence**, a typical 1930s Japanese-style house where the novelist spent the last three years of his life.

Statue, Lu Xun's Tomb

🏠 **Lu Xun's Former Residence**
9 Dalu Xincun, Shanyin Rd.
Open 9am–4pm daily.

⓵ Soong Qingling's Former Residence
宋庆龄故居

1843 Huaihai Middle Road. Ⓜ Hengshan Road. **Tel** (021) 6474 7183. **Open** 9am–4:30pm daily.

At the southwestern edge of the city is the fine villa that was the residence of Soong Qingling, wife of the revolutionary leader Dr. Sun Yat Sen. All the Soong siblings – three sisters and a brother – came to wield a lot of influence in China. Of the three sisters, Soong Meiling married Chiang Kai Shek, the head of the Nationalist Republic of China from 1928 to 1949; Ailing married H H Kung, the director of the Bank of China, and Soong Qingling married Sun Yat Sen. Her brother, known as T V Soong, became Chiang Kai Shek's finance minister. Soong Qingling stayed in China once the Communists took over and became an

⓶ Xujiahui Catholic Cathedral
徐家汇堂

158 Puxi Road. **Tel** (021) 6438 2595. Ⓜ Xujiahui. **Open** 1pm–4pm Sat, Sun.

The red-brick Gothic Cathedral of St. Ignatius that stands at a southwestern corner of Shanghai has long been associated with foreign nationals. The land originally belonged to a member of the Xu clan, Xu Guangqi (1562–1633), who was converted to Catholicism by Matteo Ricci. Upon his death, Xu left land to the Jesuits for the building of a church, seminary, and observatory. The cathedral, with its 164 ft (50 m) twin towers, was built in 1906. It was partly destroyed during the Cultural Revolution, but was rebuilt, and now holds Sunday services. The interior is an interesting mix of traditional Catholic decoration and Chinese embellishment. Xu Guangqi is buried nearby in Nandan Park.

Soong Qingling's Former Residence – a charming early 20th-century villa

㉓ Longhua Cemetery of Martyrs
龙华烈士陵园

2887 Longhua Road. Ⓜ Shanghai
Stadium then taxi. **Tel** (021) 6468
5995. 🚌 No. 41. **Open** 6am–4:30pm
daily. 🚻 Longhua Temple: 2853
Longhua Road. **Open** 7am–4:30pm
daily. 🚻

This site honors those who died
for the Communist cause before
the People's Republic was
established in 1949. At the
center is a Memorial Hall, while
many commemorative
sculptures dot the park. The
cemetery is situated on the site
of the Nationalist Party's execu-
tion ground, where hundreds of
Communists were put to death
by Chiang Kai Shek.

Nearby is **Longhua Temple**
and an octagonal pagoda. A
temple has existed on this site
since AD 687, and a pagoda
since AD 238–251. The
foundations of the current
pagoda, with its upturned
eaves, date to AD 977, while
the temple buildings were built
during the late Qing era.

㉔ World Expo Site (2010)
中国2010年上海世博会官方网站

Pudong. Ⓜ Shibo Ave & Lupu Bridge.

Spanning the banks of the
Huangpu River on each side
of the Lupu Bridge, the 2010
World Expo site hosted over
200 nations with spectacular
pavilions showcasing culture,
technology, gastronomy, and
art. The site reopened as the
Shanghai Convention Center
in 2011 but a handful of the
original venues remain,
including the China Pavillion
and the Expo Performance
Center, rebranded as the
Mercedes Benz Arena.

In addition, the Shanghai Art
Museum, renamed the China
Art Museum, has relocated here.
The former Urban Future
Pavilion has been converted
to the state-owned Shanghai
Museum of Contemporary Art.

Commemorative statue at the Longhua Cemetery of Martyrs

㉕ She Shan
佘山

22 miles (35 km) SW of Shanghai.
Ⓜ She Shan. 🚌 from Wenhua
Guangchang bus stop or Xi Qu bus
station in Shanghai.

She Hill, or She Shan, a mere
328 ft (100 m) high, is sur-
mounted by a grand, red-brick
Catholic church, **Our Lady of
China**. In the 1850s, European
missionaries built a chapel here.
Later, a bishop took refuge in the
area and vowed to build a
church. The basilica was built
between 1925 and 1935.
Services, often in Latin, take
place on Christian holidays
and particularly in May, when
pilgrims stream here. The route
to the top represents the Via
Dolorosa (The Way of Suffering),
the road that Christ took to his
crucifixion. It is a pleasant walk
past bamboo groves, but there is
also a cable car. The hill also has
an ancient observatory that
houses an earthquake-monitor-
ing device of a jar with dragon
heads around the outside and a

pendulum inside. Each dragon
has a steel ball in its mouth.
When an earthquake occurred,
the pendulum would swing,
knock a dragon, causing its
mouth to open and a ball to
drop out and thereby point
out the quake's direction.

㉖ The Long Museum at West Bund
龙博物馆西外滩

3398 Longteng Avenue Ⓜ Longhua
Middle Road. **Tel** 6877 8787. **Open**
10am–6pm Tue–Sun (last admission
4pm). 🌐 **thelongmuseum.org**

The larger of Shanghai's two
Long Museums (the other is in
Pudong), this enormous edifice
covers over 8 acres (33,000 sq m)
with exhibitions spread over four
stories. It showcases an ever-
changing array of contemporary
paintings, sculpture, installations,
and new media works. There is
also an exhibition hall for children
and a river-view restaurant.

㉗ YUZ Museum
余德耀美术馆

35 Fenggu Road. **Tel** 6426 1901. Ⓜ
Yunjin Road. **Open** 10:30am–5:30pm
Tue–Sun. 🌐 **yuzmshanghai.org**.

Part of the YUZ foundation, a
non-profit organization, this
museum serves to promote the
exhibition, development, and
understanding of contemporary
art. Formerly an aircraft hangar,
the magnificent space highlights
the contrasts between old and
new Shanghai, forming an ideal
backdrop for the large-scale
installations it often displays.

Exterior of the grand She Shan church, Our Lady of China

FARTHER AFIELD

Despite Shanghai's vast sprawl, it is not too difficult to escape to greener and more pleasant spots. The spongy landscape of the surrounding region is laced with canals and dotted with picturesque towns and villages, each claiming to be the "Venice of China." The best known and largest of these canal towns is Suzhou, which is a 30-minute "bullet" train ride from Shanghai. Once a favored abode of retired scholars and officials, it combines the attractions of boat rides and ornamental gardens with centuries of history. Suzhou was also once a center for the production of one of China's most famous exports – silk. The trio of nearby, smaller canal towns of Tongli, Wuxi, and

Zhouzhuang all boast pleasant waterways as well. The towns are fast developing but still continue to retain their charm.

Hangzhou, the delight of poets for centuries, perhaps now lacks the peace they once associated with it, and even boasts a sprinkling of noteworthy modern buildings, not to mention showrooms for the likes of Ferrari sports cars. The real joy of the poets was around the West Lake, where narrow causeways still provide today's visitor with tranquility. And there is always the option of escape onto the water – with a few sweeps of the oars of a hired boatman, the roar of traffic becomes no more than a gentle murmur.

Sights at a Glance

Towns and Cities
1. Tongli
2. Zhouzhang
3. Wuxi
5. *Suzhou pp148–9*
6. *Hangzhou pp154–5*

Lakes and Areas of Natural Beauty
4. Tai Hu

Key

░░ City limits

═ National highway

▬ Major road

═ Minor road

— Railroad

– – Shanghai Province border

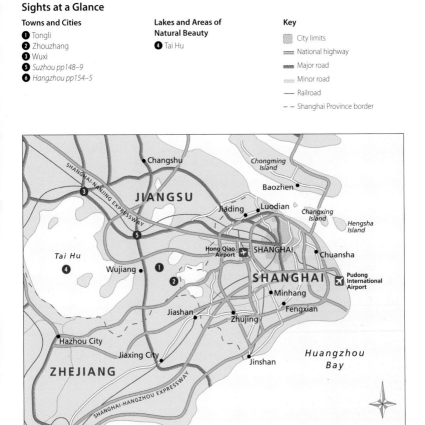

◀ Waterside pavilion in the Humble Administrator's Garden, Suzhou

For keys to symbols *see back flap*

Houses fronting canals in Zhouzhuang's old town

❶ Tongli
同里

16 miles (25 km) SE of Suzhou.
🚆 45,000. 🚌

A pretty little water town typical of the region, Tongli gives visitors a good idea of what Suzhou must have been like in its heyday. All its houses open out on to a network of canals that are spanned by dozens of stone bridges and are busy with transportation and trading boats. Some of its buildings are open to the public, such as **Jiayin Hall**, the former home of Liu Yazi, an early 20th-century actor renowned for his rather bizarre collection of gauze caps. The other interesting sight is **Tuisi Yuan**, a classical garden dating from the late Qing period.

🏯 **Tuisi Yuan**
Open 7:45am–5:30pm daily. 🅿

Sightseeing boats on one of Tongli's numerous canals

❷ Zhouzhuang
周庄

12 miles (20 km) W of Shanghai.
🚆 32,000. 🚌 Shanghai, Suzhou.
🚤 to Tongli. Old Town: tickets from Quangong Road.

A small town on the Jinghang Canal, which links Suzhou and Shanghai, Zhouzhuang was once a flourishing port, specializing in silk, pottery, and grain. It attracted scholars and officials who built fine bridges and houses between the Yuan and Qing eras. The charming **Old Town** can be explored on foot or via a boat tour on the canals. Among the sights are the Ming-era Hall of Zhang Residence with 70 rooms, and the Hall of Shen's Residence, with 100 rooms connected to the main hall. The Chengxu Temple, located near the museum, is a Song-dynasty Daoist shrine.

❸ Wuxi
无锡

25 miles (40 km) NW of Suzhou.
🚆 4,320,000. 🚌 🚕 🚤 services to Hangzhou & Suzhou. 🛈 88 Chezhan Road. **Tel** (0510) 401 6081.

The highlights of a trip to Wuxi are the scenic Tai Hu (Lake Tai) and the Grand Canal. According to legend, the town was established 3,500 years ago as the capital of the Wu Kingdom and was a center for the production of tin. When the mines ran dry (Wuxi means "without tin"), the capital moved west, but Wuxi remained significant due to its location on the Grand Canal.

Xihui Park in the west of town was established in 1958, and houses the Jichang Yuan garden. At the park's entrance, a path leads to the Dragon Light Pagoda on top of Xi Shan. A cable car connects Xi Shan to nearby Hui Shan. The **Wuxi Museum** has exhibits dating back 6,000 years, and includes some Qing-dynasty cannons.

🏯 **Xihui Park**
Huihe Road. **Open** 6am–6pm daily. 🅿

🏛 **Wuxi Museum**
71 Huihe Road. **Open** 9am–4pm daily. 🅿

The scenic cable car ride, Xihui Park, Wuxi

❹ Tai Hu
太湖

3 miles (5 km) SW of Wuxi.

One of China's largest lakes, Tai Hu is famous for its rocks, an indispensable feature of a traditional garden (see pp32–3). The lake's northern shores are fringed with scenic spots including **Mei Yuan** (Plum Garden), spectacular in spring when its 4,000 fruit trees blossom. **Yuantou Zhu** (Turtle Head Promontory) is a favorite with the Chinese, with tea houses and pretty lake views. Nearby, **Sanshan Island** is a former bandit's haunt with temples and tall Buddha statues. However, none is as tall as the 289-ft (88-m) Lingshan Buddha on Ma Shan peninsula, a short bus ride from the other sights. The area also has a handful of lakeside theme parks.

🏯 **Mei Yuan & Yuantou Zhu**
Open 7am–5pm daily. 🅿

The Grand Canal

The Grand Canal, started in 486 BC, was built in sections over the next one thousand years, with the aim of linking the Yangzi with the Yellow River, and one capital with another. It remains the world's largest man-made waterway. The earliest northern section was built for military reasons but large-scale construction began in the 7th century under the Sui Wendi emperor, involving over 5 million conscripted males aged between 15 and 55, supervised by a vast and brutal police force. Linking the comparatively populous north with the southern rice-producing region, it reached Beijing only in the 13th century. In the early 20th century, a combination of the altered course of the fickle Yellow River and the rise of the railways saw its gradual demise.

This map shows the route of the 1,112 mile (1,900 km) canal from Beijing to Hangzhou. Crossing the traditional battlefields between north and south, the canal supplied food throughout the empire. The hilly terrain led to the first recorded use of double locks, in AD 984.

Key

▬ Grand Canal

The Sui Yang Di emperor is said to have celebrated the completion of his work by touring the canal with a flotilla of dragon boats hauled by the empire's most beautiful women.

Tourist boats are now the only way to enjoy a journey on the canal as road and rail transport is favored by the locals. Regular tourist boats operate overnight services between Hangzhou and Suzhou or Wuxi, whilst boats can also be chartered for day-trips between the major tourist stops.

Barges splutter their way along the canal laden with agricultural produce and factory supplies. The busiest sections are in the south and north of the Yangzi to the border with Shandong.

The canal banks are lively with people performing domestic tasks. Families, even if they have houses, may live on board the boats when they are working.

❺ Suzhou

苏州

A network of canals, bridges, and canal-side housing characterizes the city of Suzhou. Its history dates back to the 6th century BC, when the first canals were built to control the area's low water table. The construction of the Grand Canal (see p147), 1,000 years later, brought prosperity as silk, the city's prized commodity, could be exported to the north. During the Ming dynasty, Suzhou flourished as a place of refinement, attracting an influx of scholars and merchants, who built themselves numerous elegant gardens. The city has plenty of sights, and is dissected by broad, busy roads laid out in a grid.

🏯 Beisi Ta

1918 Renmin Road. **Tel** (0512) 6753 1197. **Open** 8am–6pm daily. 🖼

The northern end of Renmin Road is domi-nated by the Beisi Ta (North Pagoda), a remnant of an earlier temple complex, which has been rebuilt. The pagoda's main structure dates from the Song dynasty, but its foun-dations supposedly date to the Three

The octagonal Beisi Ta

Kingdoms era (AD 220–265). Towering 249 ft (76 m) high, it is octagonal in shape, and has sharply upturned eaves. Visitors can climb right to the top, from where there are good views of the city, including Xuanmiao Guan and the Ruiguang Pagoda.

🏛 Suzhou Silk Museum

2001 Renmin Road. **Tel** (0512) 6753 6505. **Open** 9am–5pm daily. 🖼

The Suzhou Silk Museum is a pleasure to visit, mainly because its exhibits are well-documented with English captions. It traces the history of silk production and its use from its beginnings in about 4000 BC to the present day. Exhibits include old looms with demonstrations of their workings, samples of ancient silk patterns, and a section explaining the art of sericulture. The museum's most interesting exhibit is its room full of live silk worms, eating mulberry leaves and spinning cocoons.

🏛 Suzhou Museum

204 Dongbei Street. **Tel** (0512) 6757 5666. **Open** 9am–4pm Tue–Sun. 🖼

W szmuseum.com

The municipal museum is housed in a lavish modernist reinvention of a Suzhou villa and garden designed by Chinese-American architect I M Pei, who spent his childhood summers in Suzhou. The stunning fusion of traditional and modern Chinese architecture more than makes up for a rather dry collection that concentrates on Suzhou's association with canal construction and silk production. Some of the exhibits, especially the early maps, are of interest.

🏯 Humble Administrator's Garden

See pp150–51

🏯 Shizi Lin

23 Yuanlin Road. **Open** daily. 🖼

The Lion Grove Garden is considered by many the finest in Suzhou. However, visitors unfamiliar with the subtleties of Chinese garden design may find it rather bleak, as rocks are its main feature. Ornamental rocks were a crucial element of classical gardens, and symbolized either the earth or China's sacred mountains. Dating to 1342, the garden was originally built as part of a temple. The large pool is spanned by a zigzag bridge and buildings with unusually fine latticework, while part of the rockery forms a labyrinth.

🏯 Ou Yuan

Cang Street. **Open** 8am–5pm daily. 🖼

The Ou Yuan (Double Garden) is not as busy as many of the city's other classical gardens, and is a pleasure to visit. It takes its name from its two garden areas, separated by buildings and corridors. A relaxing place, Ou Yuan has rockeries, a pool, and a fine open pavilion at its center, which is surrounded by several teahouses. It is situated in a charming locality filled with some of the most attractive houses, canals, and bridges in the city.

The charming Ou Yuan garden

Mural in the Hall of Literary Gods, Xuanmiao Guan

🏛 Museum of Opera and Theater

14 Zhongzhangjia Xiang. **Tel** (0512) 6727 3334. **Open** 9am–4pm daily. 🗭

Housed in a beautiful Ming-dynasty theater of latticed wood, the Museum of Opera and Theater (Xiqu Bowuguan) is a fascinating and highly visual museum. Its display halls are filled with examples of old musical instruments, delicate hand-copied books of scores and lyrics, masks, and costumes.

It also exhibits additional paraphernalia including a life-size orchestra and vivid photographs of dramatists and actors. Traditional Suzhou Opera, known as *kun ju*, is renowned as the oldest form of Chinese opera, with a history of about 5,000 years. The museum is the venue for occasional performances, while the adjacent teahouse stages daily shows of *kun*-style opera and music.

VISITORS' CHECKLIST

Practical Information
32 miles (50 km) NW of Shanghai.
🚇 5,750,000. 🛈 195 Shiquan Street, (0512) 6520 3131.

Transport
🚆 Suzhou Train Station.
🚌 Bei Men Station, Nan Men Station, Wu Xianshi Station.
⛴ ferries to Hangzhou.
🚢 tours of the Grand Canal.

🏛 Xuanmiao Guan

Guanqian Street. **Tel** (0512) 6777 5479. **Open** 8:30am–4:30pm daily. 🗭

The Daoist Temple of Mystery was founded during the Jin dynasty but like many Chinese temples, it has been rebuilt many times. The Hall of the Three Pure Worshipers dates to the Song dynasty, and is the largest ancient Daoist hall in China. The intricate structure of the roof in particular is worth scrutiny. Located in Suzhou's commercial center, the temple was associated with popular street entertainment, and although the musicians and jugglers have gone, it retains a casual atmosphere.

Suzhou City Center

1. Beisi Ta
2. Suzhou Silk Museum
3. Suzhou Museum
4. Humble Administrator's Garden
5. Shizi Lin
6. Ou Yuan
7. Museum of Opera & Theater
8. Xuanmiao Guan
9. Shuang Ta
10. Garden of Happiness
11. Silk Embroidery Research Institute
12. Master of the Nets Garden
13. Dark Blue Wave Pavilion Garden
14. Pan Men Scenic Area
15. Confucian Temple

For keys to symbols *see back flap*

Humble Administrator's Garden
拙政园

Suzhou's largest garden, Zhuozheng Yuan, the Humble
Administrator's Garden is also considered the city's finest.
It was established in the 16th century by a retired magistrate,
Wang Xianchen, and developed over the years as subsequent
owners made changes according to the fashion of the day.
A 16th-century painting shows that originally the garden was
less decorative than it is now. The garden is separated into
three principal parts, east, central, and west. The eastern
section has colorful flowers but is of less interest than
the other two. There is also a museum that explains the
history and philosophy of Chinese gardens.

Covered walkway – a way to enjoy the garden
even in the hot sun

★ **Mandarin Duck Hall**
Split into two equal rooms, this
arrangement allowed visitors to
enjoy the cooler north-facing
chamber in summer, and the
warmer south-facing one in winter.

KEY

① **Western section of the garden**

② **The Wavy Corridor** rises up
and down over the water as if going
over waves.

③ **The central part** of the garden
imitates the scenery of China south
of the lower Yangzi.

④ **Little Flying Rainbow Bridge**

⑤ **Entrance to the central section**

★ **Fragrant Isle**
This pavilion and terrace is supposed to resemble the deck
and cabin of a boat. As it projects out over the water, it gives
excellent views of the garden from all sides.

The Humble Administrator's Garden

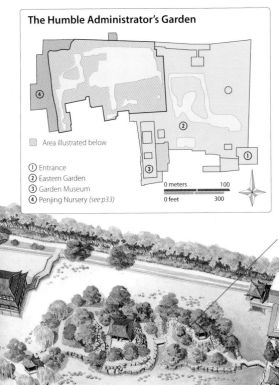

☐ Area illustrated below

① Entrance
② Eastern Garden
③ Garden Museum
④ Penjing Nursery *(see p33)*

0 meters 100
0 feet 300

VISITORS' CHECKLIST

Practical Information
178 Dongbei Street, Suzhou.
Tel (0512) 6751 0286.
Open 8am–5:30pm daily (last admission 5pm). 🖼 includes the Garden Museum. 📷 📷
🆆 szzzy.cn

Orange Pavilion
Artificial mountains, like the one this pavilion was built upon, were an important element in Chinese gardens and were ideal for quiet contemplation.

Secluded Pavilion of Chinese Parasol Tree and Bamboo
The most famous view of the garden, the "borrowed view" *(see p33)* of Beisi Ta, the Northern Pagoda reflected in the water, is visible from here.

★ **Hall of Distant Fragrance**
The main hall of the garden is named after the perfume of the large lotus pond nearby that delicately wafts in.

The octagonal Song dynasty twin pagodas, Shuang Ta

🔼 Shuang Ta

Dinghui Si Xiang. **Open** daily. 🖼

Once part of a temple, these 98 ft- (30 m-) high twin pagodas date to the early Song era. According to an inscription, they were first built in AD 982 by the students Wang Wenhan and his brother in honor of their teacher, who helped them pass the imperial civil service exams. Twin pagodas are commonly found in India but are a rarer feature of Chinese temples, as pagodas were largely built as single edifices.

🔼 Garden of Happiness

343 Renmin Road. **Open** 7:30am–4:30pm daily. 🖼

The Garden of Happiness is one of Suzhou's newer gardens, dating from the late Qing dynasty. It was built by a government official, who utilized rocks and landscape designs from other abandoned gardens. The garden appears to have originally covered a larger area; today, its central feature is a pool encircled by rockeries and spanned by a zigzag bridge. The best viewpoint is from the Fragrant Lotus Pavilion, while another pavilion that juts into the pool is known for catching cooling breezes. Look out for the calligraphy by famous scholars and poets.

🔼 Silk Embroidery Research Institute

280 Jingde Road. **Open** daily. 🖼

Housed in the Huan Xiu Shan Zhuang (Surrounded by Majestic Mountains) Garden, this institute creates exquisitely fine silk embroidery, work that is mainly done by women. In order to produce the painting-like effect of their designs, the women sometimes work with silk strands that are so fine, they are almost invisible. They specialize in double-sided embroidery – for example, a cat with green eyes on one side and blue on the other.

🔼 Master of the Nets Garden

11 Kuojiatou Xiang. **Tel** (0512) 6529 3190. **Open** 7:30am–5pm daily. 🖼

It is said that the Master of the Nets Garden was named after one of its owners – a retired official who wished to become an accomplished fisherman. Dating to 1140, it was completely remodeled in 1770 and for many people, is the finest of all Suzhou's gardens. Although small, it succeeds, with great subtlety, in introducing every element considered crucial to the classical garden (see pp32–3). It includes a central lake, discreet connecting corridors, pavilions with miniature courtyards, screens, delicate latticework, and above all, points which "frame a view", as if looking at a perfectly balanced photograph. The best known building is the Pavilion for Watching the Moon, from where the moon can be viewed in a mirror, in the water, and in the sky. Regular evening performances of Chinese opera, including local *kun ju*, take place here.

🔼 Dark Blue Wave Pavilion Garden

3 Canglang Ting Street, Renmin Road. **Tel** (0512) 6529 3109. **Open** daily. 🖼

The Dark Blue Wave Pavilion Garden – whose name is suggestive of a relaxed and pragmatic approach to life – is perhaps Suzhou's oldest garden, first laid out in 1044 by a scholar, Su Zimei, on the site of an earlier villa. His successor, a general in the imperial army, enlarged it in the 12th century, and it was rebuilt in the 17th century. It is known for its technique of "borrowing a view", allowing the scenery beyond the garden's confines to play a role in its

The Pavilion for Watching the Moon, Master of the Nets Garden

Gateway to the Confucian Temple

design. Here, it is achieved by lowering walls on the north side of some of the pavilions, allowing views across water; elsewhere, the southwest hills can be seen. The central feature is a mound that is meant to resemble a wooded hill. Gardens were ideal places for contemplation and writing poetry, a fact demonstrated by the engravings of verses dotting the area.

Pan Men Scenic Area

2 Dong Da Road. **Open** 8am–5pm daily.

This area has been extensively restored but it still contains some of the city's most interesting historical sights. Pan Men is a unique fortified gate that controlled access to the city by both land and water nearly 700 years ago, although most of the present construction is more recent. Other highlights include the graceful Wu Men Bridge and the views of the city from the 140 ft- (43 m-) high Ruigang Pagoda. The bridge and pagoda both date back to the Song dynasty, although each has been rebuilt since.

Confucian Temple

45 Renmin Road. **Open** daily.

The original Song-dynasty temple was rebuilt in 1864 after it was destroyed in the Taiping Rebellion. Its main hall, dating from the Ming dynasty, has several stone carvings including China's oldest surviving city map, depicting Suzhou, or Pingjiang as it was known in 1229. Also on display is a star chart dating from 1247 that maps the positions of stars and celestial bodies in the heavens. It is one of the earliest surviving maps of its kind.

Tiger Hill

Huqiu Road. **Tel** (0512) 6532 3488. **Open** 7:30am–5pm daily.

In the city's northwest is the popular Tiger Hill (Huqiu Shan), the burial place of He Lu, the King of Wu and founder of Suzhou. His spirit is said to be guarded by a white tiger, which appeared three days after his death and refused to leave.

The main attraction is the Song-dynasty leaning pagoda (Yunyan Ta or Cloud Rock Pagoda), built in brick, which leans more than 7 ft (2 m) from the perpendicular at its highest point. Some 10th-century Buddhist *sutras* and a record of the year that it was constructed (959–961) were discovered during one of the

Ceremonial urn, Tiger Hill

attempts to prevent it from falling. The park is quite large, with pools and flowerbeds filled with blooms in spring and early summer. One of the many boulders is split in two, allegedly the result of He Lu's swordsmanship. He is supposedly buried nearby along with 3,000 swords.

Hanshan Temple

24 Hanshansi Long. **Tel** (0512) 6533 6634. **Open** 8am–5pm daily.

First constructed in the Liang dynasty, the Cold Mountain Temple was named for a Tang-dynasty poet-monk. A stone rendition of him and his fellow monk, Shi De, is to be seen here. The temple was rebuilt in the 19th century, after it was destroyed during the Taiping Rebellion. Located close to the Grand Canal, it was immortalized by the Tang-dynasty poet Zhang Ji, who arrived here by boat and anchored nearby. His poem "Anchored at Night by the Maple Bridge" is inscribed on a stone stele, and contains the lines that made Hanshan Temple famous: "Beyond Suzhou lies Hanshan Temple; at midnight the clang of the bell reaches the traveler's boat." The bell alluded to here was subsequently lost, and the temple's current bell was presented by Japan in 1905. Nearby, a beautiful arched bridge offers views along the Grand Canal.

Incense burners in the grounds of Hanshan Temple

⑥ Hangzhou

杭州

Renowned in medieval China as an earthly paradise, Hangzhou became the splendid capital of the Southern Song dynasty between 1138 and 1279. Later, when the conquering Mongols chose what is now Beijing as their new capital, Hangzhou continued to be a thriving commercial city. Its glories were extolled by Marco Polo *(see p157)*, who allegedly visited Hangzhou at the height of its prosperity and described it as "the City of Heaven, the most magnificent in all the world." Although most of the old buildings were destroyed in the Taiping Rebellion, the attractive West Lake and its surrounding area are still worth visiting.

Entrance archway to Yue Fei Mu (Tomb of Yue Fei)

🏯 Yue Fei Mu

Bei Shan Road. **Tel** (0571) 8796 9670. **Open** 7:30am–5:30pm daily. 📷

Just north of the West Lake lies the tomb of the Song general Yue Fei, a popular Chinese hero revered for his patriotism. His campaigns against the invading Jin were so successful that his Song overlords began to worry that he might turn against them. He was falsely charged with sedition and executed, only to become a martyr whose exploits were widely celebrated in painting.

The Yue Fei Temple is a late 19th-century construction, and the tomb lies beside it. Leading to the tomb is a small avenue of stone animals. The central tumulus belongs to Yue Fei, while the smaller one is his son's, who was also executed. The kneeling figures in iron represent his tormentors – the prime minister, his wife, a jealous general, and the prison governor. It was customary to spit on them, but this is no longer encouraged.

🌳 Huanglong Dong Park & Qixia Shan

North of West Lake (Xi Hu).

This hilly area, crisscrossed with paths, has several sights of interest. Huanglong Dong Park, nestling in the hills, is very attractive with its teahouses, ponds, and flowers, and a pavilion where musicians perform traditional music in summer. To the east is **Baoshu Ta**, a 20th-century rebuild of a Song-era pagoda. Looming close by is Qixia Shan (Lingering Clouds Mountain), with the **Baopu Daoist Temple** located halfway up its slopes. This active temple has services on most days. It makes an interesting stopover, where visitors can watch pilgrims, priests, and perhaps even one of the frequent ancestral worship ceremonies.

Wood panel carving at Baopu Daoist Temple

🏛 Hu Qinyu Tang Museum of Chinese Medicine

95 Dajing Xiang. **Tel** (0571) 8702 7507. **Open** 8:30am–5pm daily. 📷

This interesting museum is housed in a beautiful old apothecary's shop. It was established by the merchant Hu Xueyan during the Qing dynasty and traces the history of traditional Chinese medicine, which goes back thousands of years. It is still an active dispensary and pharmacy.

🌊 West Lake

See pp156–7.

🏛 China National Tea Museum

88 Longjing Road. **Tel** (0571) 8796 4221. **Open** 8:30am–4:30pm Tue–Sun. 📷 🌐 english.teamuseum.cn

Tracing the history of tea production, this museum, on a working tea plantation, has lots of interesting information regarding the different varieties of tea, its cultivation, and the development of tea-making and tea-drinking vessels. Fortunately, many of the captions are in English.

🍵 Longjing Village

SW of Tea Museum. 📷

The village of Longjing (Dragon Well) produces one of China's most famous varieties of green tea. Visitors can wander around the tea terraces, catching glimpses of the different stages of production, such as cutting, sorting, and drying, and also buy the tea, which varies in price according to its grade.

Inside the main hall of the Hu Qingyu Tang Museum of Chinese Medicine

🔲 Lingyin Si

1 Fayun Long, Lingyin Road. **Tel** (0571) 8796 8665. **Open** 6am–6pm daily. 🖼

The hill area known as Feilai Feng (The Peak that Flew Here) is home to some of the city's main sights, including Lingyin Si. Founded in AD 326, this temple once housed 3,000 monks who worshiped in more than 70 halls. Though now much reduced in size, it is still one of China's largest temples. It was damaged in the 19th-century Taiping Rebellion, and then again by fire in the 20th century. It is said to owe its survival to Zhou Enlai, who prevented its destruction during the Cultural Revolution. Still, some parts of the temple are ancient, such as the stone pagodas on either side of the entrance hall, which date from AD 969. Behind this hall is the **Great Buddha Hall**, with an impressive 66 ft (20 m) statue of the Buddha carved in 1956 from camphor wood.

The **Ligong Pagoda** at the entrance was built in honor of the Indian monk Hui Li, who gave the mountain its eccentric name. Hui Li thought it was the spitting image of a hill in India and asked whether it had flown

here. Feilai Feng is known for the dozens of Buddhist sculptures carved into the rock, many dating from the 10th century.

🔲 Six Harmonies Pagoda

16 Zhijiang Road. **Tel** (0571) 8659 1401. **Open** 5:30am–6:30pm daily. 🖼

Standing beside the railway bridge on the northern shore of the Qiantang River, Liuhe Ta is all that is left of an octagonal temple first built in AD 970 to placate the tidal bore, a massive wall of water that rushes upstream during high tide. Over 197 ft- (60 m-) high, it served as a lighthouse up until the Ming dynasty.

Buddha sculptures at Feilai Feng

Hangzhou City Center

① Yue Fei Mu
② Huanglong Dong Park
  & Qixia Shan
③ Hu Qingyu Tang Museum
  of Chinese Medicine
④ West Lake
⑤ China National Tea Museum
⑥ Longjing Village
⑦ Lingyin Si
⑧ Six Harmonies Pagoda

0 km   1
0 miles   1

West Lake
西湖

Long considered one of the scenic wonders of
China, covering over three square miles (8 sq km),
West Lake (Xi Hu) is situated at the heart of Hangzhou.
Surrounded by gentle green hills, the lake's willow-
shaded causeways and fragrant cover of lotus blossoms
have long been an inspiration for artists. Originally the
lake was an inlet off the estuary of the Qiantang River,
becoming a lake when the river began to silt up in
the 4th century. The lake had a tendency to flood,
so several dykes were built, including the Bai and
Su Causeways. Hiring a private boat from the
eastern shore for an afternoon on the water is
highly recommended, as is a leisurely stroll
along the shady causeways.

★ **Three Pools Reflecting the Moon**
Three small stone pagodas rise from the
waters near Xiaoying Island. At full moon,
candles are placed within and their
openings are covered in paper to create
reflections resembling the moon.

Xi Li Hu

Huagang Garden
This garden is intended as a place
for viewing fish. Designed by a
Song-dynasty eunuch, its pools
are filled with shimmering
goldfish in a restful setting
of grasses and trees.

KEY

① **The Seal Engravers Society** is
open in the summer months.

② **Zhejiang Provincial Museum**

★ **Xiaoying Island**
Often called San Tan Yin Yue Island, referring to the three
moon-reflecting pagodas off its shores, Xiaoying Island consists
of four enclosed pools fringed by pavilions first built in 1611.
The zigzagging Nine Bend Bridge was built in 1727.

★ Su Causeway

The longer of the two causeways takes its name from the Song dynasty poet Su Dongpo, who also served as governor. Linked by six stone bridges, the causeway is a peaceful thoroughfare running along the lake's western edge.

VISITORS' CHECKLIST

Practical Information
Hangzhou. Zhejiang Provincial Museum: 25 Gushan Road. **Tel** (0571) 8798 0281. **Open** 1–4pm Mon, 9am–4pm Tue–Sun. **W** zhejiangmuseum.com

Transport
daily from eastern shore near Hubin Road. Boats for hire on Gu Shan Island.

Bridge to Quyuan Garden

This bridge leads to a stunning garden surrounded by lotus flowers. It is considered one of the ten prospects from where the lake can be seen to best advantage.

Gu Shan

Xi Hu

Bei Li Hu

Marco Polo

Whether Marco Polo ever visited China is much disputed. However, according to the book he dictated to a ghost writer, who embroidered it substantially, Polo became governor of nearby Yangzhou for three years during the Yuan dynasty. He describes Hangzhou as paradise and the finest city in the world, with fascinating markets, pleasure boats, and prostitutes. Hangzhou was indeed a cosmopolitan city, ever since the Southern Song dynasty made it their capital. *The Travels of Marco Polo*, however, may be based on earlier journeys by his father and uncle, and stories from other merchants.

Engraving of Marco Polo, 1254–1324

Bai Causeway

Named after the 9th-century poet-governor Bai Juyi, this dyke leads to Gu Shan, an island first landscaped during the Tang dynasty, and now containing a teahouse and the provincial museum.

TWO GUIDED WALKS

After the grandiose sweep of the Bund, the best routes in Shanghai are through the areas where the *shikumen*, or stone-gate houses, of ordinary people stand next to the vast European-styled villas and mansions erected in the early years of the 20th century for foreign business magnates.

Although the city is best known for its foreign influences, something even Shanghainese highlight first when talking about their home town, the Chinese side of Shanghai should not be forgotten. After the Opium Wars of the 1840s and 1850s, the original modest walled city became surrounded by swathes of foreigner-controlled territory. But it is in what survives of the Old City that the remnants of more traditional Chinese culture can still be found.

The first walk begins at the heart of this district, taking in temples, street vendors, and bustling markets of all kinds. It ends with a look at a successful modern attempt to recycle the city's traditional buildings with the shopping, dining, and entertainment district of Xintiandi ("New Heaven and Earth"), which recreates the buildings of Old Shanghai for more modern purposes.

West of Xintiandi, the French Concession district offers some of the best of the surviving colonial-era villas and mansion blocks. Some have now become hotels or restaurants and bars, and some have been preserved through the accident of having at some point been occupied by those the ruling Communist Party promotes as "Great Men."

The second walk visits some of the more notable examples of Concession architecture. It traces a century's worth of history written in brick and stone, from the party town that was Shanghai in its 1930s heyday, through the rather more dour Party decades post-1949, to the rebirth of the city, as most visibly exemplified by the high-end international retailers now crowding fashionable Huaihai Road. The walk also includes the lively, artsy Tianzifang neighborhood, packed with cafés and souvenir stalls (of varying quality) in the tiny lanes.

| 0 kilometers | | 2 |
| 0 miles | 1 | |

Key

··· Walk route

◀ The busy shopping street of Nanjing Road, with classical buildings dwarfed by new high-rises

A 90-Minute Walk through the Old City

Although the city walls of the original Chinese settlement were pulled down early last century, their former path is still clearly visible on maps, marked by a perfect circle of road. Within this ring you will find everything from bustling produce markets full of pajama-clad vendors and shoppers, to some delightful old timber and brick architecture. The Old City is also home to the famous Yu Gardens, and to places of worship of every shape, size, and religious persuasion. After time spent observing backstreet reminders of Shanghai's history, the walk ends with the ultra-fashionable Xintiandi.

⑦ Dajing Road food market

② Fangbang Middle Road

Key

• • • Walk route

Fangbang Middle Road

The walk begins on Fangbang Middle Road at the southern entrance to the Yu Gardens and Bazaar complex. Just inside is the **City Temple** ①. Once much larger, the temple is now squeezed by tall mock-traditional department stores, but it remains a popular place of worship and is fascinating to visit. After seeing the temple, return to **Fangbang Middle Road** ② and walk west past dealers in "antiques," along with sellers of tea, furniture, peasant art, and traditional blue-and-white batik-style cloth. The shops are worth browsing, but they are also prone to over-charging anyone who does not know better.

Where the bazaar comes to an end, turn right and head north towards the large **decorative gate** ③, or *pailou*. However, before reaching it turn left and then take the first right;

this will take you by the long, mustard-colored wall of the **Chengxiang Ge Buddhist Temple** ④. Turn left at the top of the alley and dodge the enthusiastic pearl vendors whose shops cluster near the temple entrance. The three

large halls that make up the complex remain home to a sizeable community of nuns.

Continue west a short distance to the **Fuyou Road Mosque** ⑤, Shanghai's oldest place of Islamic worship (1868) – a green sign indicates its location down a tiny alley.

Dajing Road

At Henan South Road, turn left and pass beneath another

④ The courtyard of the Chengxiang Ge Buddhist Temple

⑬ A lively street café in popular Xintiandi

⑧ Dajing Tower museum

gaudy **reconstructed arch** ⑥. Continue south for a little while before turning right into Dajing Road, which soon becomes a bustling **food market** ⑦.

Depending on the time of day, you'll see groups of wizened ladies sorting through leafy piles of greens, chefs tossing blackened woks full of noodles and traditional Shanghai dumplings, and fishmongers scaling the catch of the day. Stay on this road until you reach the junction with Renmin Road, which is where you'll find the **Dajing Tower** ⑧. Originally part of the city's defences and then an active temple, the tower now houses an interesting small museum with a model of the old city walls and an exhibition of black-and-white photos.

Sadly, there is virtually nothing left of the original city walls. This whole area, especially the fringes where any remaining bits of wall once were, are fast being redeveloped.

Liuhekou Road
Cross busy **Renmin Road**, which follows the line of the walls that formerly encircled the Old City. Despite Shanghai's growing number of cars, it still resembles a cycle track during rush hour. Enter **Shouning Road** ⑨, one of the few remaining food streets. Locals come here for fresh seafood and shellfish cooked to order on outdoor barbecue grills, plus tasty pastry and Chinese dessert stands. Turn left onto Xizang South Road, then take a right into Liuhekou Road, where there's an indoor **bird and flower market** ⑩, full of cricket enthusiasts (the insect, not the game) who gather with their jars of chirping creatures. A little further on, the **Dongtai Road** ⑪

⑫ Birds in Huahai Park

bric-a-brac market is no more, but a few pricey antiques stores still remain.

Xintiandi
Head north up Dongtai Road and turn left on Chongde Road, following the street until it turns right into Taicang Road. This borders **Huaihai Park** ⑫ for a bit, and then a few hundred yards farther west is **Xintiandi** ⑬, an area of *shikumen* (stone tenements) redeveloped into a smart shopping, dining, and hotel complex. This district has been completely redesigned and transformed into a lively area by day and night.

Tips for Walkers

Length: 2 miles (3.2 km).
Getting there: Take a taxi to the Yu Gardens Bazaar.
Yu Gardens: Open 8:30am–5:30pm daily.
Chengxiang Ge: Open 7am–4pm daily.
Dajing Tower: Open 9am–4pm daily.
Bird and Flower Market: Open 8am–6pm daily.
Stopping off points: Huxinting Teahouse in the Yu Gardens is the most famous spot at which to take a break for tea and snacks, and the Nanxiang Steamed Bun Restaurant has Shanghai's most famous dumplings, but both may have long queues. Having finished the walk at Xintiandi, try Crystal Jade for a dim sum lunch, the KABB for beers, wines, and cocktails, Element Fresh for cakes and salads, or T8 for a reasonably priced set lunch.

For keys to symbols *see back flap*

A 90-Minute Walk around the French Concession

In 1843, the British negotiated a deal with the Chinese that led to the creation of the International Concession, a zone of self-rule for foreign powers in Shanghai. The French, however, declined to join. They made a separate deal to found their own concession, beginning with a narrow finger of land between the old Chinese city and what is now Yan'an Lu, and later spreading to cover a large area to the west. Redevelopment is constantly removing the old villas and apartment buildings that formerly made this area of Shanghai resemble a typical French provincial town, but there remains much to see and this is a very walkable part of town.

⑥ Taikang Road

Ruijin No. 2 Road and Taikang Road

Start by taking a taxi to 27 Shaoxing Road for morning coffee or Chinese tea at the **Old China Hand Reading Room** ①. This is a quiet café with elegant period furnishings that also sells books on the old architecture of Shanghai and elsewhere produced by the team of American-born but long-time Shanghai resident Tess Johnston and local photographer Deke Erh. From

the café, head off east along Shaoxing Road, a lovely street with a number of small galleries. Turn right down **Ruijin No. 2 Road** ② and look above the modern shop fronts for hints of the city's Art Deco past, and other oddities such as the particularly **Germanic mansion** ③ at No. 152. Cross the junction with Jianguo Middle Road, take the next left into **Taikang Road** ④, and pass under an arch leading into Tianzifang, lined with art shops with foreigner-pleasing watercolors, and tailors happy to make traditional *qipao* dresses. At Zui Zhu Zhai (No. 322), framed calligraphy by a living master is available from about ¥600 – much cheaper than in Xintiandi or elsewhere.

Cross over the road for a fascinating **wet market** ⑤, full of live fish, frogs, eels, and snakes, then

pass under an arch leading into **Taikang Road** ④. This is a labyrinth of lanes lined by cafés, craft shops, boutiques, and galleries. Side turnings are lined with fine examples of *shikumen*,

the houses with stone-framed entrances that are this city's counterpart to Beijing's *siheyuan* dwellings.

Sinan Road

At the top of the alley, turn right along Jianguo Middle Road, then left into Sinan Road, past mansions with hints not only of

① Café-cum-bookshop-cum-library: Old China Hand Reading Room

⑭ Cafés and bicycles on Maoming North Road

Tips for Walkers

Length: 2.4 miles (4 km).
Getting there: Take a taxi to the Old China Hand Reading Room.
Old China Hand Reading Room: Open 9:30am–midnight daily.
Taikang Road wet market: Open 6am–4pm daily.
Stopping off points: There is a variety of cafés and restaurants among the rapidly expanding boutiques and galleries in Tianzifang. Kommune Café in the central courtyard and Indian restaurant Lotus Land are popular choices. Grandmother's Noodles on Sinan Road, by Nanchang Road, is invariably packed with locals perched on plastic stools slurping some of the city's best noodles. At 30 Sinan Road, Cha's recreates an old-time Hong Kong diner.

France, but Spain and Germany too. These were spacious enough to attract senior figures from both the rival Nationalist and Communist parties in their day. On the right you come to the **Former Residence of Zhou Enlai** ⑦ *(see p136)*, Premier and Foreign Minister under the People's Republic. The spartan interior of the residence is left furnished much as it was in Zhou's time. Just on the corner of Sinan Road and Fuxing Middle Road is the **Sinan Mansions** ⑧, a cluster of 1930s mansions that have been redeveloped as bars, cafés, and restaurants. Sample Boxing Cat Brewery for a craft ale and American comfort classics with pavement seating. Hotel Massenet, a boutique hotel housed in a series of restored mansions, is also located here. The hotel gets its name from the street's French Concession-era name, Rue Massenet. Farther along is the **Sun Yat Sen Memorial Residence** ⑨ *(see p136)*. Many of Sun's personal items are on display here.

Huaihai Middle Road

Immediately east of the Sun Yat Sen residence is the French-created **Fuxing Park** ⑩ *(see p136)*, worth a detour before returning to Sinan Road via Gaolan Road and a visit to the onion-domed former **Russian Orthodox Church of St. Nicholas** ⑪, built in 1933 and dedicated to the last Tsar. Continuing north brings you to **Huaihai Middle Road** ⑫. Once the French Concession's principal boulevard, this is one of the city's premier shopping streets, mixing international big brand names with an array of smaller boutiques. Walking west, after a short time you'll see the spire-topped Art Deco exterior of the **Cathay Theater** ⑬ over on the north side of the road. Built in

⑨ Sun Yat Sen, founder of the Nationalist Party

⑦ Former Residence of Zhou Enlai

the 1930s, it is still in use as a cinema and is one of the host venues for the Shanghai International Film Festival in June *(see p39)*.

Turn right into **Maoming North Road** ⑭. A short way along this road there are two heritage buildings, facing each other. On the left is the **Okura Garden Hotel** ⑮, formerly the Cercle Sportif Français (French Sports Club). Built in 1926, the original colonnaded building remains a spectacular sight. Opposite is the **Jinjiang Hotel** ⑯, which houses the Art Deco Grosvenor Mansions apartment block. The Shanghai Communiqué was signed by Mao Zedong and the then US President Richard Nixon in the hotel's Grand Hall in 1972.

CHANGLE ROAD
CHENGDU SOUTH ROAD
HUAIHAI MIDDLE ROAD ⑫
SI SOUTH ROAD
N RD ⑪
NANCHANG ROAD
⑩
NGSHAN RD
⑨
FUXING PARK
KING MIDDLE ROAD
⑧
CHONGQING SOUTH RD
TH ROAD
⑦
ANGUO DDLE RD

| 0 meters | 500 |
| 0 yards | 500 |

Key

• • • Walk route

SHOPPING IN SHANGHAI

Where Beijing boasts a thousand-plus years of imperial history and asssociated monuments, Shanghai reigns supreme when it comes to the modern passions of eating and shopping. With the latter, the enticements begin with the likes of Chinese cotton slippers, sold two pairs for a dollar at the street market, and run all the way up to high-fashion labels such as Gucci and Prada at the glitzy new iAPM Mall, Jing'an Kerry Centre, and ifc Mall in Pudong. The former main shopping street of Nanjing East Road is being redeveloped, but its flagship, the No. 1 Department Store remains, where you can buy Mao-label tea and cigarettes in a packet emblazoned with a golden Oriental Pearl TV Tower. Shanghai shoppers also throng Huaihai Road, lined with high-gloss malls at its eastern end, with boutique shopping farther west. One block south, the Xin Tiandi mall is housed in reconstructed *shikumen* stone tenements. Markets are thinner on the ground than in Beijing but, even so, only the most morose opponent of consumerism could fail to find fun shopping in Shanghai.

Practical Information

Most shops are open seven days a week from around 10am through until 9pm or even later. Markets will start and finish earlier. Credit cards are not as widely accepted as you might expect; some places only take local cards and many don't take any form of plastic at all. You need to carry cash. If you run short, ATMs are not hard to find.

Shopping Etiquette

When bargaining at any market that sees plenty of foreign shoppers – Fangbang Road, for example – don't listen to advice that says half or one-third of the first offer made by the vendor is reasonable. This first-named price may easily be five, ten, or even fifteen times what any local would consider a reasonable sum. A counter-offer of only half the vendor's price marks you down as easy prey. Offer far less – maybe as little as

A Western fashion house advertises in the windows of a Shanghai mall

Modern twists on classic Chinese fashion at Shanghai Tang

10 per cent of the price you were quoted. Your first counter-offer says, "I'm not as stupid as you think. And maybe I'm not that interested anyway." It's hard to make an offer that's too low, and you also have nothing to lose. Either the vendor will dramatically lower his or her price, or he or she will let you walk away, in which case you can improve your offer. Your second offer should be no more than a fraction higher than your first.

It is worth remembering that since there is nothing original or truly antique in Shanghai's markets, there is little that is unique either. You should always try your luck with a number of vendors before settling on any purchase. Always do everything in a friendly way and with a smile and bear in mind that refunds are impossible, so be certain that you have what you want before you pay.

Antiques

Buying genuine antiques in Shanghai is a tricky business. Even if you do manage to ferret out a prize from all the fakes on offer, you'll still have to negotiate the government's strict laws on exporting antiques out of China.

The demise of Dongtai Road in 2015 has left Shanghai with one less outdoor street market and scattered the repro-antique peddlers. They should eventually regroup in some fashion but for the time being your best bets for Mao-era and faux ancient knick-knacks are nearby **Fuyou Road** (open Sunday only) and **Fangbang Road**. Fangbang Road's **Hubao Building Basement Market**, part of the busy Yu Gardens Bazaar complex, is the city's largest indoor antiques market. Over in the French Concession, **Madam Mao's Dowry** is a curiosity store of odd bits and pieces of recent heritage collected by its magpie owners, from vintage clothing to Socialist-Realist posters. Everything here is the genuine article – no repros. Serious collectors can check out **Green Antiques**, a huge warehouse with antiques and reproductions as far as the eye can see. Friendly English-speaking staff will help you distinguish your Ming from your Qing and can also arrange professional export and shipping.

Other stores worth a visit include the state-run **Shanghai Antique & Curio Shop**, just off the Bund, which is something of an antique itself, having been around for over a hundred years, while over in the Hongkou district **Duolun Road** has a row of shops selling antiques and curios.

Art

The Shanghai equivalent of Beijing's 798 Art District is the M50 art hub on Mogan Shan Road. This is a street just to the north of Jing'an District, not far from the train station on the west bank of Suzhou Creek. Here, an area of light industrial buildings has been taken over by artists' ateliers and workshops and a number of commercial galleries. These include the

well-respected **ShanghART**, as well as **Art Scene China**, which represents over 20 of China's leading contemporary artists.

In the French Concession, **Art Labor** has cutting-edge contemporary works of art by Chinese and international artists. Jewelry, home accessories, and other creations by Chinese contemporary designers can be bought at the **Shanghai Museum of Contemporary Art (MOCA)** shop, in the heart of People's Square.

For something a little more edgy, **Tianzifang** on Taikang Road is an attempt to foster a district of arts, crafts, boutiques, and cafés based around a former candy factory and several lanes of old *shikumen* houses. There are a handful of art galleries, plus some handicraft workshops and interesting jewelry and ethnic clothing boutiques. The area is visited on one of the Shanghai Guided Walks *(see p162)*.

Antique radio for sale at a street market

Books

Shanghai beats Beijing hands down for English-language books. Like its counterpart in the capital, the state-run **Foreign Languages Bookstore** has a reasonable selection of English-language novels, as

Mao's "Little Red Book" – still widely available in Shanghai

well as plenty of souvenir picture books. **Garden Books**, at the heart of the French Concession, combines bookselling with a pleasant café and ice-cream counter, while the **Shanghai Museum Shop** is as good as it gets when it comes to books about not just Shanghai, but China as a whole.

The **Confucius Temple** in the Old City has a book market every Sunday that makes for fun browsing. There are also bookstores in shopping malls such as the top floor of **CITIC Square** mall on Nanjing Road and Xujiahu's **Grand Gateway Plaza**, where Xinhua sells a small selection of English-language books.

Chinese Pharmacies

If you know your Chinese medicine, speak Chinese, or are just plain curious to see dried seahorses and the like, **Tong Han Chun** is a venerable example of a traditional Chinese medicine store – one reputedly established in 1783. Claiming even older roots, **Lei Yun Shang Pharmacy** first opened in Suzhou in 1662 but is a relative newcomer to Shanghai, having arrived only in 1860. It still maintains its old-fashioned wooden interior. For modern pharmacies, the Hong Kong pharmacy retailer Mannings now has several outlets across downtown Shanghai.

One of the many curio stores in Shanghai

Boutique clothes store on Huaihai Middle Road, French Concession

Clothes and Textiles

Most major fashion brands from Europe, the US, and Japan are represented in Shanghai. Although there are some bargain clothes items, with factories originating in China, some shops have prices in line with or higher than in Europe and the US, due to high taxes. The main shopping streets are **Huaihai Road** in the French Concession and **Nanjing Road** west of People's Square, where you will find modern, high-end malls such as CITIC Square and Jing'an Kerry Centre.

For something a bit different, Xinle Road and Changle Road, particularly between Shaanxi South Road and Fumin Road, have some stylish boutiques, as does Anfu Road. Styles are Western, although sizes are Eastern (small). Many specialize in factory seconds of items by well-known designers.

Those interested in the latest lines by exciting upcoming Chinese and Asian fashion designers should check out the Xintiandi Style Mall on Madang Road, next to the Xintiandi mall. Both Xintiandi and Maoming Road have a branch of **Shanghai Tang**, the glamorous retro-Asian, Hong Kong high-fashion store which can also be found in Pudong. Shaanxi North Road also has several boutiques representing Chinese designers.

The city has revived its tradition of fine tailoring. Maoming Road, on either side of Huaihai Road, is famous for its strip of tailors selling custom-made *qipao* dresses, which were high fashion in the 1920s, and still worn by elegant, high-society women. **W.W. Chan & Sons Tailor Ltd.** is noted for high quality at fair prices. Fabrics by the meter or the bolt are sold at the **Shanghai Nan Waitan (South Bund) Textile Market**. Filling four floors, it resembles a provincial shopping mall, but it sells only fabric. Most stalls also have a resident tailor ready to whip up made-to-measure cashmere coats, cotton shirts, or silk dresses. They can follow any pattern provided, or even make copies from pictures clipped from a fashion magazine. It typically takes a week for garments to be made but rush jobs can be done for a little more. A shirt will cost the equivalent of around $10, trousers $20.

Crafts

It is never good practice to shop near sites with a high volume of tourist traffic, and as you might imagine, there is a lot of trash for sale at the shops around the **Yu Gardens Bazaar** *(see pp134–5)*. But even Shanghainese visit the quieter corners of the complex for items such as tea, teapots, and tea sets. For porcelain in general, some of the best buys are the fine reproductions of classic designs available at the gift shop of the **Shanghai Museum** *(see pp130–33)*. The

Silk embroidered coasters

shop also has lots of other beautiful items, from calligraphy to carved jade, jewelry, and silk slippers. Although expensive, the work sold here is of better quality than almost anything else on the market. Handicrafts made by some of China's myriad ethnic minorities, as well as by people of neighboring countries, including Nepal, are available at shops dotted along Nanjing Road.

Department Stores and Malls

The Shanghainese have caught the mall craze and multi-story retail plazas have sprung up everywhere. Two of the newest and glitziest are **Jing'an Kerry Centre** above Jing'an Temple subway station on Nanjing Road and **iAPM** on Huaihai Road. Other excellent malls include the **Shanghai ifc Mall** and the **Superbrand Mall**, both near the Lujiazui metro station in Pudong. **Hong Kong Plaza** on Huaihai Road is another trendy mall. All these places are full of luxury-brand Western goods (at significantly higher than Western prices). Another upscale shopping district in Shanghai is **Xintiandi Shopping Mall**, housed in rebuilt 19th-century *shikumen* buildings. Visitors can browse brand-name shops, eat in world-class restaurants, or simply take in the scenery.

Plaza 66, one of three adjacent modern malls on Nanjing West Road

Electronics

There are no bargains to be had on computers or other electronic items. Almost everything is imported and so costs as much, if not more than, in the US or Europe. There are a few exceptions such as Sony shortwave radios, made in China for export, which may be bargained down to decent prices. Cheap Chinese MP3 players or DVD players are often multi-lingual and multi-voltage, but there's no warranty except with a very few global Chinese brands. Accessories and media such as disks, tapes, leads, and

Nanjing East Road, once Shanghai's main shopping street

convertors, all made in China, are cheaper than the identical item packaged up for sale at

home. There are multiple Apple Stores in downtown Shanghai, including iAPM Mall, Hong Kong Plaza, and ifc Mall in Pudong.

Pearls and Jewelry

Jewelry shops abound all over the city, particularly in the Old City around the Yu Gardens Bazaar and along pedestrianized Nanjing East Road. Pearls are a specialty, both fresh- and saltwater. One of the best shops is **Shanghai Pearl City**. Prices are competitive, but you do need to know what you are looking at.

DIRECTORY

Antiques

Fuyou Road Market
Cangbao Road, Fangbang Middle Road 457, Old City. **Map** 2 C4.

Green Antiques
4877 Middle Jiasong Road, Qingpu District.
Tel (138) 1832 6863.

Hubao Building Basement Market
Fangbang Road, Old City.
Map 2 C4.

Madam Mao's Dowry
207 Fumin Road, French Concession.
Tel (021) 5403 3551.

Shanghai Antique & Curio Shop
218–226 Guangdong Road, by Jiangxi Middle Road, Huangpu District.
Map 2 C3.
Tel (021) 6321 4697.

Art

Art Labor
Building 4, 570 Yongjia Road. **Map** 1 E5.
Tel (021) 3460 5331.
w artlaborgallery.com

Art Scene China
2/F, Building 4, 50 Mogan Shan Road, Putuo District.
Tel (021) 6277 4940.
w artscenechina.com

Shanghai Museum of Contemporary Art (MOCA) Shop
231 Nanjing West Road.
Map 2 A3.
Tel (021) 6327 9900.
w mocashanghai.com

ShanghART
Building 16, 50 Mogan Shan Road, Putuo District.
Tel (021) 6359 3923.
w shanghart.com

Tianzifang
Taikang Road Shopping District.
Map 1 F5.

Books

Confucius Temple Book Market
215 Wenmiao Road, Old City. **Map** 2 B5.

Garden Books
325 Changle Road, French Concession.
Map 1 E4.
Tel (021) 5404 8728.

Foreign Languages Bookstore
390 Fuzhou Road, Huangpu District.
Map 2 B3.
Tel (021) 6322 3200.

Shanghai Museum Shop
201 People's Avenue, People's Square.
Map 2 A3.
Tel (021) 6372 3500.

Chinese Pharmacies

Lei Yun Shang
2 Huashan Road, Jing'an District. **Map** 1 D3.
Tel (021) 6217 3501.

Tong Han Chun
20 Yuyuan Xin Road, by Jiuxiao Road, Old City.
Map 2 C4.
Tel (021) 6355 0308.

Clothes and Textiles

Shanghai Nan Waitan (South Bund) Textile Market
399 Lujiabang Road, Huangpu District.

Shanghai Tang
Lane 333 Huangpi South Road, Xintiandi North Block. **Map** 2 A4.
Tel (021) 6377 3333.

W.W. Chan & Sons Tailor Ltd.
129 Maoming South Road, by Huaihai Middle Road, French Concession.
Map 1 E4.
Tel (021) 5404 1469.

Crafts

Yu Gardens Bazaar
Fuyou Road, Old City.
Map 2 C4.

Department Stores and Malls

Hong Kong Plaza
Corner of Huaihai Middle Road and Songshan Road.
Map 2 B4.
Tel (021) 2327 8888.

iAPM
999 Huaihai Middle Rd.
Map 1 E4.
Tel (021) 6391 5517.

Jing'an Kerry Centre
1515 Nanjing West Road, Jing'an District.
Map 1 D3.
Tel (021) 6087 1515.

Shanghai ifc Mall
8 Century Avenue, Pudong. **Map** 3 E3.
Tel (021) 6311 5588.

Superbrand Mall
168 Lujiazui West Road, Pudong. **Map** 3 E3.
Tel (021) 688 7788.

Xintiandi Mall
Huangpi South Road, Old City. **Map** 2 A4.
Tel (021) 6311 2288.

Pearls and Jewelry

Shanghai Pearl City
3721 Hongmei Road, Hongqiao.

ENTERTAINMENT IN SHANGHAI

It is frequently said that Beijing produces the art and culture, and Shanghai sells it. There is some truth in this. Beijing has the happening music scene; its film academy has produced almost every director of note of recent times; and it is the home of traditional art forms such as Beijing Opera. But in the last decade, Shanghai has pulled ahead in building arts and entertainments venues, including theaters, concert halls, and galleries. The city prides itself on being cosmopolitan and, as a result, venues tend to host Western shows such as *Cats*. However, this is changing and centers now showcase Chinese and Asian musicians and orchestras.

Shanghai's modern nightlife once existed in the shadow of the reputation of the famously wild 1920s and 1930s. Many of the hotel bars and seedier expat hang-outs played on this reputation, with female wait staff dressed in the figure-hugging *qipao* dresses of old, live jazz, and cocktails. Today, the city's nightlife is thriving, diverse, and improving all the time.

Shanghai Grand Theater, the city's premier venue for performing arts

Practical Information

For details of what's on in town pick up one of the English-language listings magazines, such as *Time Out Shanghai*, *City Weekend*, and *That's Shanghai*. These publications are available free in hotel lobbies and at restaurants and bars.

Tickets are generally bought at the venue box offices and paid for in cash. At small music clubs, pay on the door. Most hotel concierges can usually help with securing seats at the theaters.

Classical Music and Performing Arts

The major theaters – which include the **Shanghai Grand Theater**, **Shanghai Concert Hall**, **Majestic Theater**, **Oriental Art Center**, and **Shanghai Culture Square** – put on large-scale concerts of Chinese and foreign music and Western musicals, as well as some home-grown dance and musical spectaculars. Other theaters put on more traditional Chinese Opera performances, notably the **Yifu Theater**. The 2010 World Expo Site's handful of permanent attractions includes the oyster shell-shaped **Mercedes-Benz Arena**, which hosts concerts, theater, and large stage shows.

Shanghai is most famous for its acrobatic shows. Although most performances are now constructed with tourists in mind, complete with theatrical lighting and sequined costumes, this makes them no less valid or spectacular. Lissom adults and children who seem more fluid than solid make towers out of themselves and assortments of tables, chairs, and umbrellas, and disappear into objects the same size as carry-on luggage.

Bars and Pubs

Shanghai's image in the West links it inextricably to the cocktail, and certainly there are now many suitably luxurious locations in which to drink one. Hotel bars offer the most dramatic settings and include the Park Hyatt's dizzying 91st-floor **100 Century Avenue** bar, the Hyatt on the Bund's **Vue** skydeck bar, with views of the Bund, Huangpu River, and the Pudong skyline, the expensive 14th-floor outdoor terrace of **Sir Elly's** at the Peninsula Hotel on the Bund, and **The Long Bar** at Waldorf-Astoria Shanghai on the Bund, which recreates a 1930s bar of the same name. These bars all offer views that may quickly induce the slightly colonial feeling of being master of all you survey.

International sophistication spreads well beyond the big hotels. **Bar Rouge**, with snooty patrons awash in Veuve Cliquot, is one of the few places in China where a dress code is enforced. If you're anything less than "smart casual" look elsewhere, although it's a shame to miss the terrace overlooking the Huangpu. **Barbarossa** offers a

Cotton's, one of the city's many watering holes

North African theme with sequinned pillows and a terracotta-tiled rooftop terrace overlooking a small lake in central People's Park. In the up-and-coming Rockbund heritage enclave just behind the Bund, **The Nest** opened in 2014 and has quickly become a fashionable place to party. The chic gastro-lounge feels like stepping into a 1960s New York apartment. A collaboration between popular Chinese club MUSE and French vodka brand Grey Goose, it combines a cocktail bar, raw seafood bar and Nordic-inspired restaurant. A sixth-floor terrace looks out over heritage rooftops.

The Fuxing Road area of the French Concession has become something of an after-dark hotspot with cool cocktail lounges like **The Apartment** and **El Coctel**, plus microbrewery pub **Boxing Cat Brewery**. Another popular bar is the Yunnan-themed **Mask**, which forms the first floor of Lost Heaven restaurant.

As an alternative to the cocktail scene, there is no shortage of down-to-earth pubs. In the French Concession district, **Sasha's** bar and grill is set in a historic mansion with a beautiful patio garden. This stalwart of Shanghai was one of the city's first real international standard bars. It is particularly popular for its weekend brunch and it also makes good wood-fired pizzas. In the same grounds, **Zapata's** is a Mexican bar, restaurant, and club that targets a younger, more clubby crowd than Sasha's. Directly across Hengshan Road, **Shanghai Brewery** is another popular brewhouse spread over two large floors with an extensive menu, sports on big screens and a pleasant sidewalk terrace. The **Paulaner Brauhaus** on the Pudong riverfront brews its own, expensive ale, with schnitzels and wurst to help it down, and views of the lights coming on along the Bund in the early evening. **Cotton's** is a big old house with rooms galore, each furnished with a grand fireplace.

Just north of Nanjing West Road, Tongren Road has the Canadian-owned **Big Bamboo Sports Bar**, the city's best venue for watching international soccer and other sports matches. Another popular sports bar, especially for Australian sports, is **The Camel** on Yueyang Road. Upscale

Xintiandi has a good selection of pubs including **Kabb**, a trendy bar and grill, great for sophisticated cocktails, or try classy wine bar **Dr Wine**, on Fumin Road, a perfect spot to start a night on the town.

Clubs

You're unlikely to travel to China just to go clubbing, but Shanghai regularly attracts big-name foreign DJs and hip-hop acts. A glimpse at nouveau riche Chinese partying is on offer at **Diva**, a large, lavishly designed mix of club, karaoke house, and late night bar. VIPs recline on the fringes drinking Chivas and green tea (and that's in the same glass). It's loud and decadent but great fun. Down the road, French club **Le Baron** draws a well-dressed mix of foreigners and locals, though you first need to get past the selective door bouncers. Close to the Bund, **M1NT** is one of Shanghai's clubbing stalwarts. The cavernous club, with its famous shark tank and open-air rooftop, packs the party people in.

Film

Cinemas in Shanghai suffer the same handicaps as movie houses in Beijing, namely heavy censorship, a strict limiting of the number of foreign movies that can be screened, and the fact that you can get any new release on DVD for less than a dollar long before it reaches the big screen. For all these reasons,

A superb hotel bar, some 80 floors above street level

The foyer of the Cathay Theater, one of Shanghai's 1930s cinemas

Shanghai possesses far fewer cinemas than you would expect. The most modern and high-tech venue is the **Palace Cinema** at the iAPM mall on Huaihai Road, with IMAX and 3-D screens. The **UME International Cineplex** is also well placed for visitors at Xin Tiandi and screens English language movies. Buy tickets ahead as sessions frequently sell out. For a taste of cinema-going of old, visit the 1930s Art Deco **Cathay Theater** in the French Concession. It often screens international movies with Chinese subtitles.

Shanghai is also the venue for an international film festival, held every June (see p39). Film screenings are open to the public and the movies shown are not subject to the usual censorship.

Jazz

The last living relic of the "Whore of the Orient" era, the nonagenarian band at the **Fairmont Peace Hotel Jazz Bar**, is more novelty act than any kind of serious musical proposition, although concierges and guide books will usually direct you to them. Serious blues lovers head for the **Cotton Club**, which has been around long enough to garner a good reputation and is typically packed at weekends. Try also **Club JZ**, a regular venue for visiting overseas jazzers and sessions of improvization. It is also where you may see famous local singer Coco. Nearby, live jazz venue **Heyday** is an inti-mate, semi-circular vintage lounge seating only 50 patrons at a squeeze and hosting a nightly roster of Shanghai's leading jazz musicians from 9:30pm, accompanied by barrel-aged classic cocktails. The **House of Blues and Jazz**, located on Fuzhou Road, two blocks back from the Bund, is bluesier, and also features

many touring bands from overseas, many of whom have played in top clubs in cities like New York. Drink prices at all these venues tend to be high.

Rock and Pop

Beijing claims the crown when it comes to live contemporary music, but Shanghai is trying its best to catch up with the capital. There are still relatively few live music bars in the city, but the scene is starting to pick up. A popular choice among locals is the hip underground bar and club **The Shelter**, which features regular live music and DJs playing everything from reggae to IDM and electro to hip-hop at high volume.

The **Mercedes-Benz Arena** in Pudong and its more intimate Mixing Room host big-name international pop acts, including Ed Sheeran and Katy Perry.

Teahouses

Normally the traditional Chinese teahouse offers a respite from the crowds of the city, but Shanghai's most famous, the **Huxinting** or "mid-lake pavilion," is set amid the bedlam of the Yu Gardens and its attendant shopping, and is anything but calm. However, its 200-year-old willow pattern looks, with access only via a ghost-thwarting zig-zag bridge (ghosts can only travel in straight lines), makes it the most popular place to experience a Chinese tea ceremony. Past visitors have included the likes of Queen Elizabeth II, Bill Clinton, and other heads of state.

Fangbang Middle Road, the street that runs to the south of the Yu Gardens complex, has several similar operations of greater modernity, most selling tea as well as providing a place to drink it.

The Fairmont Peace Hotel, home of Shanghai's oldest jazz band

DIRECTORY

Classical Music and Performing Arts

Majestic Theater
66 Jiang Ning Road, Jing'an District.
Map 1 E2.
Tel (021) 6217 3311.

Mercedes-Benz Arena
1200 Expo Avenue, Pudong.
Map 3 E5.
Tel (086) 400 181 6688.

Oriental Art Center
425 Dingxiang Road.
Tel (021) 6854 1234.

Shanghai Concert Hall
523 Yan'an East Road.
Map 2 A4.
Tel (021) 6217 2426.

Shanghai Culture Square
225 Shanxi South Roadd.
Map 1 E5.
Tel (021) 5461 9961.

Shanghai Grand Theater
300 Renmin Avenue, Renmin Square.
Map 2 A3.
Tel (021) 6386 8686.

Yifu Theater
701 Fuzhou Road, Huangpu District.
Map 2 B3.
Tel (021) 6351 4668.

Bars, Pubs, and Clubs

100 Century Avenue
91/F Park Hyatt Shanghai, Century Boulevard, Pudong. **Map** 3 F4.
Tel (021) 6888 1234.

The Apartment
3/F 47 Yongfu Road, French Concession.
Tel (021) 6437 9478.

Bar Rouge
7th Floor, Bund 18, 18 Zhong Shan Dong Yi Lu, The Bund.
Map 2 C2.
Tel (021) 6339 1199.

Barbarossa
Nanjing West Road 231, inside People's Park.
Map 2 A3.
Tel (021) 6318 0220.

Big Bamboo Sports Bar
132 Nanyang Road, Jing'an District.
Map 1 D3.
Tel (021) 6256 2265.

Boxing Cat Brewery
82 Fuxing Road, French Concession.
Tel (021) 6431 2091.

The Camel
1 Yueyang Road, French Concession.
Map 1 D5.
Tel (021) 6437 9446.

Club JZ
46 Fuxing West Road, French Concession.
Tel (021) 6431 0269.

Cotton Club
1428 Huaihai Middle Road, French Concession.
Map 1 E4.
Tel (021) 6437 7110.

Cotton's
132 Anting Road, Xuhui District.
Tel (021) 6433 7995.

Diva
2/F, 291 Fumin Road, French Concession.
Map 1 D4.
Tel (021) 6136 0288.

Dr Wine
177 Fumin Road.
Map 1 D4.
Tel (021) 5403 5717.

El Coctel
2/F 47 Yongfu Road, French Concession.
Tel (021) 6433 6511.

Fairmont Peace Hotel Jazz Bar
20 Nanjing East Road, The Bund.
Map 2 C2.
Tel (021) 6138 6883.

Heyday
50 Tai'an Road.
Tel (021) 6236 6075.

House of Blues and Jazz
60 Fuzhou Road, French Concession (Nanjing East Road metro).
Tel (021) 6321 1214.

Kabb
181 Taicang Road, XinTiandi. **Map** 2 A4.
Tel (021) 3307 0798.

Le Baron
7/F, 20 Donghu Road.
Map 1 D4.

The Long Bar
Waldorf-Astoria Shanghai on the Bund, 2 The Bund.
Map 3 C3.
Tel (021) 6322 9988.

Mask
38 Gaoyou Road, French Concession.
Tel (021) 6433 5126.

M1NT
24/F, 318 Fuzhou Road.
Map 2 C3.
Tel (021) 6391 2811.

The Nest
6/F, Rockbund, 130 Beijing East Road.
Map 2 C2.
Tel (021) 6308 7669.

Paulaner Brauhaus
Binjiang Avenue, by Pudong Shangri-La.
Map 3 D3.
Tel (021) 6888 3935.

Sasha's
11 Dong Ping Road & Hengshan Road, French Concession.
Tel (021) 6474 6628.

Shanghai Brewery
15 Dongping Road.
Map 1 D5.
Tel (021) 3461 0717.

The Shelter
5 Yongfu Road, near Fuxing West Road.
Tel (021) 6437 0400.

Sir Elly's
13/F, The Peninsula Shanghai Hotel, 32 The Bund.
Map 3 D2.
Tel (021) 2327 2888.

Spot Bar
331 Tongren Road, Jing'an.
Map 1 D3.
Tel (021) 6247 3579.

Vue
32–33/F, Hyatt on the Bund Hotel, 199 Huangpu Road, near The Bund (north).
Tel (021) 6393 1234.

Zapata's
5 Hengshang Road, French Concession.
Tel (021) 6433 4104.

Film

Cathay Theater
Huaihai Middle Road 870, French Concession.
Map 1 E4.
Tel (021) 5404 2095.

Palace Cinema
6/F, iAPM Mall, 999, Huaihai Zhong Lu
Tel (021) 5109 3988

UME International Cineplex
2nd Floor, Lane 123, Xingye Road, Xintiandi.
Map 2 A4.
Tel (021) 6373 3333.

Teahouses

Huxinting
257 Yu Yuan Road, Old City.
Map 2 C4.
Tel (021) 6355 8270.

SHANGHAI STREET FINDER

The map references listed for sights, hotels, restaurants, shops, and entertainment venues described in this chapter refer to the following maps only. The first figure of the map reference indicates which map to turn to, and the letter and number that follow are the grid reference. The key map below shows which parts of Shanghai's city center are covered in this Street Finder and

the symbols used in the Street Finder are listed below. A complete index of street names follows the maps. In contrast to Beijing street names, which still use Pinyin, Shanghai street names now use the English term for their suffixes and directionals: "lu" is now road, "dong" is east, "bei" is north, "nan" is south, "zhong" is middle, "jie" is street, and "dadao" is avenue.

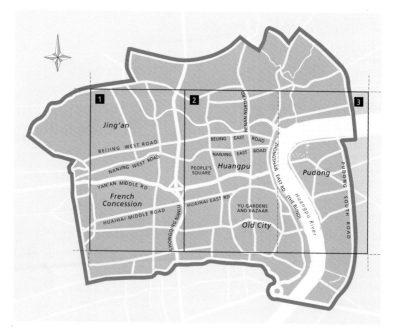

Key to Street Finder

▪	Major sight	ℹ️	Tourist information
▪	Place of interest	➕	Hospital
▪	Other important building	🏛	Temple
🚢	Ferry teminal	✝	Church
🚢	River boat pier		
Ⓜ	Subway station		

Scale of map above

0 kilometers   2

0 miles   1

Scale of maps 1–3

0 meters   500

0 yards   500

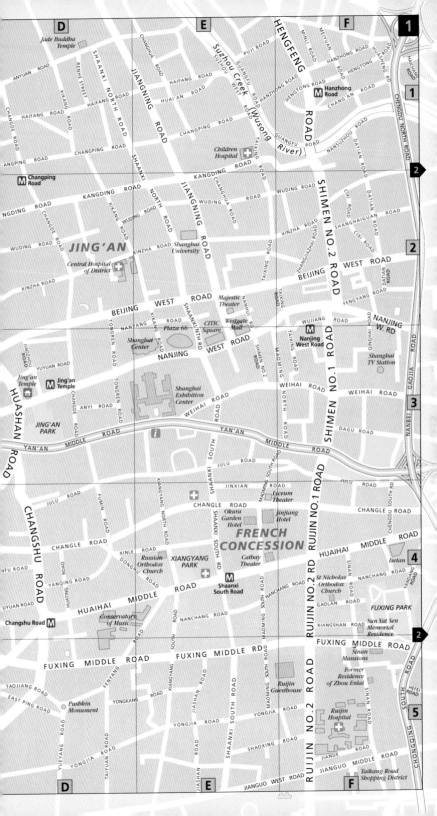

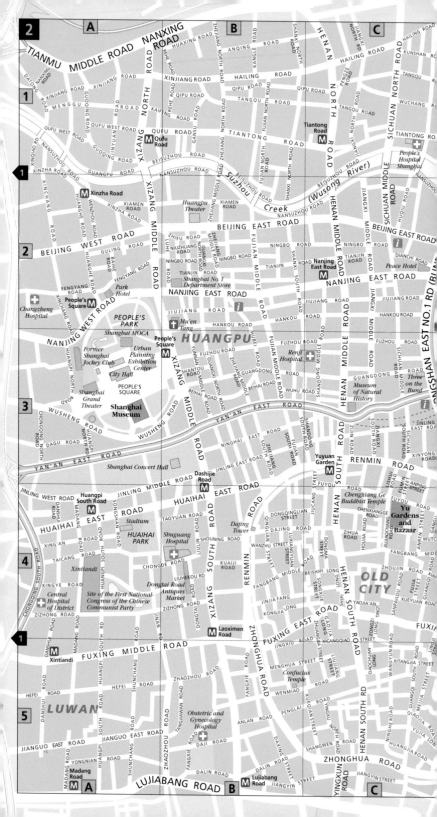

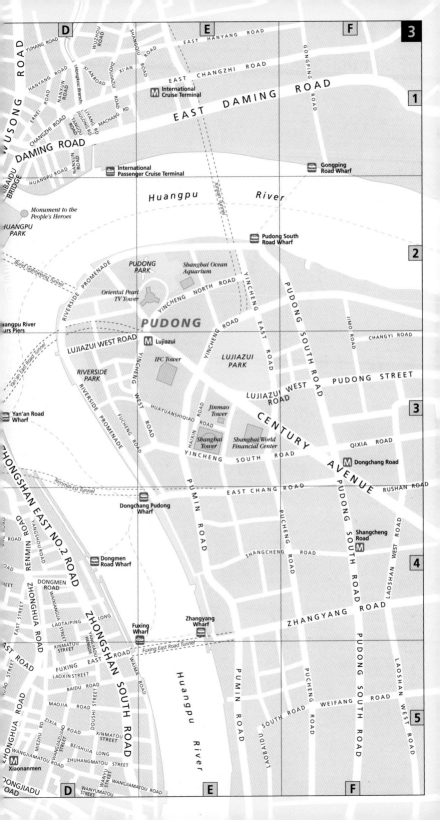

Shanghai Street Finder Index

TRAVELERS' NEEDS

WHERE TO STAY

Beijing and Shanghai together offer the most glamorous hotels in mainland China, and some of the most historic too. Four- and five-star hotels, many belonging to foreign chains, are plentiful. Boutique hotels can now be found in both cities. Beijing also has a number of "courtyard" hotels, which are conversions of traditional old Chinese homes, and Shanghai has some old lane houses that have been converted into boutique hotels and bed-and-breakfasts. There are plenty of other comfortable mid-range choices, and for budget travelers, dirt-cheap need not mean dirty.

Hotels on Shanghai's historic Bund are often architecturally splendid

International and Chinese-Run Hotels

Visitors in search of international standards of comfort and service should stick either to five-star hotels managed by familiar Western chains, or the Singapore- and Hong Kong-based luxury companies. Increasingly, however, larger Chinese-run hotel groups are successfully emulating Western operations and hospitality standards across all price ranges.

The Chinese star system of grading hotels does not follow international norms, and some hotel grades can be overstated. Rather than be involved in the star-rating system, some international hotels choose to go starless, but can be far superior to neighboring Chinese-run "five-stars". As a general rule for Chinese-run hotels, the newer the hotel, the better the facilities.

Budget Hotels and Other Options

It's easy to find somewhere good to stay in Beijing and Shanghai on a budget, including dorm beds from ¥50. Neither city has any sort of official camping grounds. If you want to stay with a local and get a real feel for the city, the online hosting service Airbnb has plenty of options in both cities, from budget stays to luxury apartments.

Booking a Hotel

In China, the real price of a hotel room is what the customer is willing to pay. Locals will always ask for a discount and you should too.

For most foreign-run hotels and newer Chinese hotels, the best available price will be on the hotel's own website. Prices can drop nearer to the planned day of stay, but it can be risky to wait too long as demand at international hotels is often high, particularly in Shanghai.

Be wary of websites advertising Chinese hotels, some of which quote a wildly inflated rack rate. Specialist websites often claim to offer huge discounts, so it is best to stick to reputable sites such as elong. net and english.ctrip.com.

Most non-budget hotels will accept international credit cards but many charge a transaction fee. Foreign exchange facilities in hotels are becoming less reliable, and holders of travelers' checks in particular may be sent to the nearest large branch of the Bank of China. Particularly in more modest Chinese hotels, always be prepared to pay in local currency. Wherever you stay, you will always be asked for a credit card or cash deposit to cover hotel extras.

Hidden Costs

The prices quoted by major international hotels do not include their service charges. Many Chinese-run, upper-end hotels levy service charges of between 5 and 15 percent, plus 3 percent VAT (Value Added Tax). Most Chinese customers refuse to pay the charges, and hotels rarely insist, but ask before you check in. Only a modest service charge is added to the cost of any international phone calls made from your hotel room.

Luxurious bedroom at the Ritz-Carlton, Pudong in Shanghai

◄ Grand Hyatt Shanghai, looking down multi-story atrium to patio below

Seasonal Demand

The busiest travel periods are during the week-long national holiday around October 1, and during the Spring Festival or Chinese New Year *(see p42)*. But most of the travel is away from the big cities, and so demand for hotel rooms is more greatly affected in Suzhou and Hangzhou than in Beijing and Shanghai. Exhibitions and conferences pose more of a problem, though tend to affect upper-end accommodations only. The primary conference seasons in both cities are March–June and September–late November (excluding October holiday). The April dates of Shanghai's Formula One Grand Prix should also be avoided.

General Observations and Precautions

It is common for Chinese-run hotels to request payment for the room in advance. Check-out is usually noon (some hotels charge for late check out).

Some cheap business hotels in China advertise facilities such as night clubs and karaoke bars, but these are often fronts for prostitution. Be wary of calls to your room offering massage.

Courtyard hotels such as the Duge are often the most atmospheric *(see p184)*

Facilities for Children and the Disabled

Most hotels allow under-12s to stay with their parents free of charge. Most will also add an extra bed for an older child for a nominal (and negotiable) fee.

In general, China is not well-prepared for the disabled. Only the newest and best international hotels provide wheelchair access, or fully adapted rooms.

Tipping

Traditionally, there is no tipping in China, but because of the increasing number of visitors

that do tip regardless, this is starting to change. This is most particularly true in hotels in heavily touristed areas and in more upmarket establishments.

Recommended Hotels

The hotels chosen on pages 182–5 are in six categories: Boutique, Budget, Business, Historic/Courtyard, Luxury, and Modern. Luxury and business hotels are self-explanatory, but travelers on a limited budget should also check out Modern hotels for inexpensive and stylish chains. China's boutique hotel industry is booming, and this category can include everything from slick and trendy city operations to rural homestays with just a few rooms. And despite China's fondness for the wrecking ball, there are many historic options for visitors to choose from, from Art-Deco gems in Shanghai to historic *hutong* hotels in Beijing.

Throughout, hotels highlighted as DK Choices are extra-special places, highly recommended for one or even several reasons, be it a stunning setting, a great spa, an arresting design, or a highly regarded restaurant.

DIRECTORY

Hotel Chains

Crowne Plaza
Tel 1-800 801 881 (US).
0800 8222 8222 (UK).
W ichotelsgroup.com

Fairmont
Tel 1-800 257 7544 (US).
0800 0441 1414 (UK).
W fairmont.com

Four Seasons
Tel 1-800 819 5053 (US).
0800 6488 6488 (UK).
W fourseasons.com

Grand Hyatt
Tel 1-800 233 1234 (US).
0845 888 1234 (UK).
1-800 481 034 (Ireland).
W hyatt.com

Hilton
Tel 1-800 774 1500 (US).
0800 4488 22073 (UK).
W hilton.com

Holiday Inn
Tel 1-800 465 4329 (US).
0800 405 060 (UK).
W ichotelsgroup.com

Howard Johnson
Tel (+86 21) 6886 8840.
W hojochina.com

Hyatt Regency
Tel 1-888 591 1234 (US).
0845 888 1234 (UK).
W hyatt.com

InterContinental
Tel 1-800 801 881 (US).
0800 1800 1800 (UK).
W ichotelsgroup.com

Marco Polo
Tel +852 2118 7232
(Hong Kong). W marco
polohotels.com

Marriott
Tel 1-888 721 7033 (US).
0800 1927 1927 (UK).
W marriott.com

Novotel
Tel 1-800 666 0835 (US).
W novotel.com

Park Hyatt
Tel 1-877 875 4658 (US).
0845 888 1234 (UK).
1-800 481 034 (Ireland).
W hyatt.com

Peninsula
Tel 1-866 382 8388 (US).
0800 2828 3888 (UK).
W peninsula.com

Radisson
Tel 1-800 805 164 (US).
0800 374 411 (UK).
1-800 557 474 (Ireland).
W radisson.com

Ritz-Carlton
Tel 1-800 542 8680 (US).
0800 234 000 (UK).
1-800 145 004 (Aus).
W ritzcarlton.com

St. Regis
Tel 1-800 325 3589 (US).
0800 3257 8734 (UK).
W starwood.com

Shangri-La
Tel 1-866 565 5050 (US).
0800 028 3337 (UK).
W shangri-la.com

Sheraton
Tel 1-888 625 5144 (US).
0800 3253 5353 (UK).
W starwood.com

Sofitel
Tel 1-800 763 4835 (US).
0871 663 0625 (UK).
1300 884 400 (Aus).
008 133 388 (China).
W sofitel.com

Westin
Tel 1-888 625 5144 (US).
0800 3259 5959 (UK).
W starwood.com

Where to Stay

Boutique
Beijing

DK Choice

The Orchid Gulou ¥¥
65 Baochao Hutong
Tel *(010) 8404 4818* **Map** 2 A2
[W] theorchidbeijing.com
A stylish boutique hotel set in a renovated courtyard in the increasingly hip Baochao Hutong. The rooftop bar and lounge affords fine views over the *hutongs*.

3 + 1 Bedrooms ¥¥¥
17 Zhangwang Hutong, Jiu Gulou Dajie, Dongcheng district
Tel *(010) 6404 7030* **Map** 2 A2
[W] 3plus1bedrooms.com
This tiny boutique injects minimalist chic into the courtyard hotel scene. The stark whiteness of the rooms is a counterpoint to the colorful local street life.

Red Capital Residence ¥¥¥
9 Dongsi Liutiao, Dongcheng district
Tel *(010) 8403 5308* **Map** 2 3C
[W] redcapitalclub.com.cn
This five-room guest house in a gorgeous courtyard, decked out with antique furniture and Communist Party memorabilia, is a funky place to stay.

Beijing Farther Afield

Red Capital Ranch ¥¥
No. 28 Xiaguandi Village
Tel *(010) 8401 8886*
[W] redcapitalclub.com.cn
Ten rustic stone cottages, each filled with artifacts. A quiet stretch of the Great Wall is walking distance away. Closed Dec–Feb.

The Schoolhouse ¥¥
12 Mutianyu Village
Tel *(010) 6162 6506*
[W] theschoolhouseatmutianyu.com
Guests needing a break from the smog can stay at the eco-resort or hire one of the converted village homes and enjoy amazing views of the Great Wall.

Brickyard Inn ¥¥¥
Beigou Village, Huairou District
Tel *(010) 6162 6506*
[W] brickyardatmutianyu.com
Small and friendly bed-and-breakfast created from an old glazed-tile factory. The 16 Queen rooms, all with private terraces, contain reminders of the past.

Shanghai

Quintet ¥¥
808 Changle Lu, Jing'an district
Tel *(021) 6249 9088* **Map** 1 D4
[W] quintet-shanghai.com
Tasteful and charming; the rooms have king-size beds dressed with luxurious white linens.

Cachet Shanghai ¥¥¥
931 Nanjing Xi Lu, Jing'an district
Tel *(021) 6217 9000* **Map** 1 E3
[W] cachethotels.com
Philippe Starck-designed hotel in an unbeatable location. Rates include extras such as evening cocktails, breakfast, and laundry.

Les Suites Orient ¥¥¥
1 Jinling Dong Lu
Tel *(021) 6320 0088* **Map** 2 C3
[W] lessuitesorient.com
Hotel fusing Art Deco design with traditional Oriental style, with an iconic view over the river. Rates include breakfast.

Shanghai Farther Afield

Hotel Soul Suzhou ¥¥
27-33 Qiaosikong Xiang, Suzhou
Tel *(0512) 6777 0777*
[W] hotelsoul.com.cn
A good, inexpensive but stylish base from which to explore the city, with pleasant rooms and helpful staff who speak a little English.

Tonino Lamborghini Boutique Hotel Suzhou ¥¥¥
168 Xinggang Street, Suzhou
Tel *(0512) 6285 9999*
[W] tlhotelsgroup.com
Part of a small chain; the bright, spacious rooms don't come with

Tonino Lamborghini Boutique, a stylish, modern base in Suzhou

the famous cars, unfortunately. Upgrade to a garden view room and enjoy your own courtyard.

Budget
Beijing

Downtown Backpackers ¥
85 Nanluoguxiang, Chaoyang district
Tel *(010) 8400 2429* **Map** 2 B2
[W] backpackingchina.com
This cheerful hostel fills Beijing's pressing need for low-priced, well-placed rooms. It is located halfway down the city's most funky *hutong*.

Red Hotel ¥
10 Taipingzhuang, Chunxiu Lu
Tel *(010) 6417 1066* **Map** 3 E2
[W] red-hotel.com
Rooms feature faux-antique furnishings and multi-jet capsule showers. Minutes' walk from the entertainment district of Sanlitun.

Shanghai

Ling Long Hotel ¥
939 Yanan Xi Lu, Changning district
Tel *(021) 6225 0360*
This small hotel feels more like a private residence. The slightly old-fashioned decor only adds to the charm.

Phoenix Hostel ¥
17 Yunnan Road, Huangpu district
Tel *(021) 6328 8680* **Map** 2 B3
Walking distance from Shanghai Museum and the Bund. Rooms are simple and clean; there are lovely views from the rooftop.

DK Choice

Magnolia B&B ¥¥
36 Yanqing Lu, Xuhui district
Tel *(138) 1794 0848* **Map** 1 D4
[W] magnoliabnbshanghai.com
Great for giving guests a taste of Shanghai living thanks to its back alley location, the 1920s lane-house makes an interesting and intimate place to stay. Rooms are minimalist but with everything one needs. The husband-and-wife managers are friendly and hospitable.

Shanghai Farther Afield

West Lake Youth Hostel ¥
62–3 Nan Shan Lu, Hangzhou
Tel *(0571) 8702 7027*
W westlakehostel.com
Hostel full of character with a
great location on the banks of
the lake near Leifeng Pagoda.
Rooms are bright and spacious.

Business

Beijing

Aloft ¥¥
Tower 2, 25 Yuanda Road
Tel *(010) 8889 8000*
W starwoodhotels.com
Situated in the lively university
district near the Summer Palace
and Olympic Stadium, offering
affordable loft-style rooms.

**Crowne Plaza Beijing
Wangfujing** ¥¥
48 Wangfujing Dajie
Tel *(010) 5911 9999* **Map** 2 B5
W crowneplaza.com
Comfortable, good-value rooms
within walking distance of the
subway and the Forbidden City.

China World Summit Wing ¥¥¥
*1 Jianguomenwai Avenue,
Chaoyang district*
Tel *(010) 6505 2299* **Map** 3 F5
W shangri-la.com/beijing/
chinaworldsummitwing
Guests enjoy superb views from
the China World Trade Center.
Tasteful, ultra-modern interiors
marry traditional Chinese aes-
thetics with Western chic.

East, Beijing ¥¥¥
22 Jiuxianqiao Road
Tel *(010) 8426 0888*
W east-beijing.com
Part of the Indigo complex, this
new property is aimed at business
people with style. Restaurants are
a cut above standard hotel fare.

Fairmont Hotel Beijing ¥¥¥
*8 Yong An Dong Li, Jianguomen Wai
Dajie, Chaoyang district*
Tel *(010) 8511 7777* **Map** 5 E1
W fairmont.com/beijing
Glamorous without being gaudy.
North-facing rooms have great
views over the city and extras
include Bose technology.

Hilton Beijing Wangfujing ¥¥¥
*8 Wangfujing Dong Dajie,
Dongcheng district*
Tel *(010) 5812 8888* **Map** 5 D1
W hilton.com
Located within easy walking
distance of Tian'an Men Square
and the Forbidden City, with

Understated elegance at China World Summit Wing

spacious rooms and warm
service. The pool and spa area are
great refuges from sightseeing.

**InterContinental Financial
Street Beijing** ¥¥¥
11 Jinrong Jie (Fucheng Men Nan Dajie)
Tel *(010) 5852 5888*
W intercontinental.com
Although far from tourist sights,
spacious rooms are good value
with plasma TVs, impressive
bathrooms, and tasteful, modern
decor throughout.

JW Marriott Hotel Beijing ¥¥¥
83 Jianguo Lu, Chaoyang district
Tel *(010) 5908 6688*
W marriott.com
With a great selection of food
and beverage outlets, the JW is
popular with locals. Located in
the CBD with good facilities, it's
also good for business travelers.

Park Hyatt Beijing ¥¥¥
*2 Jianguomenwai Dajie,
Chaoyang district*
Tel *(010) 8567 1234*
W beijing.park.hyatt.com
In one of the city's tallest skyscrapers, this hotel overshadows
its competition in service and
style. Rooms are chic, understated,
and filled with amenities.

The Peninsula Beijing ¥¥¥
8 Jinyu Hutong, Dongcheng district
Tel *(010) 8516 2888* **Map** 2 B5
W beijing.peninsula.com
The *grande dame* of Beijing's
luxury hotel scene is within
walking distance of Tian'an Men
Square and the Forbidden City.
Superb service.

Sofitel Wanda Beijing ¥¥¥
*93 Jianguo Lu, Tower C, Wanda
Plaza, Chaoyang district*
Tel *(010) 8599 6666*
W sofitel.com
Expect sober, stylish rooms
where everything is controlled

with a push of a button. Excellent
staff who understand what
business travelers want.

Waldorf Astoria ¥¥¥
5–15 Jinyu Hutong
Tel *(010) 8520 8989* **Map** 2 B5
W waldorfastria3.hilton.com
Opened in 2015, offering sizeable,
well appointed rooms, some
overlooking the Forbidden City.
Rates include butler service.

Shanghai

Purple Mountain Hotel ¥¥
778 Dongfang Road
Tel *(021) 6886 8888*
W pmhotel.com.cn
Close to Shanghai's convention
centre, this five-star hotel offers
spacious, stylish rooms and great
views of Pudong.

**Hotel Indigo Shanghai
on the Bund** ¥¥¥
585 Zhongshan 2 Road
Tel *(021) 3302 9999* **Map** 3 D4
W shanghai.hotelindigo.com
Set on the iconic waterfront,
this hotel makes the most of its
location with reclaimed artifacts
from Shiliupu Dock in the lobby.

Park Hyatt Shanghai ¥¥¥
100 Century Avenue, Pudong
Tel *(021) 6888 1234* **Map** 3 E3
W shanghai.park.hyatt.com
One of the tallest hotels in the
world, occupying floors 79–93 of
the SWFC, with giddying views
of the city. There is a great pool
and spa, and morning *tai chi*
sessions are offered.

Pudong Shangri-La ¥¥¥
33 Fucheng Road
Tel *(021) 6882 8888* **Map** 3 D3
W shangri-la.com
Comprising a stately tower and
newer river wing, this is one of
the largest hotels in the city.
Exceptional butler service.

For more information on types of hotels *see pp180–81*

Soothing neutral tones at the Waldorf Astoria Shanghai on the Bund

Le Royal Meridien ¥¥¥
789 Nanjing Dong Lu, Huangpu district
Tel *(021) 3318 9999* **Map** 2 B2
W starwoodhotels.com
Despite a confusing layout, this is a pleasant hotel, with open-plan bedrooms featuring stunning floor-to-ceiling windows.

Shanghai Farther Afield

Shangri-La Suzhou ¥¥
168 Tayuan Lu, Suzhou
Tel *(0512) 6808 0168*
W shangri-la.com
Impeccable five-star service and a great central location. Rooms are enormous, with stunning bathrooms and oversized showers.

Xihu State Guest House ¥¥¥
8 Yanggongdi, West Lake
Tel *(020) 8600 9099*
W xihustateguesthangzhou.com
A peaceful and well-appointed house on the banks of the famous lake. Popular so book ahead.

Historic/Courtyard
Beijing

4 Banqiao ¥
4 Banqiao Hutong, Beixinqiao, Dongcheng district
Tel *(010) 8403 0968* **Map** 2 C2
W 4banqiao.com
In Beijing's most historical *hutong* area. Rooms are furnished to a high standard with antiques and handmade bedspreads.

Courtyard 7 ¥
7 Qiangulouyuan Hutong, Nanluoguxiang, Xicheng District
Tel *(010) 6406 0777* **Map** 2 B2
W courtyard7.com
A tastefully converted 300-year-old courtyard hotel set back off one of Beijing's most interesting *hutongs*. Rooms have been sympathetically modernized.

For key to prices *see p182*

Red Lantern House ¥
5 Zhengjue Hutong, Xinjiekou Nandajie, Xicheng district
Tel *(010) 8328 3905* **Map** 1 E2
W redlanternhouse.com
This cute, family-run hostel/hotel may be hard to find, but persevere if you want to stay in a traditional and excellent-value *siheyuan*.

Duge Courtyard Hotel ¥¥¥
26 Qianyuanensi Hutong, Nanluoguxiang, Dongcheng district
Tel *(010) 6406 0686* **Map** 2 B2
W dugecourtyard.com
Exclusive and flamboyantly colorful, this luxurious hideaway was part-designed by a jeweler; each of the ten rooms is unique.

Shanghai

Astor House Hotel ¥¥
15 Huangpu Lu
Tel *(021) 6324 6388* **Map** 2 D2
W astorhousehotel.com
Shanghai's longest-running hotel is a glorious timewarp with basic but comfortable rooms. Great location minutes from the Bund.

Broadway Mansions ¥¥
20 Suzhou North Road
Tel *(021) 6324 6260* **Map** 2 C1
W broadwaymansions.com
This historic brick building looms over Suzhou Creek off the Bund. Eight room types at varying prices.

Taiyuan Villa ¥¥
160 Taiyuan Road
Tel *(021) 6471 6688* **Map** 1 D5
W ruijinhotelsh.com
Perfect for history buffs; past guests include Ho Chi Minh. Polished wood and curios abound and outside is a delightful garden.

InterContinental Ruijin ¥¥¥
118 Ruijin 2 Road
Tel *(021) 6472 5222* **Map** 1 F5
W ihg.com
Few hotels have such grand history as this – it was once the

headquarters of the Communist Party in Shanghai. Chairman Mao and Zhou Enlai both stayed here.

DK Choice

Mansion Hotel ¥¥¥
82 Xinle Lu, Xuhui district
Tel *(021) 5403 9888* **Map** 1 D4
W chinamansionhotel.com
In a 1930s mansion built for one of Shanghai's most powerful vice lords, this beautifully renovated, very expensive hotel in the heart of the French Concession captures the essence of old Shanghai. Rooms are understated but opulent.

Waldorf Astoria Shanghai on the Bund ¥¥¥
88 Sichuan Zhong Lu
Tel *(021) 6322 9988* **Map** 2 C3
W waldorfastoria3.hilton.com
Award-winning hotel situated on the Bund, offering unparalleled service, luxury amenities, and spectacular skyline vistas.

Waterhouse at South Bund ¥¥¥
3 Maojiayuan Road, Huangpu district
Tel *(021) 6080 2918* **Map** 3 D5
W waterhouseshanghai.com
This 1930s warehouse is now a swanky boutique hotel filled with designer furniture. The restaurant is a destination in itself.

Luxury
Beijing

DK Choice

Aman at Summer Palace ¥¥¥
1 Gongmenqian Jie, Haidian district
Tel *(010) 5987 9999*
W amanresorts.com
Fit for an emperor, this stunning hotel consists of converted Summer Palace courtyards to sleep in, linked up by covered walkways in stunning grounds. Guests enjoy private access to the UNESCO heritage site as well as a cinema, stylish spa, and subterranean swimming pool. The restaurant – like the hotel – is impressively expensive.

Rosewood Beijing ¥¥¥
Jinguang Centre, Hujialou, Chaoyang district
Tel *(010) 6597 8888* **Map** 2 F4
W rosewoodhotels.com
Elegantly styled hotel featuring eye-catching modern Chinese design and artworks, and offering exquisite service and fine dining.

Temple Hotel ¥¥¥
23 Shatan North Street
Tel *(010) 8401 5680*   **Map** 2 B4
ⓦ thetemplehotel.com
Formerly a Tibetan Buddhist temple, years of restoration work have transformed this into the city's most luxurious art hotel.

Beijing Farther Afield
Sunrise Kempinski ¥¥¥
8 Jia, Yanshui Road, Yanqi Lake
Tel *(010) 6961 8888*
ⓦ kempinski.com
With great views of the Great Wall and nine bars and restaurants, this lakeside resort aims to be the perfect retreat from the city.

Shanghai
Hyatt on the Bund ¥¥¥
199 Huangpu Lu, Hongkou district
Tel *(021) 6393 1234*   **Map** 3 D1
ⓦ shanghai.bund.hyatt.com
Offers "casual luxury" at the north end of the Bund. Contemporary flair and the latest mod cons, with a great spa and restaurant.

The Peninsula Shanghai ¥¥¥
32 Zhongshan Dong Yi Lu, near Beijing Dong Lu, Huangpu district
Tel *(021) 2327 2888*   **Map** 2 C2
ⓦ peninsula.com
Regularly voted one of the world's best business hotels, the Pen combines 1930s elegance with 21st-century amenities.

DK Choice
The Puli Hotel and Spa ¥¥¥
1 Changde Road, Jing'an district
Tel *(021) 3203 9999*   **Map** 1 D3
ⓦ thepuli.com
Sleek "urban resort", with over 200 spacious rooms featuring complimentary Wi-Fi and mini bars, a knockout restaurant, and glamorous spa. A calm oasis in a bustling part of Shanghai.

The Ritz-Carlton Shanghai, Pudong ¥¥¥
Shanghai ifc, 8 Century Ave, Pudong
Tel *(021) 2020 1888*   **Map** 2 E3
ⓦ ritzcarlton.com
Luxe high-rise with modern art-deco interiors, floor-to-ceiling views in the rooms, and one of Pudong's hippest rooftop bars.

Shanghai Farther Afield
Suzhou Pan Pacific ¥¥
259 Xinshi Road, Suzhou
Tel *(0512) 6510 3388*
ⓦ panpacific.com/suzhou
The architecture is impressive, reflecting the heritage of old

Suzhou; the central building is based on the Panmen Gate. Inside are all mod cons including a luxury spa; many rooms have outstanding views of the tranquil, traditional gardens.

Amanfayun ¥¥¥
22 Fayun Jie, Xi Hu Jie, Hangzhou
Tel *(0571) 8732 9999*
ⓦ amanresorts.com
An ultra-expensive resort hidden in a picturesque valley and surrounded by beautiful tea fields.

Fuchun Resort ¥¥¥
339 Jiangbin Dongdadao, Dongzhou Jiedao
Tel *(0571) 6341 9500*
ⓦ fuchunresort.com
With its traditional architecture and state-of-the-art facilities, this lakeside resort, about 30 minutes' drive from Hangzhou, is impressive. The private villas are its crowning glory.

Modern
Beijing
Emperor Beijing Forbidden City ¥¥
33 Qihelou Jie, Dongcheng district
Tel *(010) 6526 5566*   **Map** 2 B4
ⓦ theemperorbeijing.cn
Injecting some contemporary style into the Forbidden City area, this hotel has modern, colorful rooms and stylish modular furniture.

Nuo Hotel Beijing ¥¥¥
2A Jiangtai Road, Chaoyang district
Tel *(010) 5926 8888*
ⓦ nuohotels.com
Elegant new hotel blending modern comforts with Ming-themed design, and a stunning Chinese art collection displayed throughout, curated by world-famous artist Zeng Fangzhi.

The **Opp**osite House ¥¥¥
1 Sanlitun Bei Lu, Chaoyang district
Tel *(010) 6417 6688*   **Map** 3 F3
ⓦ theoppositehouse.com
Part club, part hipster hotel, with three restaurants and a great café. The contemporary green glass exterior is more *Blade Runner* than traditional Beijing.

W Hotel Chang'an ¥¥¥
No. 2 Jianguomennan Avenue
Tel *(010) 6515 8855*   **Map** 5 E1
ⓦ starwoodhotels.com
Very recently opened, with all the latest must-haves including fully wired technology and a tranquil Bliss® Spa.

Beijing Farther Afield
Commune by the Great Wall ¥¥¥
Badaling Expressway Exit 20, Shuiguan Section
Tel *(010) 8118 1888*
ⓦ commune.com.cn
A popular retreat for Beijing-based expats, offering rooms and suites in striking, architect-designed villas set in spectacular natural surroundings, with private access to a part of the Great Wall.

Shanghai
Andaz Xintiandi ¥¥¥
88 Songshan Road
Tel *(021) 2310 1234*   **Map** 2 A4
ⓦ shanghai.andaz.hyatt.com
Part of the Hyatt chain, this new hotel has tech-savvy rooms with complimentary Wi-Fi, iPad docking, and customizable colored LED lighting system.

Urbn Hotel ¥¥¥
183 Jiaozhou Lu, near Beijing West Road, Jing'an district
Tel *(021) 5153 4600*   **Map** 1 D3
ⓦ www.urbnhotels.com
China's first carbon-neutral hotel, blending sustainable credentials with elegant design, chic styling, and high-tech amenities.

Shanghai Farther Afield
Pinjiangfu Suzhou Hotel ¥¥
60 Bai Ta Dong Lu, Suzhou
Tel *(0512) 6770 6688*
ⓦ pingjiangpalace.com
Traditional yet contemporary retreat surrounded by the classic gardens of Suzhou. Smart, contemporary interiors.

The stunning Skyrise atrium at the Hyatt on the Bund

For more information on types of hotels see see pp180–81

WHERE TO EAT & DRINK

Once you dine in Beijing or Shanghai, you may start to question your prior conceptions of Chinese food. The local restaurants in these two cities serve up cuisines of such variety and delight that it will quickly dissolve memories of the pale imitations of Chinese food experienced back home. Beijing's slender wheat noodles, *jiaozi* dumplings, and roast duck are vastly different from Shanghai's rope-like noodles, *shengjian* fried buns, and braised crabs. But both cities also offer the best of China's regional cuisines, from fiery Sichuanese and Hunanese, and subtle Cantonese (quite different from that served at home), to the lesser-known sweet and fruity tastes of Yunnan in the southwest, the vinegary noodles of Shanxi, and the hard-to-define but always excellent dishes of the Hakka (Kejia) minority of the southeast. Chinese consider the opportunity to sample different foods one of the main reasons to travel, and so should you.

Elegant interiors of Crystal Jade *(see p201)*, a popular Cantonese restaurant

Types of Restaurant

Whether you are looking to eat in the splendor of an imperial pavilion in Beijing or a chic Shanghai emporium, you will find a restaurant boom taking place in China. Entrepreneurs are thinking up tempting new ways to indulge in the country's favorite pastime. You never have to walk far to find restaurants in China and when you do, do not let first appearances put you off – many gourmet restaurants boast simple decor and harsh lighting. Look instead for happy crowds of diners and a different concept of atmosphere: in Chinese eyes, the more lively and noisy *(renao)* a restaurant is, the better.

Open All Hours

You can breakfast on the street by 6am, but all hotels should serve breakfast until 10am. Lunch is typically from 11am until 1pm, after which some restaurants shut until the evening shift starts around 5pm. However, there are plenty of restaurants that are open all day and some that offer 24-hour dining. It's always wise to book well-known restaurants in advance, particularly in Shanghai, but unnecessary at the cheaper, hole-in-the-wall type joints.

Hotel Food

If you are tired and hungry, and staying at one of China's more expensive hotels, then room service can provide the usual international fare, and un-challenging made-for-foreigners Cantonese one-dish meals.

In Beijing and Shanghai, it used to be the case that all the best restaurants were in hotels but these days, diners who venture outside the comfort of four- or five-star hotels will reap handsome dividends.

Street Food

Street-food vendors are a vital part of the everyday life of China, selling cheap and popular foods such as dough sticks *(youtiao)* and beancurd *(doujiang)* for breakfast, or snacks like scallion pancakes *(jian bing)*, sweet potatoes *(shanyu)* roasted in old oil drums, deep-fried beancurd cubes *(zha doufu)*, and local fruits. A reliable way to locate delicious street food is to stroll through a night market *(ye shi)*, a culinary and visual feast where clouds of vapour escape from bamboo steamers, and the sky glows red from the flames of oil-drum stoves. The sizzle of cooking and clamor of vendors should stir your appetite, and if deep-fried scorpions or cicadas prove too exotic, plenty of other foods will take your fancy. If the food is hot and freshly cooked, hygiene problems are rare. The market off Wangfujing Street *(see p76)* in Beijing is the most famous of the night markets.

Scorpion *kabobs* (kebabs) – cooking renders the sting ineffective

Steaming food on the street – simple, fast, and efficient

Little Eats

Cheap and nourishing snacks such as those found at night markets are known collectively as *xiao chi*, or "little eats." Restaurants that specialize in them are called *xiao chi dian*; they sell different types of noodles or dumplings, stuffed buns, or pancakes. Open early for breakfast, they may serve simple stir-fried dishes too, and shut only when the last guest leaves. The setting is usually basic, but the food is hearty, tasty, and very reasonably priced.

The very visible success of Western fast-food restaurants (McDonald's and KFC are everywhere) has led to local restaurant chains adopting the same style to serve native Chinese fast-food dishes and snacks. These are generally far tastier and healthier than their Western counterparts.

The Other China

Beijing and Shanghai show-case not only regional cuisine from all over Han China, but also a whole range of ethnic specialties belonging to the 55 minority nationalities, from the Korean border to the Tibetan plateau. Minorities' restaurants are an "exotic" attraction for Chinese as well as foreign tourists. In some Dai restaurants, offering the Thai-like cuisine of southern Yunnan, guests are greeted with scented water, given a lucky charm, and may later be invited to join in the singing and dancing. In more upmarket Uighur restaurants, serving lamb-heavy dishes from the Muslim northwest, belly dancing is sometimes included as part of the entertainment.

Vegetarian Surprise

Rice and chopsticks

The Chinese understanding of a good life is inextricably associated with meat. They find it hard to understand why someone who could afford to eat meat would choose not to. Nevertheless, you will find an increasing number of vegetarian restaurants in Beijing and Shanghai. Some use soya protein to imitate meat with extra-ordinary authenticity. Others simply use Chinese cooking methods to bring out the best in pulses and vegetables. Ordinary restaurants can lay on good vegetarian meals too, as long as you can repeat, "Wo shi chi su de. Wo bu chi rou," ("I'm vegetarian. I don't eat meat").

International Food

Almost all kinds of foreign food, from Brazilian to Indian can be found in Beijing and Shanghai. Italian is probably the most popular of Western cuisines, ravioli and spaghetti being easy concepts for the dumpling- and noodle-loving Chinese to appreciate. Some have justifiably earned wide acclaim, such as Mercante in Beijing, and Mercato in Shanghai. Other Asian cuisines, namely Korean, Japanese, Indian, and Thai, are also well represented, and more readily accepted by the chopstick-wielding Chinese.

Recommended Restaurants

In our restaurant recommend-ations (pp196–203), we've aimed to choose as wide a selection as possible, from inexpensive to upscale, and while majoring on the various Chinese cuisines, there are also plenty of options, from great cafés to Western fare with an Asian twist. The extra-special eateries we've selected as DK Choices are the best of the best – whether they offer an amazing atmosphere, sophisticated wine list, or the freshest and most delicious food available, you can be sure that they are well worth a visit.

Eating together, an important aspect of Chinese social life

Dining Etiquette

The Chinese are quite informal at meal times. Confucius may have been renowned for his silence while eating, but these days a busy Chinese restaurant can be a deafening place as waiters crash plates about and diners shout orders at the waiters. It may seem daunting but just join in and expect praise for your chopstick skills – even if you struggle, your willingness to try will be appreciated.

Dinner in a private room, a popular Chinese way of doing business

Earning Some Face

The Chinese do not expect visitors to be fully versed in proper banquet etiquette, but awareness of a few essentials can earn "face" both for yourself and your host, whatever the occasion. The other guests will appreciate that you have some respect for Chinese culture and traditions.

When attending, or hosting, a formal meal, note that the guest of honor is usually placed on the seat in the middle, facing the door. The host, who was traditionally positioned opposite the guest, now more often sits to his or her left.

If you come as a guest, be punctual and do not sit down until you are given your seat – seating arrangements can be very formal and based on rank. Once seated, do not start on the food or drink before your host gives the signal. Some of the delicacies on offer may test your courage but it is an insult if the food is untouched. Leave some food on the plates: empty bowls imply that the host is too poor or mean to lay on a good spread. In addition to

the above, there are further rules that should be kept in mind. If you are applauded as you come into the room, don't feel shy about applauding back. Reply to any welcome toast with your own (short) speech and toast. In your speech and any subsequent conversation avoid broaching sensitive subjects, in particular Chinese politics.

Show respect to your elders and superiors by ensuring that the rim of your glass is lower than theirs when clinking glasses, and drain your drink in one swift movement.

The Art of Ordering

If you are someone's guest, you may be asked to order something, or state some sort of preference – if you do not do so, a ten-course banquet could soon appear. Feel free to name your favorite dish, or point at the object of your desire, possibly something swimming in a fish tank at the entrance to the restaurant. Freshness is all-important in Chinese cuisine.

A meal might begin with cold starters such as pickled vegetables, seasoned jellyfish, or cold roasted meats. Main courses should be selected for harmony and balance. A typical order would be a variety of different meats and vegetables, cooked in different and complementary ways. The last dish, or *cai*, is usually soup. Then comes *fan*, a grain staple such as rice, noodles, or bread *(mantou)*, without which a Chinese diner may feel they have not eaten. At informal meals, you can have rice at the start of the meal – although you may want to remind the waiting staff of this – but not at a banquet, or your host will assume his dishes are inadequate.

English-language menus are becoming more common. An increasing number of restaurants actively encourage visitors to get out of their chairs and choose ingredients from tanks, cages, and super-market-type shelves. Your Chinese friends (and waiters and onlookers) will likely be delighted by any interest you show

A variety of dim sum dishes – no need to finish them all

in the whole experience. In the end, when language or phrase book fail, simply look around and point at whatever appeals on other tables, or even head into the kitchen to find what you want.

Invited to Dinner

A formal meal often takes place in a private room and usually begins with a toast. The host serves his guest with the choicest morsels, and then everyone is permitted to help themselves. Simply watch others for guidelines on when to use serving utensils, and when, more informally, your own chopsticks will suffice.

Only in restaurants regularly frequented by lots of foreigners, or which also have Western dishes on the menu, will knives and forks be available.

Seafood – abundant in Beijing and Shanghai

The host almost always orders more dishes than is necessary. While it is, as stated earlier, polite to try everything, it is far from necessary to finish it all.

Dos and Don'ts

The Chinese are fairly relaxed about table manners. Slurping shows appreciation, enables better appreciation of flavor, and sucks in air to prevent burning the mouth. Holding your bowl up to your mouth, to shovel rice in, is another practical solution. You may happily reach across your neighbors, but do not spear food with your chopsticks, and do not stand them upright in a bowl of rice either, as this looks like an offering to the dead. If you have finished with the chopsticks, lay them flat on the table or on a rest. You shouldn't suck greasy fingers, or use them to pick bones out of your mouth – spit bones or shell onto the table, into the saucer that was under your bowl, or

How to Hold Chopsticks

1 Place the first chopstick in the crook of your thumb and forefinger. Support it with the little and ring fingers, and keep it there with the knuckle of the thumb.

2 Hold the second chopstick like a pencil, between middle and index fingers, anchored by the pad of your thumb.

3 When picking up food, keep the lower stick stationary and the tips even. As the index finger moves up and down, only the upper stick should move, using the thumb as an axis.

Third finger acting as a rest for the lower stick

Thumb and first finger controlling the top stick

more delicately into a napkin. Toothpicks are ubiquitous, but do cover the action with your free hand. And generally don't be shy about shouting for attention as enthusiasm for food is much appreciated. Eating alone is alien to the Chinese way of thinking. They believe that eating in a group – sharing both the dishes and the experience – significantly increases the enjoyment.

The End of the Meal

A platter of fresh fruit and steaming hot towels signal the end of the meal is coming. In more formal meals, just as you should await the start of a meal, do not stand up before your host, who will rise and indicate that the dinner has ended and ask if you've had enough. The correct answer is always "yes."

Dining outdoors in Shanghai, possible for much of the year

The person who invited you usually shoulders the full weight of the bill, so accept graciously. Offering to pay is fine, even polite; insisting too hard suggests that you doubt the host's ability to pay.

Prices are fixed and written down in most restaurants, and on bills. Tipping is not necessary and the only places that include a service charge are the upmarket restaurants within hotels. These are also the only places likely to take international credit cards.

Party Food

In a culture that is obsessed with both symbolism and eating, many foods have earned special meaning and must be consumed on set occasions. Round mooncakes, dotted with moon-like duck egg yolks, are a must at Mid-Autumn Festival. At Spring Festival, the whole family cooks *tangyuan*, round sweet dumplings made of glutinous rice flour, because *yuan* can also mean "reunion." Fish is auspicious, because the character for fish (*yu*) sounds like the one for "abundance" and offers the hope of good fortune in the year ahead. Meat dumplings (*jiaozi*) are another New Year favorite as their shape is said to resemble the symbol for prosperity. Birthdays are often celebrated with noodles, a symbol of longevity, while red beans are a metaphor of longing and love. To celebrate new arrivals, parents hand out eggs painted red for luck – an even number for a boy, an odd number for a girl.

What to Eat in Beijing

Communities developed beside the Yellow River before 6000 BC, but it is not until about 1500 BC, when written records started, that a picture of the dietary habits of the ancient Chinese becomes clear. They kept pigs and grew millet, wheat, barley, and rice and even fermented their grain to make alcoholic beverages. Later (around 1100 BC), soybeans were added to the Chinese diet, then byproducts such as soy sauce and beancurd (tofu). Late-founded Beijing had no distinctive cuisine of its own, but as the center of a mighty empire, it imported elements and influences from a variety of sources.

Chinese leaf, also known as Tianjin cabbage

Candied apples, a common Beijing street food

The Palace Kitchen

Kublai Khan made Beijing the capital in 1271 and brought simple Mongolian influences to the imperial kitchens – lamb, roasting, and the hotpot. These were foods that did not require a lot of equipment, ideal for pastoral nomads and armies on the move. Elaborate preparation

and expensive ingredients – shark's fin, bird's nest soup, and abalone, all imported from the south – feature as well as artistic presentation and poetic names. Beijing cuisine can be summed up as the distillation of the creations of generations of Imperial Palace chefs over almost a millennium.

Mongolian and Muslim Cuisine

One highly successful alien invader is the Mongolian hotpot, a simple one-pot dish. Although Buddhists, the Mongol minority within China are not vegetarians – their traditional nomadic lifestyle made vegetable

Marinated roast duck

Steamed pancakes

Scallions

Sliced cucumber

Special duck sauce

A whole Peking duck with traditional accompaniments

Regional Dishes and Specialties

Peking duck – an Imperial meal – must be the best-known dish in north Chinese cuisine. The duck, a local Beijing variety, is carefully dried, and then brushed with a sweet marinade before being roasted over fragrant wood chips. When ready, it is carved by the chef and eaten wrapped in pancakes with a special duck sauce, and slivered scallions and cucumbers. To accompany the duck, diners might also be served duck liver pâté, and duck soup to finish. Beijing is also known for a wide variety of cold dishes that start a meal, for stuffed breads and pastries, and for *jiaozi* (dumplings). Look out for *zha jiang mian* (Clanging Dish Noodles), in which ingredients are added at the table to a central bowl of noodles, the bowls loudly clanged together as each ingredient goes in.

Duck pears – like a duck's head

Mu xu pork: stir-fried tiger lily buds, scrambled egg, black fungus, and shredded pork – eaten with pancakes.

growing impractical, and the hotpot is served with a choice of finely shaved lamb or beef, or sometimes more exotic meats. Modern Beijing has a great many dedicated hotpot restaurants, and it is one of the cheapest ways of group eating.

Chinese Muslims are treated as a separate ethnic minority in China, known as the Hui, with enclaves in every major city. Beijing also has small pockets of Turkic Uighur people from the Xinjiang region of the Northwest, also Muslim, so none eat pork. Xinjiang men, originally from the far north-west of China, can often be found hunched over troughs of coals at the streetside, selling *kao rou chuan*, or lamb kabobs dusted with cumin. Another Uighur specialty, widely available in Beijing, are thick *lao mian* or "pulled noodles" made by endlessly doubling, twisting, and stretching a rope of dough.

Some of the wide variety of foods on display at a night food market

The art of pouring tea, exhibited in a Beijing restaurant

Shandong

Shandong is the birthplace of Confucius, and its cuisine is generally regarded as the oldest and best in China. Shandong has produced the largest number of famous master chefs, and it is said that the iron wok originated here. Most of the Chinese influences in Beijing cooking come from this province. As one of the most important agricultural areas of China, Shandong supplies Beijing with most of its ingredients – its main crops are wheat, barley, sorghum, millet, and corn. Additionally, fisheries are widely developed along the Yellow River and the north China coast, particularly the Shandong peninsula where the specialties are all kinds of fish, shrimp, shellfish, abalones, sea slugs, and sea urchins.

ON THE MENU

Drunken empress chicken
Supposedly named after Yang Guifei, an imperial concubine overly fond of her alcohol.

Stir-fried kidney-flowers
These are actually pork kidneys criss-cross cut into "flowers" and stir-fried with bamboo shoots, water chestnuts, and black fungus.

Fish slices with wine sauce
Deep-fried fish fillet braised in a wine sauce.

Phoenix-tail prawns King prawn tails coated in batter and bread crumbs, then deep fried.

Lamb in sweet bean sauce
Tender fillet of lamb sliced and cooked in sweet bean paste with vinegar to give it that classic sweet and sour taste.

Hot candied apples
A popular Chinese dessert.

Lamb and scallions: sliced lamb rapidly stir-fried with garlic, leeks or scallions, and sweet bean paste.

Mongolian hotpot: thinly sliced lamb, vegetables, and noodles dipped in boiling water and an array of sauces.

Sweet and sour carp: the quintessential Shandong dish, traditionally made with Yellow River carp.

What to Eat in Shanghai

Shanghai draws its population from neighboring provinces, and these people have brought with them their regional tastes and preferences. The surrounding provinces are traditionally referred to as the "Lands of Fish and Rice," and indeed the Yangtze River delta is one of the country's leading agricultural regions with some of the most fertile land. Both wheat and rice are grown here as well as barley, corn, sweet potatoes, peanuts, and soybeans. Freshwater fisheries abound in the network of lakes and rivers, while deep-sea fishing has long been established on the coast.

Garlic chives
and bok choi

Market stall displaying the wide variety of dried goods available

Shanghai

The characteristics of Shanghai cuisine are summarized as "exquisite in appearance, rich in flavor, and sweet in taste." A favorite ingredient is the hairy crab from the Yangzi estuary (although overfishing means they actually come from elsewhere nowadays) and the eel. The sweetness and oiliness of many Shanghai dishes is balanced by lighter elements from neighboring older

schools of cuisine – Huaiyang and Suzhe. Among the dishes Shanghai is famous for are its thick fried noodles, *shengjian mantou*, which are bread dough balls stuffed with meat and "steamed in oil," and *xiao long bao*, little pasta sacks filled with pork, crab meat, and scalding soup. Calling both of these *mantou* rather than *bao* as elsewhere in China marks you out as a local. The distinctive pungent smell of *chou doufu*, or "stinky" tofu, invented not far away in Shaoxing, is also found gusting around Shanghai streets.

Lotus root | Dried bean curd skin | Fine bean noodles

White fungus

Black fungus | Hair moss | Dried mushrooms | Tiger lily buds

Eight-Treasure Buddha's Special ingredients

Regional Dishes and Specialties

Two of the area's great cities, Nanjing and Hangzhou, were at different times dynastic Chinese capitals. Whenever there was a change of capital, the vast imperial kitchens changed location, bringing the staff with them, resulting in a cross-fertilization of recipes and methods from one region to another. One favorite imperial dish, despite its lowly name, is Beggar's Chicken – a whole chicken is stuffed with vegetables and herbs, wrapped in lotus leaves, and encased in clay before being baked. The clay container is then broken at the table, releasing the beautifully concentrated aromas. (For hygiene reasons, top hotels find clayless solutions to achieve the same delicious result.) Another specialty is *Dongpo rou*, a soya pork dish named for the Song poet exiled to Hangzhou. Freshwater crabs are best during the months of October and November.

Fermented bean curd

Lions' heads: pork meatballs braised with Chinese leaf – meant to look like lions' heads and manes.

Huaiyang and Suzhe

Based specifically around the deltas of the Huai and Yangzi Rivers, Huaiyang cuisine is most famous for its excellent fish and shellfish – the freshwater crabs from the waters of Tai Hu are superb. Suzhe cuisine, however, covers a wider area – the provinces of Jiangsu and Zhejiang – and includes culinary centers such as Nanjing and Hangzhou, which both once served as capital cities. Along with stews flavored with a light stock, the region is famous for its "red cooking" – food braised in soy sauce, sugar, ginger, and rice wine. "Chinkiang Vinegar" is black rice vinegar from Zhenjiang, Jiangsu, and is acknowledged to be the best rice vinegar in China.

The province of Zhejiang, of course, produces China's best rice wines from Shaoxing and top quality hams from Jinhua. It is also worth trying the Long Jing (Dragon Well) green tea grown around West Lake in Hangzhou.

Park cafés – popular places to snack on some filled dumplings

Hairy crabs, a Shanghai delicacy

Anhui

Shanghai is also influenced by the little known Anhui cuisine, from farther inland. Despite being landlocked, Anhui still enjoys a fish-rich diet thanks to its extensive network of lakes and rivers. The province is also another of the key agricultural regions in China, and it produces a great number and variety of crops and vegetables. One of Anhui's most famed ingredients are its tender white bamboo shoots. These crisp shoots feature large in the vegetarian cuisine prepared in the Buddhist mountain retreats and are often combined with a variety of exotic woodland mushrooms. Finally, the world-famous Keemun red tea comes from the hills of Yimeng in south Anhui.

ON THE MENU

Beggar's chicken A whole chicken stuffed with flavorings and cooked in a clay pot.

Fried prawns in shells Prawns still in their shells are rapidly fried and then braised in a soy and tomato sauce.

Three-layer shreds Steamed shredded ham, chicken, and pork with bamboo shoots and black mushroom – should be called five-layer shreds.

Freshwater crabs Simply steamed with scallions, ginger, soy, sugar, and vinegar.

Steamed belly pork with ground rice Also known as Double-Braised Pork, this long-cooked dish literally melts in the mouth.

Eight-Treasure Buddha's Special A generic name for a delicious vegetarian dish which can actually contain any number of different ingredients.

Tofu casserole: tofu with sea cucumbers, ham, prawns, mushrooms, bamboo shoots, and bok choi in a stew pot.

Squirrel fish: a bream is filleted, coated with batter, deep-fried, and served with a sweet-and-sour sauce.

Sweet and sour spare ribs: deep-fried, bite-size pork spare ribs braised in soy, sugar, and vinegar.

What to Drink

Tea, of course, is the most popular drink in China. There are countless arguments for drinking the infusion of the bush *Camellia sinensis*, and just as many legends about its origin. But if tea is the most popular drink, there is a wide range of others for the visitor. Beer is popular with meals and wine is available in many upscale restaurants. Chinese spirits can range from the extremely pleasant to the almost dangerous. Likewise, approach the "health tonics," like snake wine, with caution – as if the reptilian "sediment" in the bottle isn't enough, they can be fiercely alcoholic.

Tea may be served both during and after a meal

Types of Tea

Green is the most common tea, baked immediately after picking. Flower tea is a mixture of green tea with flower petals. Black tea colors during the fermentation process and the reddish brew that results explains its Chinese name – red tea. The most highly prized is oolong, a lightly fermented tea, and Longjing tea from Hangzhou. Brick tea is black or green, pressed into blocks. Eight Treasure tea, *babaocha*, has many ingredients including dates, dried longan, and wolfberry, and Tibetans enjoy yak butter tea.

Gaiwan or three-piece tea cup

Lid keeps leaves in the cup, not the mouth

Saucer to prevent fingers burning

Black: *hongcha*, actually called "red tea" in Chinese.

Green: *lucha*, uses leaves dried without fermentation.

Pu'er: from Yunnan, is compressed into "bricks."

Flower: *huacha*, a mix of petals – jasmine, rose, and chrysanthemum.

The famous "Hairy Peak" green tea

Coffee: as café culture enters China, coffee drinking is fashionable among the middle classes. Starbucks may have an outlet inside the Forbidden City, but freshly-ground coffee is rare outside major hotels.

Tea and coffee drink: those who want a fashionable coffee drink but cannot do without their daily shot of tea can try this blend of tea and coffee.

Soft drinks

Even as a cold drink, tea is dominant. Iced tea is very popular, especially with the young. Besides the usual array of fruit juices, there is hawthorn juice in Beijing, pomegranate juice from Xinjiang, and lychee and sugar cane juice from down south. As well as the global drink brands, local challengers include Tianfu Cola, and the energy drink Jianlibao, made with honey. As China overcomes its dairy aversion, milk and yoghurt drinks multiply, as well as soya-bean (*doujiang*) and coconut milk.

Bamboo cane juice

Iced green tea

Coconut milk drink

Beer

The Germans first introduced beer to China in the early 20th century, giving Tsingtao beer the reputation it has today; in the 21st century, China has taken over as the world's biggest brewer. Both Beijing and Shanghai have their own local breweries.

Tsingtao beer

Yanjing beer

Wine

Although grape seeds traveled the Silk Roads, China has historically preferred grain alcohol. The quality is rapidly improving, but red wine is still a safer order than white – considered good for the heart, and a lucky color too.

Great Wall

Dragon Seal

Spirits

For millennia the Chinese have been distilling grains into *baijiu* or "white spirits" ranging from strong to deadly. They are classified into three types: the *qingxiang*, or light bouquet, group includes Fenjiu from Shaanxi; Guizhou's famous Maotai is a classic *jiangxiang*, soy bouquet; *nongxiang*, strong bouquet, is championed by Sichuan giant Wuliangye.

Maotai, "eight times fermented and seven times distilled," is favored for toasts at banquets. At the other end of the scale, *erguotou* is cheap and effective – the people's drink.

Rice wine

Despite being called "wine," some care is required as this can vary in strength from a mild 15–16% alcohol, to the double- or triple-fermented wines at up to 38% ABV. Good rice wine is best drunk warm and goes well with cold starters.

Shaoxing rice wine

Maotai

Erguotou

Shaoxing: this is among the best of the *huangjiu* (yellow spirits), noted for its moderate alcohol content (about 16%) and mellow fragrance.

Strong rice wine

Drinking Culture

Chinese youth drinking in a local modern teahouse

Teahouses are enjoying something of a revival in China, as appreciation of traditional tea culture recovers after years of proletarian austerity. While *cha* (tea) stimulates quiet contemplation, *jiu* (alcohol) lubricates noisy celebrations. Despite reveling in the drunkenness of their poets such as Li Bai *(see p24)*, the Chinese have not been as badly affected by alcoholism as many other societies. Public drunkenness is frowned upon – except maybe in the ever more popular karaoke (known as KTV) bars. Traditionally only soup was drunk with meals, but this is changing, especially when eating with foreigners. "Gan bei!" or "dry the cup" is the repeated clarion call to toasting bouts and drinking games. Beware the legendary drinking capacity of the northeast Chinese, and don't drink alone or on an empty stomach.

Where to Eat and Drink

Beijing

Baoyuan Dumpling Restaurant ¥
Regional Chinese
6 Maizidian Jie
Tel *(010) 6586 4967*
Beijing's most colorful dumplings – the skin is colored with vegetable and fruit juices. Try the crispy rice and pork.

Bellagio ¥
Regional Chinese   Map 3 E3
6 Gongti Xilu, south of the Gongti 100 Bowling Alley
Tel *(010) 6551 3533*
The best-known Taiwanese food chain in Beijing. The *sanbei* chicken is to die for, as are the smashed-ice desserts. Open until 5am.

Biteapitta ¥
Middle Eastern   Map 3 F3
201 Tongli Studio, 43 Sanlitun North, Sanlitun Houjie
Tel *(010) 6467 2961*
Hummus, tasty pittas, and other Middle Eastern fare are offered by this bright Sanlitun eatery.

The Corner Melt ¥
Café   Map 3 E3
55 Xingfucun Zhonglu
Tel *(010) 6415 3713*
A hip dive bar dedicated to grilled cheese sandwiches. Look out for the funky graffiti outside the venue. Sandwiches come with comforting sides like tomato soup for dipping.

Crescent Moon Xinjiang Restaurant ¥
Regional Chinese   Map 2 C3
16 Dongsi Liutiao, 100m (300ft) west of Chaonei Beixiaojie
Tel *(010) 6400 5281*
Possibly the best Xinjiang cuisine in town, thanks to the chunky lamb kebabs, hearty chicken stews, and home-made yoghurt.

Ding Ding Xiang ¥
Regional Chinese
D6006, 6th floor, Shin Kong Place, 87 Jianguo Lu
Tel *(010) 6530 5997*
One of the most famous hotpot chains in Beijing. The Thai soup-base pot and the rib soup are the best known. Try the sesame dip sauce and traditional Beijing baked sesame cake.

Donghuamen Night Market ¥
Regional Chinese   Map 2 B5
Dong'anmen Da Jie
This touristy and fun market sells snacks from all over China from

Healthy US-style breakfast dishes are servered at Moka Bros café

the ordinary (dumplings and chicken skewers) to the bizarre (starfish and bugs on a stick). Prices are very reasonable.

Element Fresh ¥
Café   Map 3 F3
S8-31, Sanlitun Taikoo Li South, 19 Sanlitun Nan Lu
Tel *(010) 6417 1318*
Great service, inexpensive Western classics and good coffee make this bright and sleek restaurant busy from breakfast time to evening. The fresh and healthy salads are a must.

Han Cang ¥
Regional Chinese   Map 2 A3
12 Qianhai Nanyan, Houhai
Tel *(010) 6403 5866*
This rustic venue serves food from the Hakka ethnic minority, who settled in southern China. In the evenings, Han Cang attracts crowds keen for its earthy, hearty specialties like prawns on a stick baked in salt.

DK Choice

Huajia Yiyuan ¥
Regional Chinese   Map 2 C2
235 Dongzhimen Nei Dajie
Tel *(010) 6405 1908*   **Closed** CNY
For a fun, genuine *renao* experience (busy and noisy – just how the locals like it) this is a great destination for Beijing staple dishes. Beijing duck is a good choice, as is the spicy crayfish – be sure to use the plastic gloves that staff will hand you, as it's messy stuff. There are often performances from live Chinese opera shows or magicians.

Jin Ding Xuan ¥
Regional Chinese   Map 2 C1
77 Hepingli Xijie
Tel *(010) 6429 6699*
A famous Cantonese restaurant near Lama Temple which is open 24 hours a day. Despite having three floors of seating, there's often a queue. The *dim sum* here is fantastic.

Kong Yiji ¥
Regional Chinese   Map 1 F2
A2, Dongming Hutong, Deshengmen Neidajie
Tel *(010) 6618 4917*
Zhejiang cuisine in a beautiful *hutong* courtyard right by Houhai. Shrimp and fish dishes are the highlights.

Let's Burger ¥
Café   Map 3 F2
B1/F, Sanlitun Taikoo Li North, Sanlitun Road
Tel *(010) 6415 2772*
Fab burgers and milkshakes served up in a fun, stylish setting – the massive array of delicious condiments and accompaniments is impressive.

Little Yunnan ¥
Regional Chinese   Map 2 B2
28 Donghuangchengge
Tel *(010) 6401 9498*
This famous courtyard restaurant near the National Art Museum serves excellent Yunnan cuisine. Try their signature mint tea shrimps and stewed beef with mint leaves.

Lotus in Moonlight ¥
Vegetarian   Map 3 E3
East gate of Workers' Stadium, Gongti Dong Lu
Tel *(010) 6268 0848*
Delicious, healthy vegetarian fare in a relaxed atmosphere with high-quality ingredients transported from Wutaishan. Specialties include Qing Liang Shan Tai mushrooms.

Middle 8th ¥
Regional Chinese   Map 3 F2
S8-40, 4th floor, Bldg 8, Sanlitun Taikoo Li South, Sanlitun Nan Lu
Tel *(010) 6415 8858*
Serves fresh-tasting and spicy Yunnanese cuisine in a lively

setting. It's famous for its mushroom dishes; try the freshly flown-in mushrooms and ribs wrapped in leaves.

Moka Bros
Café   ¥   **Map** 3 F2
B101b, South Building, Nali Patio, 81 Sanlitun Road North
Tel *(010) 5208 6079*
Organic, healthy, and hearty eats are served up at this stylish café, best-known for its freshly made granola and crepes, which you can wash down with some of the best coffee in Beijing. Decor is industrial chic.

Najia Xiaoguan
Beijing Cuisine   ¥
10 Yong'anxili, Jianguomenwai
Tel *(010) 6567 3663*
Qing dynasty-style Beijing cuisine is served at this traditional courtyard eatery, which is reassuringly popular among locals as well as being very reasonably priced. The crispy-skin shrimp is the top dish here; try the stir-fried chicken with walnuts too.

One Pot
Korean   ¥   **Map** 3 F3
B1-238, Tower 2, Sanlitun SOHO, 8 Gongti Beilu
Tel *(010) 5935 9475*
Korean street food prepared with a Western twist. The beer chicken is a signature dish, along with the ginger tiramisu. Decor is chic and industrial.

Private Kitchen 44
Regional Chinese   ¥   **Map** 1 F2
70 Deshengmen Neidajie
Tel *(010) 6400 1280*
Guizhou cuisine served in a *hutong* courtyard. The homemade rosé rice wine is popular, as is the sour-soup fish. There is a rooftop garden perfect for summertime.

The Rug
Café   ¥
1st floor, Bld 4, Lishui Jiayuan, Chaoyanggongyuan Nanlu
Tel *(010) 8550 2722*
Healthy and organic food is on offer in this chic but relaxing café. The brunch menu is the best in town. Try the homemade bagels.

Saveurs de Coree
Korean   ¥   **Map** 2 B2
128-1 Xiang Er Hutong, Jiaodaokou
Tel *(010) 5741 5753*
Top MSG-free Korean food in a lovely *hutong* setting. As well as an à la carte menu, there are two hugely popular set menus which allow guests to sample all their signature dishes.

DK Choice

Siji Minfu
Beijing Cuisine   ¥   **Map** 2 C3
32 Dengshikou Xijie
Tel *(010) 6513 5141*
For Beijing duck *par excellence*, head to this bustling eatery, which specializes in the city's most famous dish. Enjoy the theater of the glossy duck being sliced wafer-thin at your table by an expert carver. It's advisable to book way in advance as this restaurant regularly features in the media.

Susu
Vietnamese   ¥   **Map** 2 B3
10 Qianliang Hutong Xixiang
Tel *(010) 8400 2699*   **Closed** *Mon*
Locals love the Vietnamese cuisine on offer at this *hutong* venue – book ahead to secure a rooftop table with beautiful views. Must-orders include Vietnamese street food dishes such as the fresh spring rolls. Curries are also good.

The Taco Bar
Café   ¥   **Map** 3 E3
Unit 10, 4 Gongti Beilu
Tel *(010) 6501 6026*   **Closed** *Mon*
Enormously popular thanks to great food and modern and hip decor; expect to queue if you have not booked. The tacos are a popular choice. Try the sangria.

A Thousand and One Nights
Middle Eastern   ¥   **Map** 3 F3
3–4 Gongti Bei Lu
Tel *(010) 6532 4050*
Authentic Arabic cuisine with hookahs and belly dancing. The kebabs are delicious, as is the hummus. There are some Syrian dishes on the menu, too.

The Tree
Italian   ¥   **Map** 3 F3
Friendship Hostel, 43 Bei Sanlitun Nan
Tel *(010) 6415 1954*
One of the oldest Western spots in town, deservedly popular thanks to its brick pizza oven. There's also Belgian beer on tap.

Three Guizhou Men
Regional Chinese   ¥
Solana Shopping Park, 6 Chaoyang Park Road
Tel *(010) 5905 6855*
Guizhou restaurant inside the Solana mall; sour-soup fish is the most famous dish, along with the mint-and-chilli lamb. There is outdoor seating for sunny days. Look out for the creepy paintings.

The Veggie Table
Café   ¥   **Map** 2 B1
19 Wudaoying Hutong
Tel *(010) 6446 2073*
Vegan and organic food served in a cosy setting with a menu that spans the world – the Indian dishes and Middle Eastern favorites like hummus are big hits.

Vineyard Café
Café   ¥   **Map** 2 C1
31 Wudaoying Hutong, off Yonghegong Dajie
Tel *(010) 6402 7961*   **Closed** *Mon*
This converted courtyard down an obscure *hutong* is a great place to refuel on Western staples. The coffee is good, as is the comforting mac 'n' cheese.

Agua
Spanish   ¥¥   **Map** 3 F2
4th floor, Nali Patio, 81 Sanlitun Beilu
Tel *(010) 5208 6188*
Spanish Chef Jordi Valles excels at this fine dining restaurant, an outpost of the Hong Kong flagship. The suckling pig is excellent, as is the seafood.

The plush and elegant dining room at Spanish restaurant Agua

For more information on types of restaurants *see pp186–7*

Brian McKenna's sophisticated but unstuffy restaurant at The Courtyard

Da Dong ¥¥
Regional Chinese
Bldg 3, Tuanjiehu Beilu
Tel *(010) 6582 4003*
Famous for its Beijing roast duck; there is often a queue outside so book ahead. Inside, the decor may be glitzy but prices are keen.

DK Choice

Dali Courtyard ¥¥
Regional Chinese   Map 2 B2
67 Xiaojingchang Hutong, Gulou Dong Dajie
Tel *(010) 8404 1430*
One of the most beautiful courtyard restaurants in Beijing, this laid-back venue serves up spicy and unusual Yunnanese dishes. There's a fixed-price menu and no choice, aside from a separate vegetarian menu. If you're lucky, Yunnan goats cheese and cured ham will be on the menu.

Factory by Salt ¥¥
Café
Factory A1 North, 797 Middle Street, 798 Art Zone A
Tel *(010) 5762 6451*   **Closed** *Mon*
Creative fusion cuisine by the chef of the former popular SALT. White and modern interior, with a terrace looking over Lido park.

Hatsune ¥¥
Japanese   Map 3 F2
S8-30, 3rd floor, Sanlitun Taikoo Li South, 19 Sanlitun Road
Tel *(010) 6415 3939*
Where the in-crowd come to eat sushi. Purists may object to the interpretations of classic dishes, but for fresh and funky sushi, this place is unbeatable.

Huang Ting ¥¥
Regional Chinese   Map 2 B5
B2, Peninsula Palace Hotel, 8 Jinyu Hutong
Tel *(010) 8516 2888 ext. 6707*
Arguably the best *dim sum* in the city, served by stylish waitresses in *qipaos*. The slate-grey interior

is decorated with salvaged stonework from demolished courtyard houses and Ming Dynasty antiques.

Jing Yaa Tang ¥¥
Regional Chinese   Map 3 F2
B1/F, The Opposite House, 11 Sanlitun Road North
Tel *(010) 6410 5230*
Upscale, affordable venue for Beijing duck. They also have Sichuan and Cantonese cuisine for a full taste of China.

Karaiya Spice House ¥¥
Regional Chinese   Map 3 F2
S9-30, 3rd floor, Bldg 8, Sanlitun Taikoo Li South, 19 Sanlitun Road
Tel *(010) 6415 3535*
A Westerner-friendly take on spicy Hunan fare in central Sanlitun. The classic dishes here are ribs covered with spicy peanut sauce and steamed mandarin fish.

Lost Heaven ¥¥
Regional Chinese   Map 3 F5
Unit G, 23 Qianmen Dong Dajie, Dongcheng District
Tel *(010) 8516 2698*
Yunnan cuisine in the courtyard of the former US embassy. The huge terrace dinning area has a view towards the courtyard and old-style buildings. Try the famous truffle steamed cod.

Migas ¥¥
Spanish   Map 3 F2
6th Floor, Nali Patio, 81 Sanlitun Lu Chaoyang district
Tel *(010) 5208 6061*
Fun and artsy; the huge rooftop patio is the place to go in summer. The set lunch menu is good value and changes each week.

Mosto ¥¥
Café   Map 3 F2
3rd floor, Nali Patio, 81 Sanlitun Beilu
Tel *(010) 5208 6030*
Modern southern American, Mediterranean, and European light dishes on a simple

one-page menu. Warm and welcoming, with chic decor.

My Humble House ¥¥
Regional Chinese
L2-12, Parkview Green, 8 Dongdaqiao Lu
Tel *(010) 8518 8811*
Regional Chinese fusion cuisine with a modern twist, situated in the most artsy mall in Beijing.

Village Café ¥¥
Café   Map 3 F2
The Opposite House, 11 Sanlitun Road North
Tel *(010) 6410 5210*
Book ahead at this airy café inside the hip Opposite House hotel. Popular for long, leisurely weekend brunches.

DK Choice

Brian McKenna @ The Courtyard ¥¥¥
Fine Dining   Map 2 B5
95 Donghuamen Dajie
Tel *(010) 6526 8883*
A new incarnation of an old favorite thanks to the takeover of the Courtyard by one of Beijing's best-known chefs. The fun and creative menu, attentive service, and fabulous views of the Forbidden City make this a meal to remember. Don't miss the signature dessert: a chocolate Terracotta Warrior.

Capital M ¥¥¥
Fine Dining   Map 4 C2
3rd floor, 2 Qianmen Pedestrian Street
Tel *(010) 6702 2727*
Wonderful for a special dinner or Sunday brunch while soaking up the views of Tian'an Men Square. The most celebrated dishes are crispy suckling pig and the slow-baked, salt-crusted leg of lamb.

Duck de Chine ¥¥¥
Regional Chinese   Map 3 F3
1949 The Hidden City, 4 Gongti Bei Lu
Tel *(010) 6501 8881*
Head here for Beijing's leading specialty. The stylish decor attracts an arty crowd. Duck is served with non-traditional, French-style sides.

Made in China ¥¥¥
Regional Chinese   Map 2 B5
Grand Hyatt, 1 Dong Chang'an Jie
Tel *(010) 8518 1234 ext. 3608*
This sophisticated and sleek venue brings a crisp, modern sensibility to Chinese dining and is much beloved by the wealthy. The Beijing duck is a star attraction, as is the wine list.

Mercante ¥¥¥
Italian **Map** 2 A2
4 Fangzhuanchang Hutong
Tel *(010) 8402 5098* **Closed** *Mon*
The best Italian in town; the home-made pasta and stuffed gnocchi are rightly famous. The warm ambience, along with the exceptional service, keeps fans coming back for more and the wine list is considered one of Beijing's best.

Okra ¥¥¥
Japanese **Map** 3 F3
1949 The Hidden City, Courtyard 4, Gongti Beilu
Tel *(010) 6593 5087* **Closed** *Mon*
Sushi and sashimi are must-order menu choices here; both are creatively made and extremely fresh. The set menu changes according to the seasons to ensure the finest ingredients. Cocktails are pricey but worth every penny. They also make their own ice-cream.

Opera Bombana ¥¥¥
Italian
Unit 21, B2/F, Parkview Green, 9 Dongdaqiao Lu
Tel *(010) 5690 7177*
One of the few restaurants in Beijing with Michelin star chefs. Offers reasonably priced set menus at lunch time, accompanied by a fantastic wine list.

Beijing Farther Afield

Cuan Yun Inn ¥
Regional Chinese
No. 23 Cuandixia Village
Tel *(010) 6981 9788* **Closed** *CNY*
Located right inside the village. The roast leg of lamb prepared here is so famous that it regularly features on Chinese TV.

Homey decor at Mercante, deservedly popular for its Italian cuisine

Dongpo Restaurant, Simatai ¥
Beijing Cuisine
Simatai Great Wall, 100 m (300 ft) north of main entrance
Tel *(0136) 1314 3252*
Grab an outdoor table for the most incredible view of the Great Wall. The menu may be simple but the ingredients are mostly home-grown by the friendly owners. Menu in English.

Kangling Zhengde Chunbing #25 ¥
Regional Chinese
#25 Courtyard, Kangling Village, Shisanling Town
Tel *(010) 8972 1120* **Closed** *CNY*
Since the time of Emperor Zhengde, *chunbing* (spring pancake) is traditionally eaten on the first day of Spring. All of the restaurants in this village next to Zhengde's tomb sell *chunbing*, but this cute eatery is the most famous.

Paulaner Bräuhaus ¥
German
Sunrise Kempinski Hotel, 18 Jia, Yanshui Road, Yanqi Lake, Huairou district
Tel *(010) 6961 8888* **Closed** *Tue, Sun*
Located in the brand-new Kempinski Hotel. Enjoy freshly brewed beer as you eat classic German dishes such as crispy-skinned pork knuckle and its world-famous sausages.

The Schoolhouse at Mutianyu ¥
Café
Mutianyu Town, Huairou district
Tel *(010) 6162 6505*
In a renovated schoolhouse by the Great Wall. The organic, healthy dishes are made using fresh, local ingredients. A great stop for lunch if visiting the Mutianyu section of the Wall.

Xiaolumian ¥
Beijing Cuisine
130 Yingbeigou Village
Tel *(010) 6162 6506* **Closed** *Nov–March; all weekdays*
Run by the same team as The Schoolhouse. Serves traditional handmade noodles and dumplings in an authentic village house.

Green T. House Living ¥¥
Modern Chinese
318 Cuige Zhuang Xiang, Hegezhuang Village
Tel *(010) 6434 2519*
This creatively designed space is part museum, spa, hotel, and fine dining restaurant, all mixed into one. The cuisine is equally creative and guests can also enjoy fabulous views of the Great Wall. It's in the countryside and a little tricky to find, so it's worth asking the cab driver to phone ahead for directions.

The Orchard ¥¥
Italian
Behind the Beijing Riviera, Hegezhuang Village, Cuigezhuang Township
Tel *(010) 6433 6270* **Closed** *Mon*
Feel a world away from the city at this stunning place, which is also a popular wedding venue. All ingredients on the modern Italian menu are home-grown and organic.

Terrace Lounge ¥¥
International
Commune by the Great Wall, Exit 53 at Shuiguan, G6 Jingzang Highway
Tel *(010) 8118 1888*
The casual restaurant at boutique resort Commune by the Great Wall. Enjoy spectacular views of the Wall from the terrace as you munch on a burger or steak.

Fine dining and simple modern styling at Temple Restaurant Beijing

For more information on types of restaurants *see pp186–7*

Shanghai

Blue Frog ¥
Café **Map** 3 E3
Shanghai World Financial Centre,
B/F, 100 Century Avenue
Tel *(021) 6877 8668*
When you need a taste of
America, this well-run bar and
café hits the spot. There's a great
happy hour every day with half-
price drinks and food. The
burgers are their specialty.

Bohemia Café and Bar ¥
Café **Map** 2 A4
42 Lane 248, Taikang Lu
Tel *(021) 6415 0065*
Popular cosy café which offers
indoor and outdoor seating and
great people-watching on this
trendy pedestrianized street.
The coffee is worth a detour for,
as are the authentic panini.

Cha's ¥
Regional Chinese **Map** 1 F5
30 Sinan Lu
Tel *(021) 6093 2062*
Reservations aren't taken here
so expect queues no matter
what time of day. People flock
to enjoy the traditional decor of
a 1950s Hong Kong diner and
the delicious Cantonese food
on offer.

Cyclo ¥
Vietnamese **Map** 2 B1
678 Shanxi Bei Lu
Tel *(021) 6135 0150*
The colorful decor at this casual
Vietnamese eatery is appealing,
as are the *pho* and spring rolls.
A good budget option is the set
lunch with *pho* and Vietnamese
sandwiches.

Din Tai Fung ¥
Regional Chinese **Map** 2 A4
2nd floor, House 6, South Block,
Xintiandi, Lane 123, Xinye Lu
Tel *(021) 6385 8378*
Unforgettable *xiao long bao*
dumplings and other steamed
goodies combine with fab
service from this Taiwanese
chain. Unusually for China,
there's a children's play area.

Element Fresh ¥
Café **Map** 1 E3
Shanghai Centre, 1/F, 1376 Nanjing
Xi Lu
Tel *(021) 6279 8682*
This friendly local casual eatery
is one of several located across
Shanghai and serves good
Western staples like healthy
salads, sandwiches and pasta.
It's a particularly popular brunch
option at weekends.

Guyi ¥
Regional Chinese **Map** 1 D4
87 Fumin Lu
Tel *(021) 6249 5628*
Local dining institution serving
the dry-spicy cuisine of China's
Hunan province. Expect to
queue at mealtimes for moreish
dishes like the signature cumin-
dusted ribs.

Hang Yuen Hin ¥
Regional Chinese
290–292 Wanping Lu, inside
Xujiahui Park
Tel *(021) 6472 9778*
Set in a park is one of Shanghai's
best *dim sum* restaurants. On
weekends, lunchtime *dim sum* is
half-price. The crab dishes are fab,
and don't miss the egg tarts.

Hanguo Chufang ¥
Korean **Map** 2 A5
1277 Fuxing Zhong Lu
Tel *(021) 6471 1639*
Opened by a Korean couple who
wanted to bring casual Korean
dining to Shanghai. The set lunch
menus are largely black-rice-
based and make for healthy and
wholesome meals.

DK Choice

Jia Jia Tang Bao ¥
Regional Chinese **Map** 1 D5
90 Huanghe Lu, by Fengyang Lu
Tel *(021) 6327 6878*
One of the top contenders for
Shanghai's best *xiao long bao*
dumplings – here called *tang*
bao, or pork soup dumplings.
It's by no means fancy and
don't expect service with a
smile, but the dumplings make
up for the lack of atmosphere.
You may have to queue, pay in
advance, and be expected to
eat and then go, but it is more
than worth it.

Kota's Kitchen ¥
Japanese **Map** 1 E5
10 Baoqing Lu, near Fuxing Lu
Tel *(021) 6404 2899*
Shanghai's very own Beatles-
themed restaurant has a couple
of branches in the city, with an
ever-present queue of people
eager to eat at this *yakitori* joint.
The pork ramen is a winner.

Lanna Coffee ¥
Café **Map** 1 D3
8 Yuyuan Dong Lu
Tel *1801 767 8867*
The only café outlet of the
organic Lanna coffee-bean brand
from Yunnan province. Good for
takeout or a speedy lunch
perched at sidewalk tables.

Mi Xiang Yuan (Holy Cow) ¥
Shanghainese
608 Xiaomuqiao Lu
Tel *(021) 3356 6100*
Very popular among office
workers in the area looking for a
healthy and quick lunch. Dishes
are traditional Shanghainese –
try their lunch rice sets and the
xiao long bao dumplings.

Mr Pancake House ¥
Café **Map** 1 E2
877 Wuding Lu
Tel *(021) 6255 1648*
The most famous chain in
Shanghai for pancakes and waffle
sets for brunch. A recreation of a
simple American diner. Opens
early in the morning.

Shanghai Chic ¥
Shanghainese **Map** 2 C3
5th floor, 489 Henan Lu
Tel *(021) 6335 7779*
Famous spot for locals to have
wedding dinners or birthdays.
The signature dishes here are
the braised pork belly and
smoked fish.

Whisk ¥
Café **Map** 1 D4
1250 Huaihai Zhong Lu, by
Changshu Lu
Tel *(021) 5404 7770* **Closed** *Mon*
Guests with a sweet tooth flock
here for everything chocolate-
related. The espresso with hot
chocolate is fabulous, as are the
double-chocolate cupcakes.
Stylish setting.

Wishbone ¥
Western **Map** 1 E3
No. 3, 888 Changde Lu
Tel *(021) 6257 8511*
Hip yet cosy dinner spot in
northern Jing'an specializing

The striking modern interior of Crystal Jade
in Xintiandi

in fingerlicking rotisserie chicken and creative sides, along with craft beers and cocktails.

Wujie ¥
Vegetarian
392 Tianping Lu
Tel *(021) 3469 2857*
Creative fusion vegetarian cuisine that you order through an iPad. If you understand Chinese, the friendly waiters will tell you where the ingredients are from and how they make every dish.

DK Choice

Xibo ¥
Regional Chinese **Map** 1 D4
3rd floor, 83 Changshu Lu
Tel *(021) 5403 8330*
This Xinjiang restaurant has a modern and hip atmosphere with concrete walls, planters of rustling bamboo and funky music playing in the background. There's a huge outside seating area, perfect for summertime. If you're hungry, try the *da pan ji*, which literally means "huge plate of chicken."

Yang's Fry Dumplings ¥
Shanghainese **Map** 1 F2
2nd floor, 269 Wujiang Road
Tel *(021) 6136 1391*
Fried *shengjian* soup dumplings, filled with pork and sprinkled with sesame seeds, are sold here around the clock. Whatever time of day or night, there is a queue.

Yuan Yuan ¥
Regional Chinese **Map** 1 E3
4th floor, Westgate Mall, 1038 Nanjing Xi Lu
Tel *(021) 6272 6972*
Shanghainese restaurant serving flavorful and sweet dishes with efficient staff in a down-to-earth atmosphere. Book ahead as it gets packed out.

The Commune Social ¥¥
Fine Dining **Map** 1 E2
511 Jiangning Lu
Tel *(021) 6047 7638* **Closed** *Sun eve, Mon, pub hols*
Acclaimed British chef Jason Atherton's restaurant is famous for modern, creative tapas. The upstairs bar has a huge terrace. Reservations are not accepted so come prepared to queue.

Crystal Jade ¥¥
Regional Chinese **Map** 2 A4
Xintiandi, South Block Plaza, 2nd floor, 123 Xingye Lu
Tel *(021) 6385 8752*
High quality Cantonese *dim sum* from this Asian chain, which has

Glass-enclosed dining room at Xibo overlooking the outside tables

several branches in Shanghai. The prawn noodles are excellent, as are the *xiao long bao* dumplings.

Elefante ¥¥
Spanish **Map** 1 D4
20 Donghu Lu, near Huaihai Zhong Lu
Tel *(021) 5404 8085* **Closed** *Mon*
This sleek and stylish restaurant and deli is run by Spanish chef El Willy. The indecisive had better beware: the menu is enormous. Among its highlights are a vast array of cheeses and a classic tapas selection.

Garlic ¥¥
Middle Eastern **Map** 1 D5
698 Yongjia Lu
Tel *(021) 5424 3332*
Traditional Middle Eastern cuisine; while the decor is modern, there is a fireplace in the middle that makes it popular in cold weather. There's a kids play area too. The roast lamb is the best in town.

Haiku by Hatsune ¥¥
Japanese **Map** 1 D5
28 Taojiang Lu
Tel *(021) 6445 0021*
A slick and stylish California-style Japanese restaurant and sushi bar. Purists might be appalled by roll fillings such as cream cheese and Beijing duck, but it's fun, and delicious. Booking essential.

Mercato ¥¥
Italian **Map** 3 D5
6th floor, 3 on the Bund, 3 Zhong-shan Dong Yi Lu, near Guang-dong Lu
Tel *(021) 6321 9922*
Excellent-value, relaxed Italian cuisine from Jean-Georges Vongerichten. The Pizza Lounge is a major attraction, as is the Mercato Bar which features an original selection of cocktails.

Scarpetta ¥¥
Italian
33 Mengzi Lu
Tel *(021) 3376 8223*
A cosy, warm and welcoming Italian trattoria. The pasta with clams is popular, and the slow-roasted pork rib is another signature dish.

DK Choice

Shanghai Tang Café ¥¥
Shanghainese **Map** 2 A5
373 Huangpi Nanlu
Tel *(021) 6377 3333*
Fashionable and modern Shanghainese cuisine; decor is bright and colorful, as befits the fashion chain that runs it. Almost every table orders the Bird Nest decorated shrimp. There is also a rooftop terrace with lamps so you can admire the rooftops of old Shanghai. Attentive staff.

Sichuan Citizen ¥¥
Regional Chinese **Map** 1 E4
30 Donghu Lu
Tel *(021) 5404 1235*
Lively diner with red-painted interiors and cane ceiling fans that serves the chilli-laced cuisine of China's Sichuan province, renowned for being mouth-numbingly delicious. Wash it down with one of their signature basil-drop martinis.

Table No.1 ¥¥
Café **Map** 3 D5
The Waterhouse at South Bund Hotel, 1–3 Maojiayuan Road
Tel *(021) 6080 2918*
On the ground floor of a boutique hotel is the chic but casual Table No.1, the second restaurant by British Michelin-starred chef Jason Atherton. The emphasis is on large plates for sharing. Decor is hip and minimalist.

For more information on types of restaurants *see pp186–7*

Well-executed Italian classics from pizza to roasted Serrano pork at Henkes

Tsukiji Aoasora Sandaime ¥¥
Japanese   **Map** 1 E4
191 Changle Lu
Tel *(021) 5466 1817*
Authentic Japanese cuisine from the sister restaurant to a famous Tokyo eatery, popular with expats craving sushi. The standout dish is the tuna *nigiri*, but for a selection of greats, try the sushi sets.

Whampoa Club ¥¥
Fine Dining   **Map** 2 C2
5th floor, 3 Zhongshan Dong Yi Lu
Tel *(021) 6321 3737*
The only Chinese restaurant in 3 on the Bund, with a luxurious traditional Chinese interior: walls are covered with silk and ostrich skin. The view over the river and the Bund is jaw-dropping.

Ye Shanghai ¥¥
Shanghainese   **Map** 2 A4
338 Huang Pi Nan Road, Xin Tiandi
Tel *(021) 6311 2323*
This upmarket and attractively decorated restaurant, which has sister venues in Hong Kong and Tokyo, serves distinctive interpretations of Shanghai classics.

8 1/2 Otto e Mezzo Bombana ¥¥¥
Italian
6th floor, 169 Yuanmingyuan Lu
Tel *(021) 6087 2890*
Fantastic Italian cuisine near the Bund with a slinky bar. As well as a seasonal à la carte, there is a degustation menu worth trying on special occasions.

Char ¥¥¥
Steakhouse   **Map** 3 D4
Hotel Indigo, 29–31/F,
585 Zhongshan Dong Er Lu
Tel *(021) 3302 9995*
The best steaks in town. All meat is imported and brought to your table for you to choose prior to cooking. Superb views over the Bund and the river, and the upstairs bar has a terrace.

Henkes ¥¥¥
Italian   **Map** 1 E3
Reel Mall, 1601 Nanjing Xi Lu
Tel *(021) 3253 0889*
Enjoy the huge menu of Italian classics and other European dishes on offer. It's a popular destination in summer thanks to its large outdoor seating area surrounded by greenery.

Jade on 36 ¥¥¥
French   **Map** 3 D3
Pudong Shangri-La, Level 36, Grand Tower, 33 Fu Cheng Road, Pudong
Tel *(021) 6882 8888 ext. 6888*
Beautifully styled, contemporary French restaurant located on the 36th floor of the sleek Pudong Shangri-La hotel. Offers sweeping views over the Huangpu river and the Shanghai skyline from its floor-to-ceiling windows. The attached bar is great for a pre- or post-dinner cocktail, with similarly impressive vistas.

Jean Georges ¥¥¥
French   **Map** 3 D5
4th floor, 3 Zhongshan Dong Yi Lu
Tel *(021) 6321 7733*
One of the best French restaurants in town, opened by NYC celebrity chef Jean Georges. It has some seriously good views over the Bund area. Cuisine is creative French with an Asian twist.

DK Choice

M on the Bund ¥¥¥
Fine Dining   **Map** 2 C3
7th floor, Five on the Bund, 20 Guangdong Lu
Tel *(021) 6350 9988*
One of Shanghai's oldest Western restaurants never disappoints, with its sophisticated pan-European cuisine. The lunch menu features delicious dishes such as pappardelle pasta tossed with goose confit, red radicchio, and Parmesan shavings. If the weather is fine, book one of the sought-after tables on the elevated Bund-front terrace.

Man Ho ¥¥¥
Fine Dining   **Map** 2 B3
4th floor, Marriott Hotel City Centre, 555 Xizang Zhong Lu
Tel *(021) 2312 9732*
Shanghainese and Cantonese cuisine served in traditional surroundings, with waitresses wearing *qipaos*. The lunchtime *dim sum* buffet is good value.

Mr and Mrs Bund ¥¥¥
French   **Map** 3 D5
6th floor, Bund 18, 18 Zhongshan Dong Yi Lu
Tel *(021) 6323 9898*
Renovated in early 2015, the latest incarnation of one of Shanghai's best Western restaurants, with a spectacular view, is as busy as ever. Booking is essential. Dinner only.

Shintori ¥¥¥
Japanese   **Map** 1 E3
803 Julu Lu
Tel *(021) 5404 5252*
Built in a minimalist industrial warehouse with lofty ceilings and an open kitchen. There is no sign outside; just follow the bamboo path to an automatic door. Booking is advisable.

DK Choice

Ultraviolet ¥¥¥
Fine Dining
Various Locations   **Closed** *Sun, Mon*
Opened by celebrity chef Paul Pairet, this wildly expensive and whimsical restaurant offers its 20-course menu combined with a multi-sensory concept to just 10 guests a night. Diners rendezvous at and depart from sibling restaurant Mr and Mrs Bund *(see above)* to a "secret" dining location across the city Think of it as a performance rather than a simple meal.

Yongfoo Elite ¥¥¥
Fine Dining
200 Yongfu Lu
Tel *(021) 5466 2727*
In the setting of the former UK embassy, an upmarket crowd enjoy fusion Chinese fare in an ornate room filled with antique Chinese furniture. This is old Shanghai at its finest.

Shanghai: Farther Afield

Amanfayun Steam House ¥
Regional Chinese
Aman Fayun Hotel, 22 Fayun Nong, Hangzhou
Tel *(0571) 8732 9999*
Set within a picturesque village that has been transformed into a 5-star resort, Steam House provides simple Hangzhou family-oriented dishes cooked to perfection. The pork belly is simply the best and the service impeccable. There are terraces for outside dining.

The Bookworm ¥
Café
77 Gunxiufang, Shiquan Jie,
Suzhou
Tel *(0512) 6526 4720*
Part café, part wine bar, part
library, this small outpost belongs
to a small but popular chain. The
standard Western café menu
includes good brunch dishes.

Chuanfu Laozaofang ¥
Regional Chinese
*1–7 Bifengfang, Guanqian
Jie, Suzhou*
Tel *(0512) 6522 8877*
The biggest and oldest branch
of this traditional chain famous
for Sichuan food. Live opera
performances accompany
your dinner.

Deyue Lou ¥
Regional Chinese
43 Taijian Nong, Suzhou
Tel *(0512) 6522 2230*
Fantastic restaurant in Suzhou
for local dishes, boasting 400 years
of history. The squirrel-shaped
mandarin fish is the most famous
Suzhou dish and a must-order.

Green Tea Restaurant ¥
Regional Chinese
83 Longjing Lu, Hangzhou
Tel *(0571) 8788 8022*
Part of a small local chain serving
modern Hangzhou food. This
location is the biggest and most
beautiful, set by a small pond.
Expect huge queues.

Hupe ¥
Regional Chinese
Bldg A, 581 Huoju Dadao, Hangzhou
Tel *(0571) 2810 2796*
Modern and chic decor and
welcoming staff. You can find
Chinese dishes from all over the
country here, each given a
modern twist. Try their famous
braised ox tongue.

Mamala ¥
Café
#12 Loft 49, 111 Tongyi Lu, Hangzhou
Tel *(0186) 5719 8257*
Lofty and industrial-styled
Mediterranean restaurant in a
creative art zone. The crispy
flounder fish is their most
ordered dish.

Pingjiang Lodge Fusion
Restaurant (Shanfang) ¥
Regional Chinese
33 Niujia Xiang, Suzhou
Tel *(0512) 6523 3888*
An old converted mansion, this
restaurant is very popular thanks
to its location by the canals.
Diners can enjoy both local
and Western dishes. Worth
booking ahead.

Sawasdee Thai Restaurant ¥
Thai
*2nd floor, Wyndham Grand Plaza
Royale Hotel, 555 Fengqi Lu,
Hangzhou*
Tel *(0571) 8761 6888*
The best Thai food in town,
opened by a Thai lady with a
talented team. Shrimp cake
and the curry dishes are the
smart choices.

Songhelou ¥
Regional Chinese
72 Taijian Nong, Suzhou
Tel *(0512) 6770 0688*
This restaurant dates back to the
Qing dynasty and is still popular;
reservations are a must. Try the
famed squirrel-shaped mandarin
fish and enjoy the lively and
bustling atmosphere.

Weizhuang Zhiweiguan ¥
Regional Chinese
10–12 Yanggong Di, Hangzhou
Tel *(0571) 8797 0568*
Located right by West Lake
and famous for local snacks like
xiao long bao dumplings. The

back section overlooking the
lake is for sit-down meals only.

28 Hubin Road ¥¥
Fine Dining
*Hangzhou Hyatt Hotel, 28 Hubin Lu,
Hangzhou*
Tel *(0571) 8779 1234 ext. 2828*
Authentic local cuisine served
in a luxurious environment.
Dongpo pork and the intricate
desserts are must-orders.
Reservations recommended.

La Pedrera ¥¥
Spanish
*4 Baishaquan, Shuguang Lu,
Hangzhou*
Tel *(0571) 8886 6089*
Spanish cuisine for diners looking
for a change from Chinese food.
Paella and the ham platter are
signature dishes. Good wine list.

Provence ¥¥
French
*1 Baishaquan, Shuguang Lu,
Hangzhou*
Tel *(0571) 8797 6115*
Popular restaurant, now in its
seventh successful year, set in
a beautiful French-style house.
Food is classically cooked and
there is an excellent wine list.

DK Choice

Gui Yu Restaurant ¥¥¥
Fine Dining
*2–11 Manjuelong Lu, West Lake,
Hangzhou*
Tel *(0571) 8797 7677*
Located in the Longjing mountains by West Lake, this huge
restaurant is set in a mansion
in the forest. The modern
menu offers a wide range of
chinese classics and great
seafood and vegetarian
options. Private dining rooms
are also available for hire.

Ultraviolet; a multi-sensory dining experience held in various locations around Shanghai *(see p202)*

For more information on types of restaurants *see pp186–7*

SURVIVAL GUIDE

PRACTICAL INFORMATION

China has been through an explosion in both international and domestic tourism, so most accessible sights get very crowded, especially during the summer season. Due to the absence of any non-profit network of tourist information centers, visitors are often forced to ask hotels for guidance, which can be far from reliable. China International Travel Service branches, listed on page 207, can also be problematic and local competitors or private tourist companies may be better a

better option. A thorough reading of this and other books before departure is recommended. In Beijing and Shanghai, the tourist infrastructure, including transportation, hotels, and restaurants, is mostly on a par with international standards. However, communication still poses some difficulties, as English is not spoken everywhere, though standards have improved since the Olympic Games in Beijing and the World Expo in Shanghai.

When to Go

Although there are great climatic disparities within China, spring and fall are generally the best months to travel, and the time when the Chinese also take to the road in far vaster numbers than those of foreign visitors. The peak foreign tourist season, however, is during summer (June to September), best avoided if you don't like the heat – it is baking hot in Beijing, and steamy in Shanghai. Winter is fiercely cold in Beijing, and rather dank and penetrating in Shanghai. Climate and rainfall charts are found on pages 35–7. Although planning your trip to coincide with one of the major holiday and festival periods *(see pp38–41)* can lead to a fun and colorful trip, national holidays are probably best avoided as tickets for air, train, and bus transportation can be very difficult to acquire. Tourist sights

will also be swamped with local sightseers, and most hotels and guesthouses will have raised their rates.

Visas and Passports

A passport valid for at least six months and a visa are necessary to enter the People's Republic of China. However, most foreign nationals do not require a visa for entering Hong Kong and Macau where mainland visas can be purchased more easily than anywhere else. Chinese embassies and consulates around the world issue a standard single-entry, 30-day visa, although multiple-entry 60-day visas, and 90-day visas can sometimes be obtained. Long-duration multiple-entry visas are no longer easily obtainable in Hong Kong. When completing the visa application form, you must specify what

A symbol of former European influence in Shanghai

parts of China you plan to visit. Avoid mentioning Tibet or Xinjiang, even if you plan to visit these regions, as you may be questioned about your occupation and intent of visit. Any list you provide is not binding. The vast majority of China is open to visitors and you do not need any special permits for Beijing and Shanghai. Always carry your passport, as it is an essential document for checking into hotels, and the Public Security Bureau (PSB) *(see p212)* may insist on seeing it. Photocopying the visa page and the personal information page will speed up replacement if your passport is lost or stolen. When in China, you can normally get two 30-day extensions to your visa from the PSB, though the bureaucracy can be daunting and you currently need to

Snow-covered bicycles in Beijing during winter

◀ Passengers boarding the high-speed bullet train from Shanghai to Hangzhou

Communist mementos on sale in a Shanghai market

prove you have US$3,000 in a Chinese bank account. Note that heavy fines are levied if you overstay your visa.

Customs Information

When entering China, visitors are entitled to a duty-free allowance of 70 fluid ounces (2 liters) of wine or spirits, 400 cigarettes, and a certain amount of gold and silver. Foreign currency exceeding US$5,000, or its equivalent, must be declared. Items that are prohibited include fresh fruit, all animals (except cats and dogs as pets) and plants, and arms and ammunition. Chinese law specifies limits on the export of certain items, such as particular herbal medicines. Also, objects predating 1795 cannot be taken out of China, while antiques made after that date will need to have an official seal affixed. Although foreign visitors are largely left alone, it is not advisable to take in politically controversial literature, especially if it is written in Chinese.

Embassies and Consulates

Most countries have an embassy in Beijing and many also have a consulate in Shanghai. Consular offices can re-issue passports and assist in case of emergencies, such as imprisonment, hospitalization, and if you become a victim of a crime. Your hotel can put you in touch with your nearest embassy or consulate.

Tourist Information

China has yet to recognize the value of professional tourist information centers, either at home or abroad. Those that exist in Beijing and Shanghai are, in general, useless. The state-approved **China International Travel Service** (CITS), originally set up to cater to the needs of foreign visitors, today functions as any other local operator, offering nothing more than tours, tickets, and rented cars. There are a few government-run travel agencies abroad but they fail to offer professional and unbiased advice, instead steer customers toward group tours and standard hotels. The best advice tends to come from youth hostels, hotels and private companies, such as **Bespoke Beijing**, that are geared to the needs of tourists.

Hotel receptions – a useful source of tourist information

Admission Prices

Most temples, parks, palaces, and museums have an entrance fee. Temples charge anything from ¥5 to ¥50. Star sights, such as Beijing's Forbidden City, can charge up to ¥60 in summer, plus an assortment of extra charges for access to certain areas and special exhibitions. Shanghai's Oriental Pearl Television Tower costs ¥150 if all its various platforms and exhibitions are visited. Some sights offer a *men piao*, which merely allows access to the grounds, and a *tong piao*, which includes access to buildings in the price. The sale of tickets can cease up to an hour before closing time. Guides swarm around entrances to major sights but their knowledge often amounts to no more than the Party-approved information on signs.

DIRECTORY

Embassies and Consulates

Australia
21 Dongzhi Men Wai Dajie, Beijing. **Tel** (010) 5140 4111. 22/F, CITIC Square, 1168 Nanjing West Road, Shanghai. **Tel** (021) 2215 5200.

Canada
19 Dongzhi Men Wai Dajie, Beijing. **Tel** (010) 5139 4000. 8/F, 1788 Nanjing West Road, Shanghai. **Tel** (021) 3279 2800.

United Kingdom
11 Guanghua Lu, Beijing. **Tel** (010) 5192 4000. Room 301, Shanghai Center, 1376 Nanjing West Road, Shanghai. **Tel** (021) 3279 2000.

USA
55 Anjia Lu, Beijing. **Tel** (010) 8531 3000. 1469 Huai Hai Middle Road, Shanghai. **Tel** (021) 3217 4650.

Tourist Information

Bespoke Beijing
W bespokebeijing.com **Tel** (010) 6400 0133.

China International Travel Service (CITS)
Beijing: 1 Dongdan Bei Dajie. **Tel** (010) 8522 8888/8522 8445. Shanghai: 1277 Beijing Xi Lu. **Tel** (021) 6289 4510. W cits.net

Holidays and Opening Hours

The main holiday periods are Chinese New Year (Spring Festival) and October 1 (National Day). People get around a week's holiday over both periods with the actual dates announced by the government a week in advance. There are also a number of one-day holidays throughout the year as well as the longer May holiday. Accommodation prices rise as domestic tourism peaks. Restaurants, tourist sights, and shops, mostly remain open except for a short period around Chinese New Year. The majority open every day and hours are roughly from 10am until 8pm.

Language

The official language of China is Putonghua (literally "common speech"), known outside China as Mandarin. Putonghua is the native language of the north, but it is used across the country for communication between speakers of several other Chinese dialects, and can be used throughout China. More and more people speak English in hotels, shops, and restaurants though you should not assume you will be able to find an English speaker. The tonal nature of Putonghua makes it a difficult language to learn without a little serious study with a teacher. Pinyin, which is a written romanization system, helps in the recognition of sounds, but the diacritical marks to indicate tone are all too often omitted, and without tone there is no meaning. A few basic phrases in Putonghua are listed on pages 234–6.

Public Conveniences

Away from hotels and more expensive restaurants, public bathrooms are traditionally of the squat variety. In Beijing and Shanghai, they vary between

Chinese children enjoying time in a Shanghai park

being very well looked after and quite clean to horrifying. There is little privacy and toilet paper is a rarity, so carry your own. You usually have to pay around ¥0.30 to use public bathrooms. If you are unused to squat toilets, take full advantage of hotel, fast-food restaurant, and shopping mall facilities.

Travelers with Special Needs

If you are a wheelchair user, China will be hard going, though the situation has improved since the Olympics and the World Expo. Beijing's new subway lines have wheelchair access and there are a few

Road sign in both Pinyin and Chinese characters

disabled access taxis, though they must be booked in advance. In Beijing and Shanghai, crowded pavements can be a challenge, as can public transport, but many hotels and restaurants are wheelchair accessible. The re-landscaped Bund area features concrete ramps enabling wheelchair access to the elevated riverside boardwalk. However, public buildings and places of interest are rarely fitted with ramps or rails. The best advice for disabled visitors is to hire a driver and stay in a foreign-run branded hotel which will have adapted rooms. Elevators are common in most hotels over three storys high.

Traveling with Children

The Chinese love children, and they are usually welcome everywhere. Both you and your child might have to grin and bear the hair-ruffling and general enthusiastic contact that you will likely encounter on a daily basis. If it starts to get tiresome, saying that your child is very shy (ta shi hen haixiu) might result in people being more hands-off. Baby-changing rooms are extremely rare, and very few restaurants have child seats, but people will generally go out of their way to accommodate you. Supermarkets are well supplied with diapers, baby wipes, creams, medicine, baby food, and clothing. However, you are advised to buy foreign infant milk formula as Chinese brands have twice been found to be contaminated. Bring a set of plastic cutlery for your child, as most restaurants only have chopsticks. Bear in mind that a lot of taxis do not have seatbelts in the back with which to attach child seats.

Gay and Lesbian Travelers

The gay and lesbian scene is growing, and the cities of Beijing and Shanghai are gradually becoming more open. However, the country is still a highly conventional society, and homosexuality is not considered a standard lifestyle. Both Beijing and Shanghai have several gay bars and clubs, with Destination (7 Gongti Xi Lu, (010) 6551-5138) in Beijing being a long-term favorite and Red Station (4/F, 200 Taikang Road, (021) 6415 -8695) in Shanghai the place to party. Bear in mind that bars are occasionally raided by the police as homosexuality is still a sensitive subject.

Traveling on a Budget

As China goes up in the world and the value of its currency rises, so do its prices for travelers, but in general, the country is a good place to be on a budget with plenty of well-run hostels that operate tours and offer advice. However, Beijing and Shanghai are two of the most expensive cities to visit and accommodation isn't as cheap as you might hope; dorm beds never cost less than ¥50, a fortune compared to rural parts of the country. On the bright side, public transportation is very cheap, with buses in both cities costing ¥1 or ¥2, and food can be amazing value too, with a big bowl of noodles costing around ¥3 in local cafés. Unfortunately, international student cards or cards for the retired do not entitle you to any discounts in China.

What to Take

In Beijing from November until March, you will require a good, warm jacket, gloves, sweater, warm socks, thermal leggings, sturdy footwear, and lip balm. During the same period in Shanghai, you still need a raincoat, a sweater, warm clothes, and an umbrella. In summer, you only need loose-fitting shirts or T-shirts, and thin trousers. Shorts will also do. If you do not want to do any shopping for essentials, bring a first-aid kit, raincoat, sun hat, sunglasses, and a plug adapter. Make sure you have a phrase book and all the books you require for your trip.

China operates on one time zone so midday in Beijing is also midday in Shanghai

Time and Calendar

Despite its vast size, China occupies only one time zone, and there is no daylight saving time. So, China is 7 or 8 hours ahead of Greenwich Mean Time (GMT), 2 or 3 hours behind Australian Eastern Standard Time, 15 or 16 hours ahead of US Pacific Standard Time, and 12 or 13 hours ahead of US Eastern Standard Time. The Western Gregorian calendar is used for all official work; the dates for traditional festivals follow a lunar calendar.

Electricity

The electrical current in China is 220 volts. The most common plug arrangement is two flat prongs, as in North America. Sockets will not take plugs with a third earthing pin, or those with one flat blade larger than the other. Most are also designed to take European-style two round pins, while the British three square-pin arrangement is rare outside smart hotels. Bring an adapter suitable for China to avoid problems. It is best to stay clear of cheap Chinese batteries, as they are very short-lived and may leak, but be aware that the Western-brand batteries on sale are often fakes.

Plugs with two and three prongs

Responsible Tourism

It is no secret that China has terrible environmental problems. People in Beijing and Shanghai still litter with abandon, but attitudes are changing, especially amongst the younger generation. Tourists can play their part by not wasting water (Beijing has almost constant drought) and being conscious of their impact on the local environment. New hotels often play lip service to being sustainable, but there is only one hotel in Shanghai that lives up to its eco-credentials – the Urbn (see p185) – which keeps its carbon usage to an absolute minimum. Tourists can support communities by staying in locally owned hotels and taking small, low-impact tours. There are also food markets where you can buy locally grown produce. China has banned the use of free plastic bags, so bring your own. In Beijing, the Sanyuanli Market (Shun Yuan Jie) near Sanlitun is excellent for locally grown fruit and vegetables, and in Shanghai, try the Wuzhong Wet Market (328 Wulumuqi Middle Road, near to Fuxing West Road).

Conversion Chart

The metric system is used in all parts of China.

Imperial to metric
1 inch = 2.5 centimeters
1 foot = 30 centimeters
1 mile = 1.6 kilometers
1 ounce = 28 grams
1 pound = 454 grams
1 pint (US) = 0.473 liters
1 gallon (US) = 3.785 liters

Metric to imperial
1 centimeter = 0.4 inches
1 meter = 3 feet 3 inches
1 kilometer = 0.6 miles
100 gram = 3.53 ounces
1 kilogram = 2.2 pounds
1 liter = 2.11 pints (US)

Chinese measurements
When buying fruit and vegetables, use the following measurements:
1 jin: 500 grams
1 liang: 50 grams

General Etiquette

Despite rapid modernization, China remains a traditional society governed by strong family values. Beijing and Shanghai give the outward impression of Western modernity, but older generations retain a deep-seated and family-oriented conservatism. Confucian values promote respect for elders and those in positions of authority. Religious observance is not widespread, and is largely separate from mainstream social behavior. The Chinese are, above all, welcoming and generous, and visitors are often amazed at their hospitality. If invited to someone's home, a gift of chocolates, French wine, or some other imported treat will be greatly appreciated.

Worshipers praying at a shrine at one of Beijing's many temples

Greeting People

Shaking hands is common-place in big cities, and certainly considered the norm with foreign visitors. Although the Chinese are not particularly tactile in their greetings, bodily contact is quite common between friends, even of the same sex. Young men often walk arm in arm, or with their arm around another's shoulder. The usual Chinese greeting is "Ni hao" (Hello) or "Nimen hao" in its plural form, to which you reply "Ni hao" or "Nimen hao" – the polite form is "Nin hao."

The Chinese will not blanch at asking how much you earn, your age, or whether you are married. Such questions are seen as nothing more than taking a friendly interest in a new acquaintance. When proffering business cards, the Chinese use the fingertips of both hands, and receive cards in the same manner. For business travelers, cards are essential, preferably with Chinese on one side and English on the other.

Dress

The improvement in living standards is reflected by people's clothes: where once conservative fashions in black or brown dominated, now anything goes. In cities, people wear what they wear the world over: jeans, T-shirts, and skirts, and many youngsters dress provocatively and dye their hair. Don't worry too much about what you wear, but try to avoid looking scruffy. Shorts are acceptable, but having cleavage on display will attract attention. Both cities are very fashion conscious, but generally Shanghai is considered to be a more dress-oriented society and Beijing a little more casual.

Face

Reserved in manner and expression, the Chinese also harbor strong feelings of personal pride and respect. The maintenance of pride and the avoidance of shame is known as "face." Loss of face creates great discomfort and major embarrassment for Chinese, so although you may often be frustrated by bureaucracy and delays, or the incompetence of hotel staff, try not to embarrass anybody in public. Be firm but polite, and use confrontation only as a very last resort.

Chinese Hospitality

If invited out for dinner, expect to see the diners competing to pay the entire bill, rather than dividing it up between them. It is a good idea to join in the scramble for the bill, or at least make an attempt – your gesture will be appreciated, though almost certainly declined. For more on dining etiquette, see pages 188–9.

Places of Worship

Although there are no dress codes for Buddhist, Daoist, or Confucian temples, visitors to mosques should dress respect-fully – avoid wearing shorts or mini skirts – and cover your upper arms. Buddhist, Daoist, and Confucian temples are relaxed with visitors wandering about, but be considerate toward worshipers. Also, check whether you can take photo-graphs within temple halls, as this is often not permitted. Taking photos in courtyards, however, is usually not a problem. Some Buddhist and Daoist temples are active, such as Beijing's Lama Temple, and you should show respect towards the resident monks.

Annoyances

The Chinese habit of staring, especially in smaller towns and rural areas, can be a little annoying. It can also be encountered in Beijing and Shanghai, since these cities attract a lot of migrant workers and peasant tourists. However, the intent is rarely hostile. Another problem that visitors face are constant calls

Advice for burning incense

of "Hellooo!" or "Laowai!" (foreigner). It is best either to ignore them or smile, as replying often results in bursts of laughter. In Beijing and Shanghai, people sometimes strike up conversation to

A busy shopping street, stalking ground for "art student" scamsters

practice their English, but caution is necessary as increasingly these approaches are lead-ins to scams. Around Beijing's Wangfujing shopping street, Liulichang, Tian'an Men Square and the Forbidden City, and on Shanghai's main shopping streets, decline to accompany "art students" who in the guise of fund-raising will pressure you to buy hugely over-priced art. Similarly be wary of "language students" who suggest entering a nearby café or bar and who will leave you with a bill for thousands of *renminbi*. Also watch for "accidental" encounters with seemingly friendly and helpful English speakers who eventually suggest partaking in a tea ceremony.

Although more orderly queues are beginning to replace the usual mêlée at ticket offices, you still need to be prepared for a lot of pushing and shoving. Spitting is still widespread, although there is always a crackdown in the run-up to major international events. Despite the best attempts of public educators, spitting is still common on buses and trains, and it is not considered rude to spit in mid-conversation, so do not take offense.

Smoking and Alcohol

As the world's largest producer and consumer of cigarettes (*xiangyan*), China is a smoker's paradise. Despite the appearance of no-smoking zones and rudimentary anti-smoking campaigns, Beijing and Shanghai remain shrouded in a haze of nicotine clouds. Smoking is now banned on domestic flights, on trains (except in connecting passages between carriages), and on buses, but unless the latter are air-conditioned, and sometimes even then, the rule is ignored. Smoking during meals is acceptable, especially if there are other smokers present. The Chinese are very generous when it comes to offering cigarettes, so remember to be equally generous in return. They also enjoy drinking alcohol, and there is no taboo against moderate intoxication. The usual accompaniment during a meal is beer (*pijiu*), or white spirits (*baijiu*). Wine (*putaojiu*) is increasingly popular with the middle classes and China now produces its own wine. If someone raises a toast to you ("Ganbei!"), it is good form to return the toast later.

A popular white spirit, or *baijiu*

Bargaining

As a foreign national in China, it is essential to bargain (*taojia huanjia*). You may often be overcharged – sometimes by large amounts – in markets and anywhere else where prices are not indicated. Some restaurants charge higher prices on the English menu than on the Chinese one. You should bargain to reduce your hotel room rate: no one pays rack rate and substantial discounts are almost always available, especially at Chinese-run hotels. Always ask for a discount on airfares, too. Be sure to bargain pleasantly and with a smile. At markets, let the vendor speak first and don't be afraid to counter offer with 10 per cent

or less. First prices to foreigners are often as much as 15 times higher than what will eventually be accepted. Your next offer should only be fractionally higher than your first. The prices in large shops and government emporia (*guoying shangdian*) may appear to be fixed, but the Chinese will routinely ask for discounts, and frequently get them, too. Asking is normal practice, so never be afraid.

Tipping

There is no tipping in China, so do not tip guides, taxi drivers, or anyone else. In China, the price you agree for the service is the one you pay, although some restaurants in larger hotels or fine-dining venues now routinely add a service charge and away from hotels and tourist areas waitresses will pursue you down the street to return the change they think you've forgotten. The exception is five-star hotel bell boys who do now expect tips.

Begging

China's imbalanced economic progress and huge population of rural poor have resulted in large numbers of beggars, especially in Beijing and Shanghai. Foreign visitors naturally attract attention, and groups of children are often sent by their parents to extract money. The best strategy is to ignore them and walk away.

A tourist bargaining with a vendor for his purchase

Personal Security and Health

Compared to many places in the world, China is a very safe place to travel and the vast majority of visitors won't encounter any problems. A small minority may be the victims of petty crime, especially from opportunistic thieves in tourist destinations, so like anywhere, you should protect your valuables and important documents at all times. Health-wise, it pays to eat in clean places, and drink only mineral water. If you do want to eat at street stalls, choose the busiest as it will have a high turnover of food and make sure what you eat is piping hot.

Police

The police in China, or *jingcha*, are more commonly known to foreigners as the Public Security Bureau (PSB), or *gong'an ju*. However, most visitors to Beijing and Shanghai are unlikely to encounter the PSB, unless extending their visas, or reporting a loss or theft of personal items. Note that only the largest police stations (*jingcha ju*) have English-speaking staff.

Beijing PSB officer

What to Be Aware of

Traveling in China is generally safe, and foreign visitors are unlikely to be the victims of crime, apart from petty theft and occasional scams. Sadly, anyone who approaches looking to speak English with you should be treated with caution: friendly Chinese who suggest a chat over tea, or pretty girls who want to practice English over a drink, may in both cases be in cahoots with a bar or café and looking to leave you with an artificially pumped-up bill for thousands of *renminbi*. Refuse to pay, make plenty of noise, and insist on calling the police. On buses and trains, guard your camera and valuables, wear a money belt at all times, and secure your luggage to the rack on overnight train journeys.

At some sights, you will be asked to deposit your bag before making a visit. Hotels in China are reliably secure, but management will not accept responsibility should anything vanish. If you are staying in a hostel dormitory, then be very cautious. Make use of hotel safety deposit boxes and in-room safes.

Be discreet when taking your wallet out. It is best to pocket only as much cash as you need for the day and keep the rest in a money belt under your clothes, along with your passport and other valuable documents.

It is always a good idea to carry photocopies of the personal information and China visa pages of your passport, as well as any other important documents, such as insurance policies. These should be stored separately from the originals in case of theft or loss.

In an Emergency

Don't wait for an ambulance: head directly to a hospital by any means possible (taxi is usually best) as ambulances will take too long and there may be communication problems. Enlist the help of your hotel to contact police or emergency healthcare – there are emergency telephone numbers in both cities, but they are Chinese-speaking only. It is vital to have good insurance coverage as healthcare bills can rack up frighteningly quickly.

Lost and Stolen Property

As in all countries, you should keep a close eye on your belongings; although China is in general very safe, there are pickpockets in tourist spots, cafés, and other public spaces. Crowded public transportation like buses and the subway are also prime target areas. If you do have items stolen or lose something, you will need a police report for your insurance claim. Reports can be obtained from your nearest PSB; check if your insurance company requires reports in English.

Hospitals and Pharmacies

Both Beijing and Shanghai have good public hospitals which have foreigners' wings with English-speaking doctors. Healthcare at public hospitals is cheap, but if you have good insurance, the city's private hospitals and clinics, with great facilities and highly qualified staff, are preferable. Unless you have direct billing with your insurance, you will not be allowed to depart before the bill is settled. Pharmacies (*yaodian*), identified by green crosses, are plentiful and easily found. They stock both Western and Chinese medicine. Many drugs are available over the counter without prescriptions, but there have been a few cases of contaminated drugs, so it is best to take any medication you need with you.

Shu Guang, one of several public hospitals in Shanghai

Street food – only eat it when it is cooked in front of you

Stomach Upsets and Diarrhea

If you have a stomach upset, stick to plain food, such as rice, until any diarrhea subsides. Most importantly, drink lots of fluids, as diarrhea quickly leads to dehydration, and use oral rehydration salts. Do not eat salads, cut fruit, or cold dishes, or drink fresh juice bought from street stalls. Never drink tap water or brush your teeth with it – use bottled mineral water. Only eat street food that is freshly cooked in front of you.

Heat, Humidity, and Pollution

In summer, drink plenty of fluids to guard against dehydration. Wear loose-fitting cotton clothing and sandals, a sun-hat and sunglasses, and use plenty of sunscreen. Beijing and Shanghai can see chronic levels of pollution: this aggra-vates chest infections, and asthmatic travelers should always carry their medication.

Infectious Diseases

AIDS is a growing problem in China and more than 700,000 people are believed to have the disease. Hepatitis B, also transmitted through contact with infected blood, is spread through sexual contact, unsterilized needles, tattoos, and shaves from roadside barbers, but unlike AIDS it can be prevented with a vaccine. When visiting a clinic, ensure that the doctor opens a new syringe in front of you, or bring your own disposable syringe. Avoid any other procedure using needles, such as tattooing, ear-piercing, or acupuncture.

Water-Borne Diseases

Visitors should be on their guard against dysentery. Bacillary dysentery is accom-panied by severe stomach pains, vomiting, and fever. Amoebic dysentery has similar symptoms but takes longer to manifest. Pre-travel vaccination against hepatitis A, cholera, and typhoid is advisable.

Insect-Borne Diseases

Those planning visits solely to Beijing and Shanghai (and Hangzhou and Suzhou) do not need to take malarial prophylaxis. For trips to rural areas, consult a tropical medicine specialist.

Travel and Health Insurance

It is advisable to take out an insurance policy for medical emergencies, preferably including evacuation, trip cancellation, loss of baggage by airlines, and travel delay. Policies covering the theft of valuables need to be carefully examined as exclusions and deductibles often make these worthless, and caution is often both more effective and cheaper. Remember to make sure that any adventure activity or sport that you may undertake during your trip is covered by your policy. In the case of a claim, be aware that your policy may require you to have English language reports from the police or healthcare facilities.

Vaccinations

Ensure that all of your routine vaccinations are up to date, such as tetanus, polio, and diphtheria. It is advisable to also get vaccinated against hepatitis A and B, typhoid, meningo-coccal meningitis, and cholera. Visitors traveling from countries where yellow fever is endemic must provide proof of vaccination against the disease. Malaria medication is essential for those visiting rural areas, as is a Japanese encephalitis vaccination, but neither are necessary for visits to Beijing and Shanghai, nor most other major cities. For up-to-date travel-health information and more advice on immunization, visit **MD Travel Health** online.

DIRECTORY

In an Emergency

Police
Tel 110.

Fire
Tel 119.

Ambulance
Tel 120.

Hospitals and Pharmacies

Beijing United Family Hospital
2 Jiangtai Lu, Chaoyang, Beijing. **Tel** (010) 5927 7120 (24-hr).
Ⓦ ufh.com.cn

International SOS Pharmacy
Suite 105, Wing 1, Kunsha Building, 16 Xinguanli, Chaoyang, Beijing.
Tel (010) 6462 9112.
Ⓦ internationalsos. com/en

Parkway Community Pharmacy
9-B101A, Green Garden, 333 Bi Yun Road, Shanghai.
Tel (021) 3382 1382.
Ⓦ parkwaycommunity pharmacy.com

Parkway Health Shanghai Center
203–4, West Retail Plaza, 1376 Nanjing West Road.
Tel (021) 6445 5999.

Shanghai East International Medical Center
150 Jimo Road, Pudong.
Tel (021) 5879 9999.

Travel Health

Medical Advisory Services for Travelers Abroad
Tel (0113) 238 7575.

MD Travel Health
Ⓦ mdtravelhealth.com

Banking and Local Currency

Most foreign exchange transactions take place at major branches of any bank or at foreign exchange counters at airports and in major stores, or are performed by hotels for their residents only. In Beijing and Shanghai, there are plenty of ATMs that accept foreign cards, including at both airports, and these are generally the most convenient way of acquiring Chinese currency. You cannot pay for goods or services with foreign cash or traveler's checks. Foreign credit cards are accepted in larger hotels, restaurants, and retail outlets.

Banks and Exchanging Money

The **Bank of China** has the most extensive network in the country, although several other banks, including ICBC and China Construction Bank, also operate nationwide. Some banks are only open 9am–noon and 2pm–4:30pm or 5pm Monday to Friday, but others are open all day, and some on Saturdays. All banks remain closed for at least the first three days of the Chinese New Year, and for three days during the October holidays. For all foreign exchange transactions, you will need to show your passport. While the currency is still officially non-convertible, restrictions are easing and you can buy and sell *renminbi* in more and more countries these days (near neighbors, the UK, Australia, and the US, for example). Exchange rates are decided centrally and distributed nationally on a daily basis. Rates vary very little within banks so there's little point in shopping around. Never bother with the black market as you run the risk of receiving counterfeit notes. If you wish to convert any leftover *renminbi* back before you leave, do so at the airport.

Hong Kong & Shanghai Banking Corporation (HSBC) ATMs

ATMs

It is now common for ATMs to accept foreign cards. There are many ATMs in banks, shopping malls, and hotels around the centers of Beijing and Shanghai. Those machines that do accept foreign cards are part of the Maestro, Cirrus, JCB, and Visa networks. Check the back of your card for logos. Both Beijing and Shanghai have branches of **HSBC**, **American Express**, and **Citibank**, whose machines will take almost any card. Most ATMs have a limit of ¥2,500 per transaction, up to ¥20,000 in withdrawals per day. Try to withdraw the maximum amount allowed on your card per transaction to reduce the impact of fees that your bank will charge for each cash withdrawal. Although the vast majority of the time you are unlikely to have a problem, it is best not to rely solely on taking money out at ATMs as cards can occasionally be "swallowed." It is also advisable to notify your bank or credit card provider that you are going abroad ahead of traveling as they may block cards to avoid fraudulent use.

Travelers' Checks and Credit Cards

Some hotel foreign exchange counters will no longer exchange checks, and will send you to a bank. All popular foreign brands are accepted, but occasionally cashiers nervous of responsibility will reject those that look unfamiliar. Keep the proof of purchase slips and a record of the serial numbers in case of loss or theft.

Credit cards are widely accepted in upscale hotels, restaurants and shopping malls, and in large tourist shops, but always check before attempting to make a purchase that your foreign card is accepted. Note that there may also be a small

DIRECTORY

Bank of China	HSBC	Citibank	American Express
Beijing Asia Pacific Building, 8 Yabao Lu. ATMs Oriental Plaza, 1 Dongchang'an Jie. **Shanghai** Bank of China Tower, 200 Yin Cheng Road, Pudong. ATMs 23 The Bund.	**Beijing** Block A, COFCO Plaza 8, Jianguo Men Nei Dajie. ATMs The Place Mall, 9 Guanghan Road. **Shanghai** HSBC Tower, Shanghai IFC, 8 Century Ave, Pudong. ATMs Shanghai Center, 1376 Nanjing West Road.	**Beijing** 1st floor, Tower 1, Bright China Chang'an Building, 7 Jian Guo Men Nei Dajie. **Shanghai** Citigroup Tower, 33 Huayuan Shi Qiao Road, Pudong. ATMs Adjacent to the Peace Hotel, Zhongshan East Road.	**Beijing** Room 2313, China World Trade Center, 1 Jianguo Men Wai Dajie. **Shanghai** Room 455, Shanghai Center, 1376 Nanjing West Road.

surcharge added. The commonly accepted cards are MasterCard, Visa, JCB, Diners Club, and American Express. Air tickets can be bought by credit card, but train tickets have to be paid for in cash. Cash advances can be made on credit cards at banks, but it is far cheaper to use a debit card in an ATM.

Currency

The official name of China's currency is the *yuan renminbi*, literally people's currency, but it is also called *kuai* (in Shanghai) or *yuan*. One *yuan* divides into 10 *jiao*, or *mao*, which in turn divides into 10 almost worthless *fen*. The most common coins include 1 *yuan*, and 5 and 1 *jiao*. Bills in circulation are 1, 2, and 5

jiao, and 1, 2, 5, 10, 20, 50, and 100 *yuan*. The 1-*yuan* note is being phased out. It has been proposed that there should be a 500-*yuan* note but there is no news of when this will be. Counterfeiting in China is widespread, and it is not unusual for retail outlets to regularly scrutinize notes using a special machine.

Bank Notes

The more recently printed bills have Mao Zedong on one side and a well-known heritage sight on the other. The older bills depict the traditional dress of various ethnic minorities.

1-*yuan* note

5-*yuan* note

10-*yuan* note

20-*yuan* note

50-*yuan* note

100-*yuan* note

Coins

Chinese coins are not widely circulated. There are a 1-yuan coin and some jiao denominations, as well as tiny and lightweight fen.

5 *jiao*

1 *jiao*

1 *yuan*

Communications and Media

China has an efficient postal network with a variety of services, including registered post and express mail. Tele-communication systems are reasonably advanced and international telephone calls can be made from all but the cheapest hotels. The Internet is hugely popular, and access in cafés, bars, restaurants, and hotels is widespread. Broadband and Wi-Fi are available in all but the most modest of hotel rooms. The government, however, scrupulously polices the net, and many websites, including Facebook and Twitter, are blocked, although sometimes not in the best foreign hotels. Foreign newspapers and magazines are sold in five-star hotel bookstores and in some shopping malls.

A wheelchair-accessible phone booth in Beijing

International and Local Telephone Calls

VoIP services like Skype are freely accessible in China and are the cheapest way to make international calls. International (guo ji) and long-distance (guo nei) calls can also be made from most hotels and public telephones. Hotels are only allowed to add a small service charge to the cost of calls; local calls should be free. Most public phones require an IC (Integrated Circuit) card, sold in shops and kiosks wherever the letters "IC" are seen. These are available in various values up to ¥100. International calls are best made using an IP (Internet Protocol) card; you dial a local access number and enter a code hidden behind a scratch-off panel on the card. Voice instructions are in both Chinese

and English. IP cards typically come in ¥50 and ¥100 varieties. If you wish to use one at a payphone, you will still need an IC card to enable you to dial the local access number.

Useful Dialing Codes and Numbers

To call China from abroad, dial your international access code, China's country code 86, then 10 for Beijing or 21 for Shanghai, followed by the local number. When dialing long-distance from within China dial 010 and 021 respectively. Other city codes also have a leading zero. To make a local call, omit the area code.

To make an international call from China, dial 00, the country code, the area code omitting any initial 0, and the local number. Country codes include: UK 44; USA and Canada 1; Australia 61; New Zealand 64; and Ireland 353.

Mobile Phones

There are four main GSM frequencies (Global System for Mobile Communications) in use around the world, so if you want to guarantee that your phone will work, make sure you have a quad-band phone. You may also need to ask your network operator to enable your phone for roaming. Remember you are charged for the calls you receive as well as the calls you make, and you have to pay a substantial premium for the international leg of the call.

The cheapest option by far – although you must have an unlocked phone – is to buy a local SIM card from any phone shop and use the Chinese mobile phone system. SIM cards cost about ¥60, along with a deposit of ¥1000. China Mobile has the best coverage. Some SIM cards work only in the town in which they were purchased, so if you wish to use the same number in Beijing and Shanghai, make sure you have the right kind of card. Even using a Beijing number in Shanghai is vastly cheaper than using foreign companies' roaming options. ¥100 of phone credit will allow you almost 2 hours of local calls. If, however, your phone is not compatible, you can buy a basic new one for about ¥400.

Internet and Email

China is better connected than the vast majority of western countries with a huge number of cafés, bars, restaurants, and

One of many cafés offering free Wi-Fi access

hotels offering free Wi-Fi access in both Beijing and Shanghai. Unless you need to get online urgently, avoid using hotel business centers or Internet cafés aimed at tourists as they are generally overpriced.

Postal Services

The postal service in China is, for the most part, reliable and reasonably fast. It takes a day for mail to reach local destinations, two or more days to inland destinations, while the international postal service takes about one to two weeks to send airmail and postcards overseas. Visitors can send mail by standard or registered post, while EMS (Express Mail Service) is a reliable way to send packages and documents abroad and within the country. Note that before you can send a parcel, its contents will have to be examined by post office staff. Most post offices are open all day, seven days a week. Large hotels also usually have post desks. Take your mail to the post office, rather than dropping it in a mail box. It will help postal staff sort your letter if you can write the country's name in Chinese characters as many postal workers do not speak much English. Envelopes and packaging materials are available at post offices.

Courier Services

Courier services are widely available in both cities. While it is cheaper to send large, bulky items by regular land, sea, or air cargo, important letters, documents, and parcels are best sent through a courier agency. International operatives **UPS**, **Federal Express**, and **DHL** are all present in China.

Newspapers and Magazines

China Daily is China's official English-language newspaper. It is full of propaganda and little

A choice of Chinese newspapers on display at a newsstand

else. *Global Times* is better, though not brilliant. In Shanghai, *Shanghai Daily* is the state-run newspaper. An increasingly diverse selection of international papers and magazines can be found at many hotel bookstores and upscale supermarkets, although these are subject to occasional censorship. Beijing and Shanghai have a number of expat-written free entertainment and culture magazines, such as *The Beijinger*, *Time Out Beijing*, *Time Out Shanghai*, and *That's Shanghai*. These are published at the beginning of each month and are available in most bars, cafés, and hotels.

Television and Radio

The state-run Chinese Central Television (CCTV) has CCTV News as its flagship English station. Despite a style overhaul, content can still be a bit dull, as propaganda and bright-eyed promotion for China travel are the norm. ICS (International Channel Shanghai) has higher production values. Cable and satellite television with BBC and CNN is only available in top-end hotels, although some Hong Kong channels with English programming appear lower down the scale. Chinese programs range from historical costume dramas (with political bias) and tepid soaps (intended to reinforce government social messages) to domestic travel

Mail box, Beijing

(everything is perfect) and heavily biased news programs. Many Beijing and Shanghai bars subscribe to satellite sport channels that broadcast major international games and events. The Chinese radio network has only a few local English-language programs: China Radio International (CRI) is the state-run English language radio service. You will need a short-wave radio to pick up the BBC World Service and other international programs. Voice of America has been blocked.

Shanghai's iconic Oriental Pearl Tower, a TV transmitter

DIRECTORY

Useful Numbers

DHL Worldwide Express (Beijing only)
Tel (010) 5860 1076 or 800 810 8000, Beijing. (021) 5551 4777 or 800 810 8000, Shanghai.

Federal Express
Tel (010) 6438 5560 or 800 810 2338, Beijing.
(021) 5411 8333, Shanghai.

International Post Office
Jianguo Men Bei Dajie, Beijing. Sinan Road (junction with Huaihai Road), Shanghai.

United Parcels Service (UPS)
Tel 800 820 8388 nationwide or 400 820 8388 from a cell phone.
Beijing
Room 1818, China World Tower 1, 1 Jianguomenwai Avenue.
Shanghai
23/F, China Insurance Building, 166 Lujiazui East Road, Pudong.

TRAVEL INFORMATION

Most visitors to China arrive by air, though overland routes exist with train links to neighboring Russia, Mongolia, Kazakhstan, and Vietnam, and bus links to Laos and Pakistan. It is also possible to arrive by sea; there are regular ferries from Japan and South Korea to China. Once you have arrived, flying internally is straightforward. Domestic air tickets are easy to buy, so shop around for discounts on online travel agents. There are scores of flights daily between Beijing and Shanghai Hongqiao Airport, and between Beijing and Shanghai Pudong. China's high-speed rail network is increasingly fast, efficient, and comfortable, although buying tickets can seem daunting. Bus travel is improving with an increasing number of "luxury" and "no smoking" buses. Hiring a self-drive car is not possible, although hiring a car and driver is often the best way to take a trip out of town.

Arriving by Air

All major international airlines fly to China. China's own **Air China**, **China Southern**, and **China Eastern** plus Taiwan's **China Airlines** between them cover most of the world's major airports. Hong Kong's **Cathay Pacific** and its Dragon Air affiliate have an extensive international network and service standards considerably higher than those of most other carriers. China's four main international gateways are Hong Kong, Beijing, Shanghai, and Guangzhou, and all are superior in quality to most in Europe and North America.

    Beijing Capital International Airport is 12 miles (20 km) northeast of the city center. It has three terminals, with most international flights arriving at terminal 3. A free bus service connects the terminals.

    Shanghai Pudong Airport serves international flights and is 30 miles (50 km) southeast of the city center. It has two terminals which are within walking distance of each other. **Shanghai Hongqiao Airport** serves domestic flights, Hong Kong, and some Asian routes and is 6 miles (10 km) from the city center. A second terminal opened in 2010.

On Arrival

Visitors are given a form to complete for immigration and customs. This is submitted to officials between the plane and the arrivals hall, where there are foreign exchange counters, ATMs, left-luggage services, restaurants, and shops. There's usually someone at airport tourist information counters who can speak some English.

Getting to and from the Airports

In Beijing, there are multiple bus routes into the city, and the ABC high-speed light rail line links the airport with Dong Zhi Men station in the city. Taxis wait for passengers at a marshaled rank outside the arrivals hall. Ignore the touts and insist on the driver using the meter. If you already have a hotel booked, check whether it offers a courtesy airport pick-up. In Shanghai there are bus and taxi services from Hongqiao and Pudong airports and both are connected to Line 2 of the Shanghai subway system.

Internal Flights

There are currently some 12 domestic carriers operating in China. In-flight service and on-board food is of average quality. Announcements are in both Chinese and English.

    Air flight safety records are excellent now, and most airlines have new fleets. Between Beijing, Shanghai, and other major cities, the aircraft are usually brand new Airbus or Boeing planes. The baggage allowance is 44 lbs (20 kg) for economy class and 66 pounds (30 kg) for first and business class. You are also allowed up to 11 pounds (5 kg) of hand luggage, although this is rarely weighed. Excess baggage incurs charges.

    The check-in time for internal flights is an hour and a half before departure, although in practice very few passengers ever arrive that early. The ¥50 airport tax for domestic flights is added to the price of the ticket at the time of purchase.

The impressive departure hall at Beijing Capital International Airport

In-flight service on Sichuan Airlines, a domestic Chinese carrier

children. The departure tax for international flights is ¥90 and is included in the total ticket price.

If you need to change your flight, you can usually get a refund as long as you cancel before the date of departure, and return your ticket to the same agent who sold it to you. Note that discounted tickets usually carry more restrictions so if you are not sure of your dates book a flexible ticket.

Tickets and Fares

Ticket prices are most expensive between June and September. It can also be harder to find reasonably priced tickets during Chinese holidays: Spring Festival, the first week of May, and the first week of October. While flying indirectly to China via another country is cheaper than flying direct, traveling by a Chinese airline will often be the cheapest option.

International tickets can be booked online through a travel site such as www.travelocity.com or www.orbitz.com. Where possible, book internal flights online before you travel to avoid disappointment. Reservations can be made at www.ctrip.com.cn or www.elong.net, or through ticket offices, travel agents, or the travel desks of some of the better hotels – you should not be charged a booking fee. If using an international credit card, you may be charged a surcharge. Visitors are required to show their passports or give their passport numbers when purchasing tickets.

Domestic ticket prices are calculated according to a one-way fare, and a return-ticket is usually double that. Discounts on official fares are the norm, and whatever price you are first offered you should always ask for a discount. Children over the age of 12 are charged adult fares, but there are cheaper fares for younger

Package Deals

Travel websites such as www.expedia.com offer flight and hotel packages, as do some airlines such as **British Airways** – these packages can often work out cheaper than booking separately.

Online travel agents like ctrip.com and elong.net *(see above)* should be your first port of call for domestic package deals combining flights, hotel stays, and tours. This can be a very cost-efficient way of seeing other parts of China. Be aware though that you will then be part of a Chinese tour group which can be huge in size and you might have to wear something distinctive to identify you as part of the group. Some youth hostels also offer package deals.

DIRECTORY

Airports

Beijing Capital International Airport
Tel (010) 96 158.
w bcia.com.cn

Shanghai Hongqiao Airport
Tel (021) 6268 3659.
w shanghai airport.com

Shanghai Pudong Airport
Tel (021) 91 990.
w shanghai airport.com

Airlines

Air China
Tel (010) 95 583, Beijing.
w airchina.com.cn

British Airways
Tel (010) 800 744 0031, Beijing.
w britishairways.com

Cathay Pacific
Tel 4008 886 628, Shanghai.
w cathaypacific.com

China Airlines
Tel (010) 6510 2671, Beijing. Tel (021) 5237 5269, Shanghai.
w china-airlines.com

China Eastern Airlines
Tel (010) 8441 5000, Beijing. (021) 95 808 (domestic), Shanghai.
w ce-air.com

China Southern Airlines
Tel 4006 695 539, Beijing.

Emirates
Tel 4008 822 380.
w emirates.com

KLM
Tel 4008 808 222.
852 2808 2168 (overseas).
w klm.com

Northwest Airlines
Tel (010) 6505 3505,
Beijing. 4008 140 081,
w nwa.com

Qantas
Tel 800 819 0089.
w qantas.com.au

United Airlines
Tel (0852) 2810 8616, Hong Kong.
1-800-864-8331, US.
w united.com

Virgin Atlantic
Tel (021) 5353 4600, Shanghai.
0844 209 7777, UK.
1-800-821-5438, US.
1300 727 340, Aus.
w virgin-atlantic.com

Traveling by Train, Bus, and Ferry

The Chinese rail network is extensive, with tracks running over 58,500 miles (91,000 km) and still expanding. It is possible to reach every province of China by rail from Beijing and Shanghai. High-speed bullet trains, capable of traveling at 218 mph (350 km/h), operate between Beijing and the port city of Tianjin, and between Shanghai and the cities of Suzhan, Nanjing, and Hangzhan. Even faster trains began running between Beijing and Shanghai in October 2011, cutting the journey to around five hours. Along the east coast, many bus services are efficient, comfortable, and well-regulated. In other areas they vary. Driving is invariably rash, and road conditions can be bad. Only a very limited number of passenger ferries leave Shanghai for Yangzi River destinations, and there are few coastal services.

High-speed train at Beijing South train station

Trains and Timetables

Timetables are published in April and October each year, and are available at railway station ticket offices. You can find information and reserve tickets at www.chinatrain tickets.net (note that booking fees are high). An alternative timetable is also published at www.travelchinaguide.com/china-trains.

Conventional trains with numbers prefixed by the letter "T" or "K" are express (te kuai) or fast (kuai) trains, and those whose numbers have no prefix are ordinary (pu kuai) trains of varying speeds and comfort. "Z" are prestige services, including some running between Beijing and Shanghai. High-speed trains are prefixed by the letter "G." All long-distance trains have sleeper carriages.

There is no smoking permitted except at carriage junctions. Beijing to Shanghai trains have a bar and most trains have dining cars, though the food is poor and over-priced. Staff continually push trolleys through the carriages selling instant noodles, snacks, mineral water, coffee, and newspapers. The noise level in the carriages is often very high, as announcements and music are regularly broadcast over the speakers, although Soft Sleeper compartments have a volume control.

Classes

Chinese trains have four main classes. One of the more comfortable is the Soft Sleeper (ruan wo), with four berths per compartment. It offers more privacy and security than less expensive classes, but is often little cheaper than flying. The most expensive and luxurious is the Deluxe Sleeper (gaoji ruanwo) with only two berths and sometimes with shower or private bathroom. This is available on certain routes, including Beijing to Shanghai. The high-speed intercity trains have two classes – first class and economy.

Hard Sleeper (ying wo) can be an economical choice when traveling between cities overnight, especially as it also saves the cost of a night in a hotel. Carriages consist of doorless compartments with six bunks in two sets of three. Higher berths are slightly cheaper than the lower and offer more privacy. Pillows, sheets, and blankets are provided, as are flasks of boiling water. Once aboard, the inspector will exchange your ticket for a token, and return the ticket at the end of the journey.

The cheapest class is Hard Seat (ying zuo), with three people side-by-side on lightly cushioned seats. Carriages are usually crowded and dirty, the speakers blare endlessly, lights remain on at night, and compartments are filled with smoke. If you have no reserved seat, you'll likely stand for the whole trip.

Available only on certain short daytime routes, Soft Seat (ruan zuo) carriages are more comfortable.

Exterior of Beijing Zhan train station

Passengers waiting at one of Beijing's 12 long-distance bus terminals

Main Stations

Beijing's train stations are spread across the city. The main station, Beijing Zhan, links Beijing with cities in the north and north-east, while Beijing South station services the Tianjin line and the high-speed Beijing–Shanghai route. Beijing West links the capital with Xian and Hong Kong. Shanghai's main station, Shanghai Zhan, is located in the north of the city, while Shanghai Nan Zhan is in Xujiahui. Both stations are connected to Metro line 1.

Train Tickets, Fares and Reservations

On most routes, and certainly on those between Beijing and Shanghai, it is vital to buy tickets a few days before you travel. Tickets between these two cities and some other tourist destinations are for sale 20 days before departure and a week before for other destinations. You can now buy return tickets on most high-speed inter-city routes. Train fares are calculated according to the class and the distance traveled. Joining the crowds at station ticket counters can be very trying, so unless the station has a separate ticket office for foreign visitors, which is the case in Beijing and Shanghai, ask your hotel or travel agent to arrange your bookings. They usually charge a fee of ¥20–30 per ticket for this service.

Note that getting hold of tickets during Spring Festival and May and October holiday periods can be difficult.

Long-Distance Buses

Beijing and Shanghai both have several long-distance bus stations (changtu qiche zhan), so check carefully which station you want. Destinations are displayed in Chinese characters, and sometimes in Pinyin, on the front of buses.

Long-distance buses vary enormously in quality, age, and comfort. You may find that several buses are running along the same route, so make sure you are sold a ticket for the fastest and most comfortable (gaoji or haohua) bus – or the cheapest (zui pianyi) bus, if you prefer.

Ordinary buses such as those serving rural sights around Beijing, are the cheapest and have basic wooden, or lightly padded, seats. These buses stop often, so progress can be slow. They provide little space for baggage – there's no room under the seats and the luggage racks are minuscule. Backpacks are usually stacked next to the driver, for no additional charge. Sleeper buses (wopu che) speed through the night, so reach their destination in good

time. They usually have two tiers of bunks, or seats that recline almost flat. The older models can be quite dirty, but others are so clean you are required to remove your shoes as you board.

Shorter routes are served by rattling minibuses (xiao ba), which depart only when every spare space has been filled by a paying passenger. Crammed to the roof, minibus trips can be uncomfortable.

Express buses (kuai che) are the best way to travel. Most have air conditioning, and enforce a no-smoking policy. Receipts are given for luggage stowed in the hold.

Bus Tickets and Fares

Traveling by road is generally much cheaper than train travel. Tickets are sold at long-distance bus stations but book in advance where possible. Main bus stations invariably have computerized ticket offices with short queues, and tickets are also sold on board.

Ferries and Boats

An overnight ferry service runs along the Grand Canal between Suzhou and Hangzhou, and Shanghai also has services to Yangzi River ports including Nanjing and Wuhan. Several lines also link Pudong and Puxi. Note that ferry timetables change frequently and services may have been added or removed. There are also international services from Shanghai to Kobe and Osaka in Japan, and to Incheon in South Korea.

Ferry on the Huangpu River, Shanghai

City Transportation

Beijing and Shanghai both have expansive subway systems which should be your first choice where possible. Both are in the process of being further extended. City buses are slow and usually packed, but are very cheap. Taxis *(chuzu che)* are a necessity for most travelers, and, despite the language barrier and misunderstandings with drivers, they remain the most convenient way to get around. Bicycles, which once ruled the roads of China's cities, are another alternative, and those who feel confident can use a rental bike to explore the cities.

Green Travel

With China's well-documented environmental problems, it is essential for travelers to do their bit to combat the country's pollution problems. It is relatively easy to travel green in Beijing and Shanghai as the public transportation systems are comprehensive and efficient. From the airports, catching trains – either the Maglev or metro in Shanghai or the light rail in Beijing – into the two cities is very straightforward. Cycling is obviously the greenest way to travel and there are plans for city-wide cycle rental schemes, but for now you can hire bikes from independent stores or from your hotel for very low prices. The subways in both cities are also environmentally friendly and convenient, and some green buses run on hydrogen fuel cells. Online travel agent ctrip (www.ctrip.com.cn) puts some of your fee towards carbon offsetting programs. However, exploring the countryside is more difficult without hiring private transportation.

Beijing's Subway

The metro system in Beijing is undergoing development. There are currently ten lines (plus a handful of extension lines in theater surburbs), with 19 lines planned by 2015.

The metro is a swift way to get around. The system is easy to use, although walks

Sign for the Beijing subway

between lines at interchange stations can be long. There is a flat rate of ¥4 on all lines except for the airport light rail link, which is ¥25.

Buy your ticket from either a manned booth or a machine (which has an English language option) and then insert your ticket into the automated ticket gates to gain access. Stored-value *yikatong* cards, sold at subway stations, are a good option if you want to make several journeys. They require a ¥20 deposit which is refundable upon return of the card.

Shanghai's Subway

The rapidly growing Shanghai metro system is clean and efficient, with the first line built in 1995. There are now 12 lines and the system is the longest in the world. Lines 1, 2, and 3 are most useful to tourists.

Fares range between ¥3 and ¥8, depending on the number of stops traveled, and tickets can be purchased from ticket booths or machines. Stored-value *jiaotong* cards cost ¥20 and are worth buying for multiple journeys. Put your ticket into the slot at the electronic barrier and the gates will open. Retrieve your ticket on the other side of the gate and hold on to it – you will need it when you exit.

The primarily domestic Hongqiao Airport is on Line 2, and the much touted

German-designed high-speed Maglev train *(see p141)* travels from Longyang Road metro station, also on Line 2, to Pudong Airport. It runs daily between 6:45am and 10:40pm.

Buses

City bus *(gonggong qiche)* networks are extensive and cheap. Most trips within Beijing and Shanghai city centers cost a flat fare (no change given), which is clearly posted on the side of the bus; typically ¥1 or ¥2. Air-conditioned services are usually a little more expensive. Traffic jams tend to last all day in both cities, and no priority is shown to buses, which means journeys can be very slow. The buses are almost always overcrowded and provide good conditions for thieves so keep a watchful eye on your belongings. Consider using buses only for short journeys, or for suburban sightseeing.

Bus routes can also be tricky to navigate, but, increasingly, on-board announcements are made in English as well as Chinese, though destinations and schedules are sometimes listed in Chinese only.

Taxis

The best way to get to places away from subway stations is by taxi *(chuzu qiche)*. Taxis are found in large numbers in both Beijing and Shanghai, and can be hailed in the street or summoned with Uber (a taxi service controlled by a downloadable

Buses and taxis on a busy Beijing main road

mobile app. When arriving at airports, avoid the touts who immediately surround you, and head instead to the taxi rank outside where you are less likely to be overcharged. Make sure your taxi uses the meter, which drivers usually only start once the journey is actually under way – so wait a moment, then say, "*Dabiao*" (start the meter), if necessary. Taxis rarely have rear seat belts *(anquan dai)*, and those in the front may not work, although it is required by law that they be worn. Few taxi drivers speak English, so have your destination written down in Chinese by your hotel staff. Also get into the habit of picking up business cards at places in areas that you might want to return to – such as your hotel.

Fares per half mile (a kilometer) are clearly posted on the side of the car. The minimum charge in Beijing is ¥13, rising ¥2 per half mile. ¥25 should get you anywhere within the city. In Shanghai, the minimum charge is ¥14 (¥16 after 11pm) and each additional half mile is ¥2.40. Fares in both cities rise by 20–30 percent between 11pm and 5am. There is no need to tip (the driver will be bewildered if you do).

Most taxi journeys are straightforward and trouble-free, and in general only the run from the airport into town could be problematic, as less scrupulous drivers prey on new arrivals unfamiliar with the city. Note that on the run to and from Beijing's Capital Airport, you must pay the driver the road toll of ¥10 on top of the metered fare.

In addition to ignoring touts at airports and train stations, avoid cabs waiting at popular tourist sights and those that call out to you. It is also wise to ask your hotel to call a cab rather than flag

Bicycles – the traditional way to get around the city

down a passing driver, especially in peak hours or during rainstorms.

Taxis can also be hired for the day, a convenient way to see sights just out of town. This is best arranged by your hotel who can negotiate for you. Let hotel staff know the details of what you want, including date, pickup time and location, and your complete itinerary, and then get them to ask for a price. You should also expect to pay any road, tunnel, or bridge tolls.

In smaller towns, motorcycle rickshaws *(sanlun motuoche)* and bicycle rickshaws *(sanlun che)* are a fun way to get around. How-ever, be careful in both Beijing and Shanghai as they can often overcharge tourists.

Cycling

If you are not used to heavy traffic, cycling in the cities can be intimidating. However, hiring a bike is a great way to explore. Bike lanes are common

(although usually not respected by drivers) and roadside repair stalls are everywhere. Both Beijing and Shanghai are flat but Beijing is a superior place to cycle as it has more bike lanes and quieter roads, especially in the *hutong* areas. Make sure that any bike you rent has a lock provided. Bike stands are found all over and have an attendant to watch the bikes for a fee, usually ¥0.30.

Road Names

Main streets, avenues, and thoroughfares are often divided into different sections based on the four cardinal points. For example, Huaihai Lu (Huaihai Road) may be divided into Huaihai *Xi* Lu (West Road), Huaihai *Zhong* Lu (Middle Road), and Huaihai *Dong* Lu (East Road). Similarly, you may also see Zhongshan *Bei* Lu (North Road) and Zhongshan *Nan* Lu (South Road). Road names in Beijing display

Street sign in two scripts

the Pinyin translation, but in smaller towns and remote places, only Chinese is used. Apart from *lu* (road), other key words to look out for in Beijing are *jie* (street), *dajie* (avenue), and the lanes or alleyways called *hutong*.

Walking

Crossing the road can be perilous in China, so take care. Be aware that even when a "green man" is displayed, a pedestrian cannot walk across the road without fear of being hit; cars can still approach from the side or behind – and watch out for bicycles. In Beijing, the *hutongs* are the best place for a walk, while in Shanghai, the pedes-trianized Bund area is an excellent place for a stroll, as is the boardwalk on the other side of the Huangpu River in Pudong. People's Square and the French Concession are also good spots for ambling around.

A city taxi, a convenient way of traveling

General Index

Acknowledgments

Dorling Kindersley would like to thank the many people whose help and assistance contributed to the preparation of this book.

Design and Editorial
Publisher: Douglas Amrine
Publishing Managers: Vivien Antwi, Jane Ewart

Proofreader
Ferdie McDonald

Photography Co-ordinator
Amanda Mengpo Li

Map Co-ordinators
Uma Bhattacharya, Casper Morris

Revisions Team
Louise Abbott, Emma Anacootee, Shruti Bahl, Rachel Barber, Subhashree Bharati, Katie Bradley, Gary Bowerman, Iris Chan, Emer FitzGerald, Anna Freiberger, Rhiannon Furbear, Katharina Hahn, Lydia Halliday, Helena Iveson, Caroline Jackson, Yang Jie, Helen Partington, Marianne Petrou, Rada Radojicic, Marisa Renzullo, Alice Saggers, Rituraj Singh, Beverly Smart, Vinita Venugopal, Ajay Verma

Jacket Design: Tessa Bindloss, Sonal Bhatt

Additional Photography
Max Alexander, Simon Blackall, Demetrio Carrasco, Andy Crawford, Ian Cumming, Tim Draper, Gadi Farfour, Eddie Gerald, Nigel Hicks, Dave King, Stephen Lam, Ian O'Leary, Colin Sinclair, Chris Stowers, Hugh Thompson, Linda Whitwam

Photography Permissions
The Publishers thank all the temples, museums, hotels, restaurants, shops, and other sights for their assistance and kind permission to photograph their establishments.

FOTOE: 26tr; Zhang Weiqing 26bl.

Getty Images: AFP/Frederic J. Brown 216br; AFP/Liu Jin 140tl; Jon Arnold 127tl; Scott E Barbour 5tl, 19b; AWL Images/Christian Kober 64cr; China Photos 221br; Hulton 69bc; Jeff Hunter 20t; National Geographic 44cla; Photographer's Choice/John Warden 95tl; Grand Hyatt: 141bl, 169br; Sally & Richard Greenhill: 55tr; S.A.C.U. 54br, 54cl.

Henkes: 202tl; Hyatt on the Bund: 185br.

Imaginechina: 56crb, 97br; Jin Baoyuan 33tr; Adrian Bradshaw 137cla; Wu Changqing 92tr; Jiang Chao 99tl; CNS 35cr; Guo Guangyao 32cr; Jiang Guohong 36br; Zhang Guosheng 73bl; Long Hai 34bc, 35crb, 129cra; Wu Hong 37br, 65br; Wei Hui 37cr; Li Jiangsong 25crb; Wang Jianxin 35clb; Huang Jinguo 33cr; Kan Kan 26cb; Zhou Kang 130tr; Zhou Kang Pzhk 79cr; Xu Ruikang 33tc; Chen Shuyi 77br; Lin Weijian 32bl, 126cl, 126cr; Shen Yu 32br, 142br; Fang Zhonglin 134clb; Yi Zhou 127bl; Yin Zi 22–3cr; Institute of History & Philology: Academia Sinica 22cl, 22cb.

The Kobal Collection: Columbia 37tr; Tomson Films 37cla.

Mercante: 199tc; Moka Bros: Cherry Li 196tc.

Panos Pictures: 23cra; Panorama Stock 82bl, 93tl; Panoramic Stock 94cl; Photolibrary: TAO Images Limited 19b; Popperfoto.com: 54–5c; 139cr, 139cb; Portman Ritz-Carlton: 180br.

Red Gate Gallery, Beijing: 77tl; The Red Mansion Ltd.: Fang Lijun 36–7c; Zhan Wang 36clb; Cang Xin 36cla; Rex Features: Imagechina 200br; Mark Parren Taylor 161bc; Robert Harding Picture Library: 143tr; Malherbe Marcel 90; PanoramaStock 51t.

Science & Society Picture Library: Science Museum 23bl; Shanghai Museum: 130cla, 130c, 130clb, 131tc, 131c, 131cr, 132cl, 132c, 132br, 133c, 133br; Shangri-La Hotels and Resorts: 110bl; Shangri-La International Hotel Management Limited: China World Summit Wing 183tr; China Stock: 45bl, 49c, 49bl, 54clb, 55cra.

Thames & Hudson Ltd: Eileen Tweedy 24–5c; Tonino Lamborghini Boutique Hotel Suzhou: 182bc; TopFoto.co.uk: British Museum 27bc, 53bl; The Museum of East Asian Art / HIP 51bc; Transrapid: 141tr; TRB: 199br.

Ultraviolet: Limelight Studio / Scott Wright 203b.

Waldorf Astoria Shanghai on the Bund: 180cla, 184tl; Werner Forman Archive: 47c; P'yongyang Gallery, North Korea 27cla; Peking Palace Museum 48crb; Private Collection 45br, 51c, 53br; Victoria & Albert Museum 47bc. Xibo: 201tr. Yang-Tzu-Shaw 46crb.

Front Endpapers - Dreamstime.com: Chuyu br, JF123 tc.

Jacket
Front - Alamy Images: NobleImages.
Map Cover - Alamy Images: NobleImages.

All other images © Dorling Kindersley
For further information see: www.dkimages.com

Phrase Book

The Chinese language belongs to the Sino-Tibetan family of languages and uses characters which are ideographic – a symbol is used to represent an idea or an object. Mandarin Chinese, known as Putonghua in mainland China, is fairly straightforward as each character is monosyllabic. Traditionally, Chinese is written in vertical columns from top right to bottom left, however, the Western style is widely used. There are several romanization systems; the Pinyin system used here is the official system in mainland China. This phrase book gives the English word or phrase, followed by the Chinese script, then the Pinyin for pronunciation.

Guidelines for Pronunciation

Pronounce vowels as in these English words:

a	as in "father"
e	as in "lurch"
i	as in "see"
o	as in "solid"
u	as in "pooh"
ü	as the French u or German ü (place your lips to say oo and try to say ee)

Most of the consonants are pronounced as in English. As a rough guide, pronounce the following consonants as in these English words:

c	as ts in "hats"
q	as ch in "cheat"
x	as sh in "sheet"
z	as ds in "heads"
zh	as j in "Joe"

Mandarin Chinese is a tonal language with four tones, represented in Pinyin by one of the following marks ‾ ´ ˇ ` above each vowel – the symbol shows whether the tone is flat, rising, falling and rising, or falling. The Chinese characters do not convey this information: tones are learnt when the character is learnt. Teaching tones is beyond the scope of this small phrase book, but a language course book with a cassette or CD will help those who wish to take the language further.

Dialects

There are many Chinese dialects in use. It is hard to guess exactly how many, but they can be roughly classified into one of seven large groups (Mandarin, Cantonese, Hakka, Hui etc.), each group containing a large number of more minor dialects. Although all these dialects are quite different – Cantonese uses six tones instead of four – Mandarin or Putonghua, which is mainly based on the Beijing dialect, is the official language. Despite these differences, all Chinese people are more or less able to use the same formal written language so they can understand each other's writing, if not each other's speech.

In Emergency

Help!	请帮忙！	Qing bangmang!
Stop!	停住！	Ting zhu!
Call a doctor!	叫医生！	Jiao yisheng!
Call an ambulance!	叫救护车！	Jiao jiuhuche!
Call the police!	叫警察！	Jiao jiingcha!
Fire!	火！	Huo!
Where is the hospital/police station?	医院/警察分局在哪里？	Yiyuan/jingcha fenju zai nali?

Communication Essentials

Hello	你好	Nihao
Goodbye	再见	Zaijian
Yes/no	是／不是	shi/bushi
… not …	不是	bushi
I'm from …	我是 … 人	Wo shi … ren
I understand	我明白	Wo mingbai
I don't know	我不知道	Wo bu zhidao
Thank you	谢谢你	Xiexie ni
Thank you very much	多谢	Duo xie
Thanks (casual)	谢谢	Xiexie
You're welcome	不用谢	Bu yong xie
No, thank you	不，谢谢你	Bu, xiexie ni
Please (offering)	请	Qing
Please (asking)	请问	Qing wen
I don't understand	我不明白	Wo Bu mingbai
Sorry/Excuse me!	你会讲英语吗？	Baoqian/duibuqi
Could you help me please? (not emergency)	我不会讲汉语 请讲慢一点 抱歉／对不起 你能帮助我吗？	Ni neng bang zhu wo ma?

Useful Phrases

My name is …	我叫 …	Wo jiao …
Goodbye	再见	Zaijian
What is (this)?	（这）是什么？	(zhe) shi shenme?
Could I possibly have …? (very polite)	你怎样找这个东西？	Neng buneng qing ni gei wo …?
Is there … here?	这儿有 … 吗？	Zhe'r you … ma?
Where can I get …?	我在哪里可以得到 …?	Wo zai na li keyi de dao …?
How much is it?	它要多少钱？	Ta yao duoshao qian?
What time is …?	… 什么时间？	… shenme shijian?
Cheers! (toast)	干杯	Ganbei!
Where is the restroom/toilet?	卫生间／洗手间在哪里？	Weishengjian/ Xishoujian zai nali?

Useful Words

I	我	wo
woman	女人	nüren
man	男人	nanren
wife	妻子	qizi
husband	丈夫	zhangfu
daughter	女儿	nü'er
son	儿子	er'zi
child	小孩	xiaohai
children	儿童	er'tong
student	学生	xuesheng
Mr./Mrs./Ms.…	先生／太太／女士	xiansheng/taitai/ nüshi

English	中文	Pinyin
big/small	大/小	da/xiao
hot/cold	热/凉	re/liang
cold (to touch)	冷	leng
warm	暖	nuan
good/not good/bad	好／不好／坏	hao/buhao/huai
enough	够了	goule
free (no charge)	免费	mianfei
here	这里	zheli
there	那里	nali
this	这个	zhege
that (nearby)	那	na
that (far away)	那个	nage
what?	什么?	Shenme?
when?	什么时候?	Shenme shihou?
why?	为什么?	Wei shenme?
where?	在哪里?	Zai nali?
who?	谁?	Shui?

Signs

English	中文	Pinyin
open	开	kai
closed	关	guan
entrance	入口	rukou
exit	出口	chukou
danger	危险	weixian
emergency exit	安全门	anquanmen
information	信息	xinxi
restroom/toilet (men) (women)	卫生间／洗手间（男士）（女士）	Weishengjian/Xishoujian (nanshi) (nüshi)
	占用 空闲	
men	男士	nanshi
women	女士	nüshi

Money

English	中文	Pinyin
bank	银行	yinhang
cash	现金	xianjin
credit card	信用卡	xinyongka
currency	外汇兑换处	waihui
exchange office		duihuanchu
dollars	美元	meiyuan
pounds	英镑	yingbang
yuan	元	yuan

Keeping in Touch

English	中文	Pinyin
Where is a telephone?	电话在哪里?	Dianhua zai nali?
May I use your phone?	我可以用你的电话吗?	Wo keyi yong nide dianhua ma?
mobile phone	手机	shouji
sim card	卡	sim ka
Hello, this is ...	你好，我是...	Nihao, wo shi
airmail	航空	hangkong
e-mail	电子邮件	dianzi youjian
fax	传真	chuanzhen
internet	互联网	hulianwang
postcard	明信片	mingxinpian
post office	邮局	youju
stamp	邮票	youpiao
telephone booth	电话亭	dianhua ting
telephone card	电话卡	dianhua ka

Shopping

English	中文	Pinyin
Where can I buy ...?	我可以在哪里买到...?	Wo keyi zai nali maidao ...?
How much does this cost?	这要多少钱?	Zhe yao duoshao qian?
Too much!	太贵了！	Tai gui le!
Do you have ...?	你有...吗?	Ni you ...... ma?
May I try this on?	我可以试穿吗?	Wo keyi shi chuan ma?
Please show me that.	请给我看看那个。	Qing gei wo kankan na ge.
bookstore	书店	shudian
clothes	衣服	yifu
department store	百货商店	baihuo shangdian
electrical store	电器商店	dianqi shangdian
ladies' wear	女式服装	nüshi fuzhuang
market	市场	shichang
men's wear	男式服装	nanshi fuzhuang
pharmacist	药剂师	yaojishi
picture postcard	图片明信片	tupian mingxinpian
souvenir shop	纪念品店	jinianpin dian
supermarket	超市	chaoshi
travel agent	旅行社	lüxing she

Sightseeing

English	中文	Pinyin
Where is ...?	...在哪里?	... zai nali?
How do I get to ...?	我怎么到...?	Wo zenme dao ...?
Is it far?	远不远?	Yuan bu yuan?
bridge	桥	qiao
city	城市	chengshi
city center	市中心	shi zhongxin
gardens	花园	huayuan
hot spring	温泉	wen quan
island	岛	dao
monastery	寺院	siyuan
mountain	山	shan
museum	博物馆	bowuguan
palace	宫殿	gongdian
park	公园	gongyuan
port	港口	gangkou
river	江，河	jiang, he
ruins	废墟	feixu
shopping area	购物区	gouwu qu
shrine	神殿	shendian
street	街	jie
temple	寺庙	si/miao
town	镇	zhen
village	村	cun
province/county	省/县	sheng/xian
zoo	动物园	dongwuyuan
north	北	bei
south	南	nan
east	东	dong
west	西	xi
left/right	左/右	zuo/you
straight ahead	一直向前	yizhi xiangqian
between	在...之间	zai ... zhijian
near/far	近/远	jin/yuan
up/down	上/下	shang/xia
new	新	xin
old/former	旧	jiu
in	在...里	zai ... li
in front of	在...前面	zai ... qianmian

Getting Around

English	中文	Pinyin
airport	机场	jichang
bicycle	自行车	zixingche
I want to rent a bicycle	我想租一辆自行车。	Wo xiang zu yiliang zixingche.
ordinary bus	公共汽车	gonggong qiche
express bus	特快公共汽车	tekuai gonggong qiche
minibus	面包车	mianbaoche
main bus station	公共汽车总站	gonggong qiche zong zhan
Which bus goes to ...?	哪一路公共汽车到...去?	Nayilu gonggong qiche dao ... qu?
When is the next bus?	下一辆公共汽车是什么时候?	Xiayiliang gonggong qiche shi shenme shihou?
Please tell me where to get off?	请告诉我在哪里下车?	Qing gaosu wo zai nali xia che?
car	小汽车	xiaoqiche
ferry	渡船	duchuan
baggage room	行李室	xingli shi
one-way ticket	单程票	dancheng piao
return ticket	往返票	wangfan piao
taxi	出租车	chuzuche
ticket	票	piao
ticket office	售票处	shoupiao chu
timetable	时刻表	shikebiao

Accommodations

air-conditioning	空调	kongtiao
bath	洗澡	xizao
check-out	退房	tui fang
deposit	定金	dingjin
double bed	双人床	shuangren chuang
hair drier	吹风机	chuifeng ji
room	房间	fangjian
economy room	经济房	jingji fang
key	钥匙	yaoshi
front desk	前台	qiantai
single/twin room	单人 / 双人房	danren/shuangren fang
single beds	单人床	danren chuang
shower	淋浴	linyu
standard room	标准房间	biaozhun fangjian
deluxe suite	豪华套房	haohua taofang

Eating Out

May I see the menu?	请给我看看菜单。	Qing gei wo kankan caidan?
Is there a set menu?	有没有套餐?	You meiyou taocan?
I'd like ….	我想要 …	Wo xiang yao …
May I have one of those?	请给我这个。	Qing gei wo zhege?
I am a vegetarian	我是素食者。	Wo shi sushizhe.
Waiter/waitress!	服务员!	Fuwuyuan!
May I have a fork/knife/spoon?	请给我一把叉 / 刀 / 汤匙。	Qing gei wo yiba cha/dao/tangshi?
May we have the check please?	请把帐单开给我们.	Qing ba zhangdan kaigei women?
breakfast	早餐	zaocan
buffet	自助餐	zizhucan
chopsticks	筷子	kuaizi
dinner	晚餐	wancan
to drink	喝	he
to eat	吃	chi
food	食品	shipin
full (stomach)	饱	bao
hot/cold	热 / 冷	re/leng
hungry	饿	e
lunch	午餐	wucan
set menu	套餐	taocan
spicy	酸辣	suan la
hot (spicy)	辣	la
sweet	甜	tian
mild	淡	dan
Western food	西餐	xi can
restaurant	餐馆	canguan
restaurant (upscale)	馆店	fandian

Food

apple	苹果	pingguo
bacon	咸肉	xianrou
bamboo shoots	笋	sun
beancurd	豆腐	doufu
bean sprouts	豆芽	dou ya
beans	豆	dou
beef	牛肉	niurou
beer	啤酒	pijiu
bread	面包	mianbao
butter	黄油	huangyou
chicken	鸡	ji
crab	蟹	xie
duck	鸭	ya
eel	鳗	man
egg	蛋	dan
eggplant	茄子	qiezi
fermented soybean paste	酱	jiang
fish	鱼	yu
fried egg	炒蛋	chao dan
fried tofu	油豆腐	you doufu
fruit	水果	shuiguo
fruit juice	果汁	guo zhi
ginger	姜	jiang
ice cream	冰淇淋	bingqilin

meat	肉	rou
melon	瓜	gua
noodles	面	mian
egg noodles	鸡蛋面	jidan mian
wheat flour noodles	面粉面	mianfen mian
rice flour noodles	米粉面	mifen mian
omelet	煎蛋饼	jiandanbing
onion	洋葱	yangcong
peach	桃子	taozi
pepper	胡椒粉, 辣椒	hujiaofen, lajiao
pickles	泡菜	paocai
pork	猪肉	zhurou
potato	土豆	tudou
rice	米饭	mifan
rice crackers	爆米花饼干	baomihua bing'gan
rice wine	米酒	mi jiu
salad	色拉	sela
salmon	鲑鱼, 大马哈鱼	guiyu, damahayu
salt	盐	yan
scallion	韭葱	jiucong
seaweed	海带	haidai
shrimp	虾	xia
soup	汤	tang
soy sauce	酱油	jiangyou
squid	鱿鱼	youyu
steak	牛排	niupai
sugar	糖	tang
vegetables	蔬菜	shucai
yoghurt	酸奶	suannai

Drinks

beer	啤酒	pijiu
black tea	红茶	hong cha
coffee (hot)	(热) 咖啡	(re) kafei
green tea	绿茶	lü cha
iced coffee	冰咖啡	bing kafei
milk	牛奶	niunai
mineral water	矿泉水	kuang quanshui
orange juice	橙汁	cheng zhi
wine	葡萄酒	putaojiu

Numbers

0	零	ling
1	一	yi
2	二	er
3	三	san
4	四	si
5	五	wu
6	六	liu
7	七	qi
8	八	ba
9	九	jiu
10	十	shi
11	十一	shiyi
12	十二	shier
20	二十	ershi
21	二十一	ershi yi
22	二十二	ershi er
30	三十	sanshi
40	四十	sishi
100	一百	yi bai
101	一百零一	yi bai ling yi
200	二百	er bai

Time

Monday	星期一	xingqiyi
Tuesday	星期二	xingqi'er
Wednesday	星期三	xingqisan
Thursday	星期四	xingqisi
Friday	星期五	xingqiwu
Saturday	星期六	xingqiliu
Sunday	星期天	xingqitian
today	今天	jintian
yesterday	昨天	zuotian
tomorrow	明天	mingtian

Beijing Subway

The subway system in Beijing has rapidly expanded over recent years. Lines 1–10 serve the urban core of the city while the others take you to outlying suburbs. Line 1 crosses central Beijing from east to west, and the circular. Line 2 runs around its perimeter, tracing the route once occupied by the walls of the Inner City. Line 5 splices through the city, running from north to south.

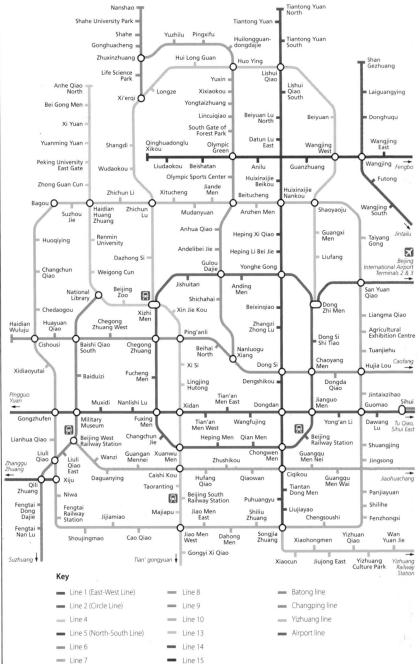

Key

Line 1 (East-West Line)	Line 8	Batong line
Line 2 (Circle Line)	Line 9	Changping line
Line 4	Line 10	Yizhuang line
Line 5 (North-South Line)	Line 13	Airport line
Line 6	Line 14	
Line 7	Line 15	